HANDS UP, DON'T SHOOT

D0468742

Hands Up, Don't Shoot

Why the Protests in Ferguson and
Baltimore Matter, and How
They Changed America

Jennifer E. Cobbina

NEW YORK UNIVERSITY PRESS
New York

NEW YORK UNIVERSITY PRESS
New York
www.nyupress.org
© 2019 by New York University
All rights reserved

Chapter 5 builds upon material previously published as Jennifer E. Cobbina, Soma Chaudhuri, Victor M. Rios, and Michael Conteh, "I Will Be Out There Every Day Strong! Protest Policing and Future Activism among Ferguson and Baltimore Protestors," *Sociological Forum* 34, no. 1 (March 2019). Copyright and reprinted here with permission from Eastern Sociological Society.

References to Internet websites (URLs) were accurate at the time of writing. Neither the author nor New York University Press is responsible for URLs that may have expired or changed since the manuscript was prepared.

Library of Congress Cataloging-in-Publication Data
Names: Cobbina, Jennifer E., author.
Title: Hands up, don't shoot : why the protests in Ferguson and Baltimore matter, and how they changed America / by Jennifer E. Cobbina.
Description: New York : New York University Press, [2019] | Includes bibliographical references and index.
Identifiers: LCCN 2018044999| ISBN 9781479818563 (cl : alk. paper) | ISBN 9781479874415 (pb : alk. paper)
Subjects: LCSH: Police brutality—Missouri—Ferguson. | Police brutality—Maryland—Baltimore. | African American men—Violence against. | Discrimination in criminal justice administration—United States. | Police-community relations—United States. | Protest movements—United States. | United States—Race relations.
Classification: LCC HV8141 .C56 2019 | DDC 363.2/32—dc23
LC record available at https://lccn.loc.gov/2018044999

New York University Press books are printed on acid-free paper, and their binding materials are chosen for strength and durability. We strive to use environmentally responsible suppliers and materials to the greatest extent possible in publishing our books.
Manufactured in the United States of America

10 9 8 7 6 5 4 3 2

Also available as an ebook

CONTENTS

PREFACE

After the killing of Michael Brown and the protests in Ferguson, Missouri, I, like many others, found myself glued to the television as I watched the story and the reaction to his death unfold. What happened in Ferguson felt personal to me. I had lived a couple of minutes from the city while pursuing my doctorate from 2004 to 2009. Thus, when Victor Rios, a colleague of mine who has done important work on policing kids, sent out an email asking if any scholars wanted to go to Ferguson to interview protesters, I jumped at the chance. Several criminologists and sociologists soon formed the Ferguson Research-Action Collaborative with the goal of studying protests and the Black Lives Matter movement. We also hoped to contribute to the struggle for racial justice in the United States.

The group talked about meeting up in October 2014 and also attending the National Day of Protest against Police Brutality. One of the local sociologists had been engaged in Ferguson protest events since early August and informed us that if we attended the protest we had to prepare for the possibility of arrest. At that time, police were arresting large numbers of protesters. We were encouraged by this local sociologist to stay on the sidewalk, wear running shoes, and write the phone number for jail support on our arms in case we were arrested and needed legal assistance. I started to grow concerned. The response from state police was also mind-boggling. I watched on CNN the various police tactics used to repress collective action on the streets, including tear gas, Long-Range Acoustic Riot Control Devices (LRAD), military-style armored tactical vehicles, police dogs, and lines of riot-geared officers. I began asking myself: "Will it be safe for me to do this research?" As a Black woman, I could be seen as a potential target for police.

With the strong desire to pursue this study but with uncertainty looming, I called my former pastor, Bishop Jesse Battle, whom I trust and respect, and who lived in St. Louis. I explained my desire to come to

Ferguson to interview residents and protesters. "But," I told him, "I'm a bit scared. Do you think it's safe?" As someone who was in the trenches and spoke out boldly against the racial injustices that were going on, he encouraged me to come. When I told him of my desire to attend the National Day of Protest against Police Brutality simply to observe, he acknowledged that I may very well be arrested just for attending. I was a bit baffled since I didn't plan on doing anything but observe the protest unfold. He told me that around that time people were getting arrested just for stepping off the sidewalk. If one happens to stay during a time police tell people to disperse, one may be arrested. He, too, confirmed the importance of wearing running shoes and writing the number for jail support on my arm. "Should I come to Ferguson given the risks?" I asked him. He responded, "Jennifer, just come." With that said, I made up my mind and went.

Introduction

On August 9, 2014, Darren Wilson, a White officer of the Ferguson Police Department (FPD), saw two young Black men, eighteen-year-old Michael Brown and his friend, twenty-two-year-old Dorian Johnson, walking in the middle of the street on Canfield Drive in Ferguson, Missouri. Ferguson is a small suburb of St. Louis where Blacks comprise 67 percent of the population.[1] Both young men had just come from a convenience store, where surveillance video captured Brown stealing several packages of cigarillos and forcefully shoving the store clerk. According to a report from the Department of Justice (DOJ), a dispatch call went out over the police radio for a "stealing in progress," thereby alerting Wilson to the theft and giving him a description of the suspects, after which he encountered Brown and his friend. According to Wilson's statement to the prosecutor and investigators, once he'd instructed the teens to move to the sidewalk Wilson suspected they were both involved in the robbery. He called for backup and parked his car at an angle to prevent Brown and his friend from walking any farther. Wilson testified that as he tried to open the door to his vehicle it closed,[2] Brown punched him and reached for his gun, and a struggle for the weapon ensued, during which Wilson fired two shots, one of which stuck Brown in the hand. The DOJ concluded that, after the shooting inside the vehicle, Brown ran and Wilson chased him and shot him after he turned around and charged at him. In total, Wilson fired twelve bullets, six of which hit Brown, two of them in the head.

Though several witnesses asserted that Brown had his hands up in an act of surrender before Wilson shot him to death, the DOJ—pointing to changing statements—determined that these accounts were inconsistent with physical and forensic evidence. The former St. Louis County Prosecutor Robert McCullough, who many protesters argued had deep ties to the police and should recuse himself, brought the case in front of a grand jury to determine whether there was probable cause to indict

Wilson for his actions.[3] On November 24, 2014, McCullough announced that the grand jury had decided not to indict. In the wake of several high-profile deaths of other Black men, including Trayvon Martin, Eric Garner, and John Crawford, the case received national attention and the grand jury announcement sparked civil unrest across the country, including in Los Angeles, New York, Seattle, Philadelphia, and Chicago. Marie, a Latina protester in Ferguson, detailed her experience protesting immediately after the fatal shooting of Brown:

> We were at the police station protesting, and the police were out there in mass with dogs. And there was a woman, and she was yelling at this line of police, saying, you know, "What if this was your child? What if this was your child?" . . . And then that night . . . like twenty-four hours after Mike Brown was shot, a little bit more than twenty-four hours, we went on West Florissant and there were—and I'm not exaggerating, like I've never seen that many cops—three hundred police in full riot gear. And I don't scare easy, but it was one of the moments in my life where I was scared because what I saw was these police, this massive police presence. And I saw unseasoned, angry, primarily young Black kids just angry and trying like some of them were throwing bottles—and then I saw the cops with their riot gear ready to engage. And I got in the middle of that. . . . I had held the line for three hours, where I had my back to the police officers and my face to the young people. . . . They were righteously mad. They had a right to protest. And when the looting started—and it did—we had to break the line to try—because there wasn't enough elders out there. There wasn't, it was all young people. We had to break the line to go and try and stop the looters. . . . [After] QuikTrip burned down . . . that's like when it started to happen, and then it was just like tanks and rubber bullets. . . . And they're teargassing the streets. . . . police [were] advancing on us in full riot gear. Police [were] advancing on us with shotguns.

Protesters across the nation rallied for months, outraged about Brown's death and the use of excessive and lethal force by law enforcement officials toward Black civilians.

Eight months following the death of Michael Brown, on April 12, 2015, officers from the Baltimore Police Department (BPD) attempted to stop and question Freddie Gray, a twenty-five-year-old Black man. After making eye contact with Lieutenant Brian Rice, Gray fled and was pursued by Rice and two other officers. After police found Gray in possession of an illegal switchblade, he was arrested; however, his request for an asthma inhaler went ignored and he was placed in a prisoner transport van without being secured, which is a violation of departmental policy.[4] En route, Gray screamed for help and one of the officers applied flex-cuffs to his wrists and put shackles on his feet. He was loaded in the prison van face down on the floor. The van made two additional stops and police provided no medical assistance to Gray even though he requested it.[5]

Approximately forty-five minutes after Gray's arrest, the city fire department received a call about an "unconscious male" at the Western District police station.[6] After paramedics arrived, Gray was transported to a hospital and underwent surgery the next day for three broken vertebrae and an injured voice box. He remained in a coma for a week and died on April 19 as a result of injuries to his spinal cord, which was determined to be 80 percent severed.[7] Civil unrest erupted over what many perceived as an unjustified homicide of another Black man at the hands of the police.[8] Less than two weeks later, Baltimore State's Attorney Marilyn Mosby filed charges including manslaughter, assault, reckless endangerment, and officer misconduct against the six officers involved in the incident (three of whom were White and three of whom were Black). In September 2015, a $6.4 million wrongful death civil settlement for Gray's family was approved by the city. However, the trials did not yield a conviction. The first trial ended in a hung jury, three more officers were acquitted after a trial before a judge, and the state's attorney dropped charges against the remaining officers who were awaiting trial. While the legal system did not convict any of the Baltimore policemen, many Black residents remain convinced that the officers were in the wrong and that these killings were part of an ongoing assault on Blacks across the United States. The death of Freddie Gray sparked protests and looting in Baltimore. Jason, a mixed-race male Baltimorean protester, described what happened at a protest he attended in the days following Gray's death:

> We were out in force, a large group of us . . . super diverse groups came out in support and it started getting tricky when they instituted the curfew, and that's when it went no holds bar[red]. We were nightly being

berated and like shoved and pushed and people were being arrested and hit and it was really traumatizing. . . . I witness[ed] a lot of police officers really overstepping their bounds and the excessive use of force when it came to the National Guard and the tear gas. I was shot with a rubber bullet protesting here. I was hit with tear gas. I was laying on the floor in the middle of Pennsylvania Avenue and North because I couldn't breathe nor see. There was smoke everywhere and all you hear is people screaming and yelling and you feel as though you are in a third world country.

Shared outrage over Gray's death became a catalyst for collective action. Though the BPD initially responded to demonstrators with restraint, in an attempt to suppress public protests and gain control over a chaotic situation, the police responded with increased aggression toward activists.

In recent years, the killings of unarmed Black men, women, boys, and girls by police officers have captured national and international attention: seventeen-year-old Trayvon Martin was shot and killed in Sanford, Florida, by a self-appointed neighborhood watchman in February 2012; twenty-two-year-old Rakia Boyd was an innocent bystander shot in the back of the head by an off-duty Chicago police officer in March 2012; Jonathan Ferrell, a twenty-four-year-old former college football player, was shot ten times and killed by a North Carolina police officer in September 2013 after seeking help following a car crash; Miriam Carey, a thirty-four-year-old woman, was fatally shot five times from behind by Secret Service agents during a Washington, DC, chase at the White House security checkpoint while her one-year-old daughter was in the car with her in October 2013; after calling the police to report a dispute between two men, Yvette Smith, a forty-seven-year-old mother, was shot dead in her home within seconds of opening the door to Texas officers in February 2014; Eric Garner, a forty-three-year-old Black man, died after a Staten Island police officer placed him in a chokehold for selling untaxed cigarettes in July 2014; twenty-two-year-old John Crawford was shot and killed in a Walmart store by a police officer in Beavercreek, Ohio, while holding a toy BB gun in July 2014; twelve-year-old Tamir Rice was fatally shot within seconds of a Cleveland, Ohio, officer approaching him as he held a pellet gun in November 2014; Walter Scott, a fifty-year-old man, was fatally shot in the back as he fled a North Charleston police officer in April 2015;

thirty-seven-year-old Alton Sterling was shot several times at close range by Baton Rouge officers while pinned to the ground in July 2016; Philando Castile, a thirty-two-year-old man who was stopped for having a broken taillight, was shot to death in July 2016 while his girlfriend and four-year-old daughter were in the vehicle; sixteen-year-old Aries Clark was killed by police while holding a toy weapon in July 2017; forty-two-year-old Keith O'Neil, a suspected carjacker, was unarmed when fatally shot by a San Francisco police officer on his fourth day of duty in December 2017; 26-year-old Botham Jean was shot and killed in his own apartment by an off-duty Dallas police officer in September 2018. Modern-day killings of unarmed Black men, women, and children have struck a conscious chord across the nation, as much of the public bears witness to the police operating with impunity.

These incidents represent only a small fraction of the deaths of unarmed Black individuals who have been killed at the hands of the police before and after Brown's and Gray's deaths. These killings, however, are hardly outliers. Rather, they are examples of racial hostility, racial bias, legalized racial subordination, and a normative police practice that targets Black individuals. But the issue of racially motivated police killings is not simply a product of individual discriminatory police officers. It is the result of deep historical forces that follow a pattern of social control over Black people that is entwined in the very fabric of the United States. Insufficient attention has been paid to the poisonous legacy of racism that infects not only Ferguson and Baltimore but communities nationwide, and is visible in America's criminal justice system. This nation has been fittingly termed the United States of Amnesia, owing to its failure to confront and repair the damage created by America's history of racial injustice.[9] Yet, as novelist Toni Morrison noted in a 1993 essay, it was on the backs of Blacks that America was built.[10] That is, the nation was founded on a system of slavery; however, it has yet to "own up to the way racial bias and legalized racial subordination have compromised our ability to implement criminal justice."[11] America's racialized past influences the way that others perceive Black people, including their treatment by the criminal justice system and the police. Without attention to this history, attempts to control crime and improve police-citizen relations will fail or be mediocre at best. In the wake of ignoring or diminishing America's history and legacy of legally sanctioned racial subordination, cities like Ferguson, Baltimore, and many others bear witness to this unacknowledged continuity between past and present.[12]

One of the goals of this book is to shed light on how historical racial oppression continues to play out in modern-day race relations and police practices. By coming to terms with the historical reality of race inequality we can better understand the racialized experiences of Black individuals in this nation. I argue that the systemic legacy of slavery and Jim Crow continues to this day to shape Black peoples' position in society and how they are perceived and treated by individuals and institutions, including the police. In this book, I will highlight parallels between modern police practices and the overpolicing that occurred in earlier eras of overt discrimination. In addition to making historical and contemporary linkages, I will detail what gave rise to the uprisings that occurred in Ferguson and Baltimore, as well as the conditions that can lead to (or stop) future unrest.

Police are the enforcement arm of government authority and they are one of the few agencies empowered to use deadly force.[13] As a result of their power, police officers are often at the forefront of controversial cases related to racially discriminatory use of force. As policing scholar Brian Withrow notes, "One of the most, or perhaps the most, intractable issue for contemporary American police administrators is race, or more specifically race-based policing."[14] Race-based policing, also known as racial profiling, is "the use of race or ethnicity, or proxies thereof, by law enforcement officials as a basis for judgment of criminal suspicion."[15]

The consequence of racial profiling can be detrimental. Such police practices can destroy the legitimacy of the police, as many individuals who are the recipients of such aggressive tactics feel distrustful of and cynical toward law enforcement.[16] In the cases of both Brown and Gray, protests and social movements (i.e., Black Lives Matter) in large cities, including St. Louis, Baltimore, Chicago, New York, and Los Angeles, were directly triggered by perceptions of race-based policing.

Race plays an important role in shaping citizens' attitudes toward the police. Studies have shown that Blacks are less inclined than Whites to believe that traffic stops are legitimate and that police behave appropriately.[17] Other studies show that, compared to Whites, Blacks are more likely to believe that the police abuse citizens, treat minorities more harshly than Whites, and are not held accountable for misconduct.[18]

Overall, Blacks tend to view police as treating them unequally and are likely to rate the police less favorably than their White counterparts.[19]

Although multiple studies demonstrate that attitudes toward police differ by race,[20] few studies account for how individuals' experiences shape these attitudes. Studies of this issue have found that Blacks undergo a wide range of harms, including disproportionate experiences with surveillance and stops, disrespectful treatment and verbal abuse, arrests, and use of force, including excessive and deadly force.[21] Research examining the relationship between perceptions and the context of citizens' interactions with police suggests that unfavorable views of the police stem from personal or indirect contact with law enforcement that is negative in nature.[22] That is, Black citizens, and especially youth, disproportionately experience a range of direct negative police behavior, such as harassment and disrespectful treatment, which, in turn, results in unfavorable perceptions of the police.[23] Some experience indirect, or "vicarious" contact, which is knowledge learned about police through family, friends, media, or others. Black individuals' perceptions of unfair treatment from the police have serious implications for police-community relations. Police stops perceived as racially motivated can very well increase the frequency of confrontations between police and Black citizens, and, consequently, generate deepening distrust of the police among those who have direct personal or vicarious contact with police.[24] Citizen distrust of the police can strain police-community relations, as police typically depend on cooperation from the public to solve crimes, and residents are more likely to cooperate when they view the police positively and with legitimacy.[25]

Since young minority males are more likely to report having negative encounters with police than young White men, young minority women, and older minority men, most studies focus their examination of police-citizen relations on Black males.[26] Yet we know less about women's encounters with the police, especially marginalized women of color, as their experiences with law enforcement remain underexamined and generally invisible in public discourse.[27] Less attention has been given to White individuals' experiences and perceptions of police, perhaps because they are less likely than Blacks to experience discriminatory policing.[28] The lack of attention to the interlocking nature of race, gender, and policing is surprising, because race and gender inequalities cannot be understood in isolation of one another, as they are intersecting structural positions that result in differences in the nature and effects of inequality.[29] Thus, another goal of this book is to shed light on these differences for race, gender, and policing.

The Communities of Ferguson and Baltimore

While there is an abundant body of research demonstrating that Blacks often bear the brunt of unwelcome police contacts, few studies have compared the relationship of police-citizen encounters across different places.[30] Thus, Ferguson and Baltimore are valuable settings in which to explore how protesters attempt to raise their voices to those inside and outside the minority community to consider how difference is perceived, treated, and reproduced. In fact, both cities are ideal sites in which to conduct this research, because they have a deep history of racial and economic disparity.

Table 1.1 compares Ferguson and Baltimore's demographic and socioeconomic indicators with their surrounding counties. Both counties have much less racial diversity than the cities of Ferguson and Baltimore—23 and 26 percent of the population in St. Louis County and Baltimore County, respectively, are Black. In contrast, in Ferguson two-thirds of the population is Black and in Baltimore this figure is approximately 64 percent. As table 1.1 shows, Ferguson and Baltimore residents are characterized by relatively high rates of female-headed households and unemployment that exceeds those residing in the county as a whole. The proportion of poverty is more than two times greater in the cities of Ferguson and Baltimore than in St. Louis County and Baltimore County. Ferguson residents have a median income nearly $20,000 lower than those in St. Louis County. Similarly, residents of Baltimore have a median income $25,000 less than those residing in the county of Baltimore. Though the city/county income gap is greater between Baltimore and Baltimore County, both Ferguson and Baltimore are characterized by the uneven distribution of individuals by income level.

Demographic transformation occurred rapidly in Ferguson. From 1900 to 1960, Ferguson grew in population from 1,015 to more than 22,149 residents, an average growth of 5 percent a year.[31] While the size

TABLE I.1. Select Neighborhood Characteristics

	Ferguson	St. Louis County	Baltimore	Baltimore County
Population Size	21,203	998,883	621,849	805,029
Median Family Income[a]	$40,660	$59,520	$41,819	$66,940
Percent Black	67.4	23.3	63.7	26.1
Female-headed Families w/ Children[b]	15.3	7.6	11.3	7.6
Percent Poverty	22.7	9.6	24.2	9.8
Percent Unemployment[b]	8.0	5.4	8.6	5.0

Source: US Census, 2010.
[a] *Source:* US Census, 2010–2014.
[b] *Source:* American Community Survey, 2010–2014.

of the population has remained steady since 1960, the racial/ethnic population has shifted quickly. The racial composition of Ferguson went from 1 percent Black in 1970 to 25 percent in 1990. From 1990 to 2010, the White population of Ferguson shrank from over 16,000 to about 6,200, even as the Black population rose to 67 percent of the town's residents.[32] As Whites left the city for White suburban communities, Ferguson soon became recognized as a "Black suburban" community.[33]

However, the growth of the Black population has been accompanied by rising unemployment rates. The city of Ferguson was generally split between Black and White with an unemployment rate of 5 percent in 2000; however, by 2010, the population was two-thirds Black, unemployment had risen to 13 percent and the number of residents who lived in poverty doubled from the previous decade.[34] As a result, the poor population in the city remains both large and highly concentrated. This is not specific to Ferguson, as the area northwest of St. Louis became predominately Black. After World War II, the number of jobs in the city of St. Louis dropped by 20 percent while those residing in St. Louis County increased by 400 percent between 1951 and 1967.[35] St. Louis residents have been in poor economic shape, due to continual disinvestments, since the region shifted from an industrial to a service-based economy.[36] Deindustrialization and disinvestments have hurt the city of St. Louis overall; however, the effects have been particularly salient for Black residents, as they were excluded from jobs or limited to low-skilled, menial, entry-level jobs.[37]

In comparison, Baltimore was once the sixth largest city in the United States. As the city grew, however, large numbers of city residents relocated to areas outside of the city limits. In the 1950s, Baltimore's population peaked to roughly 950,000 residents, yet by 1990, the population had lost 23 percent of its population and had only 736,000 residents.[38] These declines continued in the decade that followed, with the city losing nearly 80,000 additional residents (or eleven percent of its population) by the year 2000.[39] This rapid population loss is significant because it changed the demographic makeup of the city to a disproportionately high minority population. Though Blacks comprised nearly one-quarter of the population in 1970, by 1990 nearly 60 percent of the population was Black, now comprising of two-thirds of the population. In contrast, the White population went from 75 percent in 1970 to 39 percent in 1990 to 29 percent in 2010.[40]

Baltimore not only suffered population loss but massive job loss due to deindustrialization in the United States. While the economy in Baltimore historically had been dependent on jobs in manufacturing, the reduction in a number of industries since the 1970s resulted in considerable loss of available employment. Between 1950 and 2000, the US economy experienced a net loss of approximately 100,000 manufacturing jobs.[41] With the decline of manufacturing, the service-based economy came to be the dominant base of employment for Baltimore City residents. However, the shift in employment patterns worked against many inner-city residents. Numerous jobs that were created in the downtown business district emphasized high-skilled office occupations that were beyond the education and skill levels of many inner-city Blacks.[42] Those who were qualified often had difficulty accessing jobs, as retail and service jobs were located primarily in the suburbs. Many inner-city residents lacked affordable transportation and networks to connect them to suburban employment opportunities.[43] Overall, the combination of high population loss, disproportionate minority populations, and great disparities between city and suburban income levels left the poor even more socially isolated and their communities further depleted of economic resources.

Table 1.2 provides comparative data on a number of socioeconomic indicators for Blacks and Whites in Ferguson and Baltimore from 2010 to 2014 using the American Community Survey. The median income

TABLE I.2. Select Socioeconomic Characteristics by Race in
Ferguson and Baltimore

	Ferguson		Baltimore	
	Black	White	Black	White
Median Household Income	$34,103	$53,289	$33,801	$62,034
Female-headed Families w/ Children	56.0	23.5	57.7	16.6
Percent Poverty	27.4	9.7	28.3	14.4
Percent Unemployment	15.7	6.5	18.5	7.1

Source: American Community Survey 2010–2014.

of Blacks in both cities is comparable; however, the income disparity between Blacks and Whites is smaller in Ferguson than Baltimore. In Ferguson, Black residents' median income is about 64 percent of the median income of Whites, while in Baltimore, this figure is approximately 54 percent. More than half of Black individuals live in female-headed households with children in both cities; however, Blacks are two and half times more likely to live in such households in Ferguson and three and a half times more likely than their White counterparts in Baltimore. On the other hand, when we look at the other socioeconomic characteristics, we see that racial disparities are higher in Ferguson than Baltimore. The percentage of Blacks in poverty is three times that of impoverished Whites in Ferguson, while in Baltimore, Blacks are two times as likely as Whites to be poor. In both cities, Blacks are two times more likely to be unemployed than their White counterparts.

Ferguson and Baltimore are similar in that they are both troubled with high rates of poverty and unemployment. The similarities, however, do not end there. Both cities have long, strained histories between police and citizens of color. In fact, the DOJ revealed a pattern of unlawful racial bias in policing that eroded trust in the police.[44] Moreover, the racial composition of Ferguson and Baltimore is two-thirds Black. The deaths of Brown and Gray sparked a firestorm of protests, with hundreds of activists denouncing police brutality, resulting in independent federal investigations of the Ferguson and Baltimore City Police Departments. In addition, while officers involved in the deaths of both men were determined not to be criminally liable, Brown's and Gray's families were awarded civil settlements in their wrongful death lawsuits against each city. These similarities are worth consideration with regard to their influences on the nature of policing and protests.

Despite these similarities, there are distinct differences between the two cities. Ferguson and Baltimore differ in their size and composition. Ferguson is a suburban city that is part of the Greater St. Louis metropolitan area and comprised of only 21,000 residents. Located in the northern part of St. Louis County, Ferguson is one of 91 municipalities in the county. In contrast, Baltimore is the largest city in the state of Maryland, with a population of approximately 620,000.[45] The city of Baltimore is the 29th most populous[46] in the United States and is surrounded by but separated from the County of Baltimore.[47] The police departments in both cities have notably different racial/ethnic compositions. While the racial composition of Ferguson and Baltimore is predominately Black, the vast majority of Ferguson police officers are White (approximately 94 percent) while nearly half of Baltimore officers are Black (47 percent). In contrast to Ferguson, in Baltimore the city's former mayor, the former police commissioner, the state's attorney, and the judge who acquitted the three officers[48] in the Freddie Gray case were all Black. In Ferguson the grand jury made the decision not to indict Darren Wilson for Michael Brown's death; however, in Baltimore the state's attorney made a quick decision to indict the officers involved in Freddie Gray's death. In Ferguson police came under strong criticism for their use of military-grade weapons trained on unarmed civilians, while in Baltimore police initially used restrained force during the onset of protests but eventually became militarized.

In this book I bring together research on race, place, and policing, along with scholarship on social movements, with the aim of investigating how and why both Ferguson and Baltimore became highly publicized sites for protests against racially biased policing and broader structural inequalities. Specifically, my book examines how Ferguson and Baltimore residents understand their experiences with the police and the impact that those experiences have on their perceptions of the police; what galvanized Black Lives Matter as a social movement; and how policing tactics during demonstrations influenced subsequent mobilization decisions among protesters. This book does the important work of documenting the voices of individuals living under, and trying to raise their voices against, an oppressive system. Protesters are the focus here because too often their grievances, which run deep, are over-looked and are dismissed as a "mob behavior" mentality.[49] Such perceptions often seem to lump peaceful protesters with violent protesters without distinction. That is, if one bottle is thrown, one window broken, or one person chants, "Kill the police," then the whole movement is portrayed as violent "cop haters." The accounts presented here humanize people's anger, underscoring how a nationwide movement emerged to denounce both racial biases by police and the broader economic and social system that leave young Black civilians feeling the deck is stacked against them. In particular, Black people's perceptions of unfair and un-equal treatment from the police have serious ramifications for police-community relations.[50] These perceptions require policy solutions that address the nature, function, and meanings of racial inequality and offer productive strategies for ameliorating the complex and interconnected problems created by the structural inequalities faced by many Black citizens residing in economically disadvantaged communities.

Overview of the Book

I begin by focusing on police interactions with civilians. Chapter 1 examines the crossroads of race and policing as they have developed historically; it outlines the history of differential policing by reporting the purpose, consequences, and effects of slave patrols, Slave Codes, Black Codes, and Jim Crow laws. I also highlight how the systemic culture of oppression continued into the twenty-first century, illustrating that race coupled with community context shapes residents' experiences with, and ultimately attitudes toward, the police.

In chapter 2, I analyze how race and place shape police interactions, focusing specifically on direct and indirect experiences that residents had with police within their neighborhood prior to the deaths of Brown and Gray. This chapter notes both favorable and unfavorable encounters that Black and White residents have had with White officers, highlighting problematic policies and practices with police organizations. I call attention to racially biased policing in the neighborhoods of Ferguson and Baltimore, which led to the harassment and assaults of many young Black males. The chapter concludes by accounting for how residents' experiences with the police shape attitudes toward law enforcement.

Chapter 3 shifts attention from officers in general to Black officers specifically. It focuses in particular on residents' perceptions of and experiences with Black officers in Ferguson, Baltimore, and elsewhere prior to Brown's and Gray's deaths. While many commentators have proposed that hiring more Black officers would be an effective way to alleviate long-standing tension between police and Black citizens, I argue that a shared racial background in and of itself does not guarantee positive police interaction and that Black citizens can be very dissatisfied with Black officers. My findings suggest that the issue is not exclusively about the race of police officers but about the nature of police organizations and how they systematically police poor communities of color.

In the second half of the book, I shift attention from encounters with police prior to Brown's and Gray's deaths to experiences of participation in protest events. Chapter 4 provides insight into community mobilization efforts by activists. Protesters in Ferguson and Baltimore demonstrated for months in the aftermath of Brown's and Gray's deaths, many for the first time. This chapter accounts for the reasons that protesters came out in large numbers and what they hoped to accomplish, illustrating that Black activists' negative experiences with and perceptions of the police served as a starting point to participation in activism.

Chapter 5 builds from the findings in chapters 2 and 3 to focus on protesters' interactions with police, who used a range of repressive tactics while handling protests in both Ferguson and Baltimore. I concentrate on individual protesters who joined the movement with various degrees of commitment, and I examine their experiences with, and perceptions of, protest policing, as well as how such interactions shape future activism in the group.[51] The most involved and committed protesters vowed to engage in future activist efforts even after experiencing high levels of repressive police action, while, for those who were less committed, oppressive tactics by police appeared to serve as a deterrent.

Finally, chapter 6 provides an explanation for how the Ferguson and Baltimore uprisings ignited and gained nationwide attention. This chapter illustrates the complex set of social, cultural, and political factors that led to these outbreaks of public unrest in Ferguson and Baltimore, and the various conditions that can lead to subsequent uprisings in other cities.

1

Race and Policing

The More Things Change, the More They Remain the Same

Those who cannot remember the past are condemned
to repeat it.
—George Santayana, *Reason in Common Sense*

Beginning in the seventeenth century, slave traders kidnapped and enslaved millions of Africans and shipped them across the Atlantic like cattle. Not only were Blacks stolen from their homelands, but they were also made to work for no wages. The racialized caste system of American slavery originated in the Portuguese and Spanish colonies in which slaves were indentured servants—individuals who could be freed after working for a set period of time.[1] When the first Africans were brought to Jamestown, Virginia, they held the status of "servant."[2] However, as the region's economic system became dependent on forced labor, the institution of slavery in the United Stated hardened into a permanent status linked to race and lineage.[3] The goal was to create a legal structure to build an economy with cheap slave labor as its foundation.[4] Violence was a daily part of being a slave; these individuals endured horrendous conditions and were subject to physical, verbal, sexual, emotional, and psychological abuse. Historian David Baker has described the torturous punishment that African men and women suffered: "Planters often branded, stabbed, tarred and feathered, burned, shackled, tortured, maimed, mutilated, crippled, whipped, hanged, beat, and castrated slaves."[5] Racial subjugation is tied to White supremacy: a worldview declaring White superiority and Black inferiority, the racist ideology that birthed the racial hierarchy resulting in the enslavement of Africans in the New World.[6] The basis of White supremacy was the belief that Blacks were innately subordinate to Whites, and this ideology has continued to the present day. Racial oppression has merely changed forms.

The militarization of police to control protesters in Ferguson, Missouri, in 2014 and Baltimore, Maryland, in 2015 conjures up searing images of White demonstrators during the 1960s Civil Rights Movement (e.g., hosing down Black people with water, firing shots at and setting dogs on them, and even killing them), suggesting that the legacy of these attitudes is alive and well.[7]

The relationship between Blacks and law enforcement has been contentious throughout America's history. While informal police mechanisms originated in the colonial period, the origins of policing in the United States can be traced to the institution of slavery, when officers subjugated Black individuals through formal and informal mechanisms of surveillance and criminalization. Faced with the threat of slave insurrection and the chronic problem of slaves fleeing captivity, many state legislatures in the South in the 1700s passed restrictive laws controlling and regulating the movement of slaves through what was known as "slave patrol."[8] Such patrols, charged with catching, beating, and returning escaped slaves, were among the first state-sponsored police forces in the United States.[9] Imposing racially biased laws, slave patrollers were authorized to enter slaves' homes with impunity to ensure that slaves were not carrying any weapons, conducting meetings, learning to read or write, or committing criminal offenses.[10] Slave patrollers were allowed a free hand to control and dominate the slave population by restricting Blacks to certain places and monitoring their behaviors within them. The legal behavior not only approved but "sustained slavery, segregation, and discrimination for most of our Nation's history—and the fact that the police were bound to uphold that order—set a pattern for police behavior and attitudes toward minority communities that has persisted until the present day."[11]

To defend their slave property interests, Slave Codes were established and enforced by all segments of the White community. Slave Codes were state laws that defined the status of slaves and the rights of their owners, giving them absolute power to govern their slaves as chattel or property. These laws prohibited slaves from pursing a wide range of activities in which Whites were generally free to participate.[12] For example, all Whites, including slave patrollers, were conferred unlimited authority to regulate the movement of slaves and had unlimited discretion to search their lodges, break up their organized meetings, punish runaways traveling without an appropriate pass, and apprehend any slave suspected of committing criminal offenses, which led to mistrust of the police among Blacks.[13] The slave patrols constituted the most crucial component of the policing of Black bodies and served as constant reminders of slaves' inferior status.

During the early period of Reconstruction (1865–67), Southern Whites found themselves in a peculiar dilemma when the Thirteenth Amendment outlawed the institution of slavery in 1865. On the one hand, White Southerners were aware that the end of slavery could result in the collapse of the region's economy, given that slave owners were wholly dependent on Black labor to sustain economic life.[14] On the other hand, the abolition of slavery meant that for White Southerners there was no formal system in place to maintain a racial hierarchy.[15] In an effort to return Blacks to their "proper place" in society, states relied on the legal and prison system to create policies to maintain racial subordination and economically exploit emancipated Black people.[16]

The "Black Codes" were a legal tool used to control Blacks and maintain the ideology of White supremacy. Passed in 1865–66, Black Codes were criminal laws that created new offenses, such as "loitering" and "vagrancy," punishable by fines, imprisonment, and forced labor for up to one year. Many Southern states adopted vagrancy laws, making it a criminal offense not to work. Designed to regulate free Blacks and establish another system of forced labor, these discriminatory laws were applied selectively to Blacks to force them to accept employment, mostly in the sharecropping system.[17] This legal version of slavery extended the control and policing of Blacks by criminalizing what was perceived as unproductive behavior. Black Codes opened up a market for convict leasing, in which people in prison were contracted out as laborers to the highest private bidder for state profit. Relying on language in the Thirteenth Amendment that outlawed slavery and involuntary servitude "except as a punishment for crime whereof the party shall have been duly convicted," policymakers authorized the White-controlled government to lease Black individuals in prison to commercial hands.[18] Blacks who were convicted found themselves enslaved to the companies that they were leased out to, as these companies had absolute control over them.[19] Company guards had the authority to "chain prisoners, shoot those attempting to flee, torture any who wouldn't submit, and whip the disobedient—naked or clothed—almost without limit."[20] While Black people were rarely imprisoned during the era of slavery, criminalization had become the resolution for dealing with freed Blacks. Leased Black convicts faced appalling conditions; they were routinely starved and brutalized by companies, government officials, and businessmen seeking to achieve a profitable balance between the production of forced labor and the cost of sustaining them.[21] In his book *Race, Crime, and the Law*, legal scholar Randall Kennedy contends:

> When Whites had no pressing need for Black workers, Negros were permitted to move about freely to wring from the labor market whatever wages they could command. When Whites needed Black workers, however, law enforcement officials, reinforced by a panoply of byzantine statutes, limited competition for labor, deprived Negros of freedom of movement, coerced them into labor agreements, criminalized breach of contract, and compelled Black convicts to work off their "debt to society" by laboring for White employers at rock-bottom prices.[22]

Under these deplorable conditions, leased prisoners were subject to cruel and harsh treatment, and thousands lost their lives.[23] Historian David Oshinski wrote that before convict leasing was legally terminated, "a generation of black prisoners would suffer and die under conditions far worse than anything they had ever experienced as slaves."[24]

Passed by a political system in which Blacks did not have a voice, the Black Codes were enforced by all-White police and state militia forces across the South to ensure the "continued subordination of Black labor to White economic power."[25] On the whole, both Black Codes and vagrancy laws controlled the movement of freed slaves and provided justification for incarcerating them. Even after the Civil War and formal codification of emancipation, White supremacy remained deeply rooted.

During Reconstruction, the Black Codes were eventually overturned, as the nature of the codes were opposed by many in the North who contended that the codes violated the principle of free labor. As a result, Blacks saw some significant advancement during the Reconstruction era. After nearly 250 years of enslavement, slavery was abolished under the Thirteenth Amendment in 1865; Blacks were recognized as full citizens under the passage of the Civil Rights Act of 1866; Blacks were given "equal protection of the laws" in 1868, based on the Fourteenth Amendment; and in 1870 Black men were provided the right to vote based on the Fifteenth Amendment.[26]

Blacks experienced notable economic and political development during this time period, but the increase in political power and social and economic independence was accompanied by a severe backlash. Support for Reconstruction policies diminished after it was undermined by White supremacist organizations, such as the Ku Klux Klan (KKK), which often worked closely with—and was occupied by—local police.[27] In an attempt to preserve control over Black citizens, the KKK fought against Reconstruction governments and leaders, relying on bombs, mob violence, and lynchings to achieve their mission.[28] In fact, the Klan and the police—who often condoned and even participated in lynchings during Reconstruction—often worked together to actively support White supremacy.[29] Consequently, not only did federal troops withdraw from the South, thereby abandoning Blacks and others who fought for racial equality, but the federal government also stopped enforcing civil rights legislation.[30]

When the Black Codes came under legal attack, Southern states pursued racial segregation in an attempt to ensure White supremacy and Black subordination. The proliferation of Jim Crow—a term derived from a minstrel show character—grew out of economic crisis, political opportunism, and racial fear, which regulated the nature of interracial social contact.[31] Jim Crow referred to the various state laws that established different rules for Blacks and Whites in Southern and border states between 1877 and the mid-1960s. Under Jim Crow, Blacks were relegated to the status of second-class citizens, which touched every part of life: schools, housing, jobs, churches, restaurants, hospitals, hotels, restrooms, funeral homes, prisons, and virtually all other public spaces were completely segregated. Formal police departments were responsible for maintaining—and vigorously imposed—racial inequality throughout the South.[32]

The contentious relationship between police and Blacks reached a boiling point at the height of the Civil Rights Era (1954–1968), as the devastating effects of discrimination and racism continued despite the abolishment of slavery. The Civil Rights Movement, especially the Selma to Montgomery march, highlighted deeply entrenched racist policy and the role police played in maintaining discriminatory laws. Blacks, along with many Whites, mobilized to fight for social justice to gain equal rights under the law; however, with the rise of the Civil Rights Movement came more repressive policing.[33] Police in the South threatened and beat protesters, made discriminatory arrests, and failed to protect activists from violent mobs. As the movement grew more militant, it was subject to more repressive tactics. For instance, groups, most notably the Black Panthers, attracted increasing police surveillance, as the FBI sought to repress, dismantle, and discredit the movement.[34]

The legacy of slavery and dominance over Black bodies in the United States is deeply rooted and continues to affect Blacks' experiences with the police and the criminal justice system. From slave patrols and Slave Codes to Black Codes and Jim Crow laws, racially biased formal legislation was enforced for nearly 250 years. While it seems as though slavery was long ago, Black Americans were enslaved in the United States longer than they have been free—many Americans are only two to three generations removed from slavery. Blacks have endured a legacy of vicious assaults, the effects of which linger in the present day. Understanding the centrality of race in the formation and organization of policing is necessary for getting a clear picture of contemporary police practices toward racial minorities. As primary enforcers of the law, the police were in charge of upholding and enforcing racially discriminatory laws. Historically, Blacks were not viewed as citizens in need of protection but rather treated as objects of social control that were routinely surveilled by the police.[35] That current police practice may operate in the same way is not lost on Blacks, as many perceive that the police serve an oppressive function.[36] We will see how both race and community context thus shape residents' experiences with—and, ultimately, attitudes toward—the police.

Contemporary Perspectives on Race, Place, and Policing

Residents of economically distressed neighborhoods are at substantial risk of coming into direct or indirect contact with law enforcement. Negative views of the police can best be understood by taking into consideration the nature of policing in predominately Black neighborhoods.[37] Research shows that policing styles vary by location and that urban Black males are often the targets of aggressive police patrol practices and excessive use of force.[38] Police officers often face conditions in which they have limited information and available time to make decisions, resulting in their development of a "perceptual shorthand." This shorthand generally relies on stereotypical assessments of dangerousness and blameworthiness based on race, gender, and age, which cues suspicion and motivates decisions as to whom to search.[39] Such judgments can be influenced by racial typification of crime—the extent to which people associate crime with Blacks.[40] In fact, some researchers suggest that the term "criminal predator" is a euphemism for young Black males.[41] Too often, Black males are viewed as "symbolic assailants" who may represent danger to the police and the community.[42]

Consequently, Black male youths are often stigmatized and perceived by officers as suspicious. Several studies show that police are more likely to stop Blacks than Whites. For instance, in 1994 the problem of disproportionate traffic stops against Black drivers was brought to light in *State of New Jersey v. Pedro Soto,* in which the Black defendant claimed that he was stopped because of his ethnicity. Racial profiling expert John Lambert served as an expert witness. Using rigorous statistical analysis of the racial distribution of traffic stops in New Jersey, Lambert found that 73.2 percent of those stopped and arrested along the turnpike over a 3.5 year period were Black—making them 16.5 times more likely to be arrested than others. He concluded that the New Jersey State Police stop, investigate, and arrest Black motorists at rates significantly disproportionate to the percentage of Blacks in the traveling population. Recently, in their analysis of 20 million traffic stops in North Carolina, public policy scholars Frank Baumgartner, Derek Epp, and Kelsey Shoub found that young Black men in the state are the primary targets of racially disparate policing. It is well established that racial minorities are disproportionately more likely to be stopped, questioned, and arrested than Whites, suggesting that stops by the police are more likely for Blacks as a result of the race-based suspicion that is a persistent pattern of police conduct.[43]

In its seminal decision in *Terry v. Ohio* in 1968, the US Supreme Court ruled that police officers are permitted to stop, interrogate, and, under appropriate circumstances (i.e., where there is reasonable signs of potential danger), perform a "pat down" of detainees' outer clothing, provided that the officer can articulate a reasonable basis for the stop-and-frisk.[44] The court thereby set a precedent giving police formal authority to stop citizens on the street based on a standard of proof less than probable cause and to conduct pat-down searches of those citizens they stop. The effect of this ruling has been that a disproportionate number of Black individuals have been stopped and frisked by police.

While the court in *Terry v. Ohio* permitted officers to give a pat down based on suspicion rather than probable cause, in *Whren v. US* in 1996 the court declared that police can use traffic stops to investigate their suspicions even if those suspicions are unrelated to traffic enforcement and if there is no evidence of criminal activity by the driver upon which to base those suspicions. The court conceded that police could stop a motorist for virtually any reason. However, the reality is that the vast majority of drivers are unable to avoid violating some minor traffic law. On any given day, most motorists fail to signal or make a complete stop, or they drive with a malfunctioning piece of vehicle equipment, touch a lane or center line, drive too fast or too slow, or fail to display license tags and required stickers in the proper place.[45] Any minor traffic violation can support a stop and any citizen is fair game.[46] However, police use traffic codes to stop a disproportionate number of racial minorities. In *Whren*, it is constitutional to use traffic infractions as a pretext for a stop whose real motive is to discover evidence of criminal activity—no matter how minor—unrelated to the traffic violation. A consequence of the Whren decision is that police have greater leeway in using traffic laws as they please to target certain individuals. These pretextual police stops of Blacks occur so frequently that many complain about being pulled over for "driving while black."[47]

In fact, in their pivotal analysis of the causes, experiences, and effects of discriminatory police stops, scholars Charles Epp, Steven Maynard-Moody, and Donald Haider-Markel noted that it is necessary to distinguish between routine traffic stops and investigatory stops.[48] In routine traffic stops, officers target motorists who have violated traffic laws. In these stops, officers punish egregious violators (i.e., running a red light, speeding, driving while under the influence) regardless of race. Here, the driving behavior determines who is subject to these stops. On the other hand, with investigatory stops, the goal is not to enforce traffic safety laws but rather to investigate the driver with the hopes of finding evidence of a crime. Blacks are subject to a significantly higher number of such investigatory stops, which by their nature are both intrusive and punitive. Since racial minorities experience more investigatory stops, they experience being searched, handcuffed, and interrogated at a far higher rate than Whites, who are more likely to experience conventional traffic-safety stops. Consequently, Epp and colleagues argue that since investigatory stops are common, routine, and frequent among Black people, Blacks' full citizenship is denied, resulting in feelings of distrust and cynicism toward police and the criminal justice system.

While the police can catch some criminally involved individuals through the use of pretext stops, a significant number of innocent people are affected by such practices. According to law professor David Harris:

> The victims are easy to identify because they are the great majority of black people who are subjected to these humiliating and difficult experiences but who have done absolutely nothing to deserve this treatment—except to resemble, in a literally skin-deep way, a small group of criminals.[49]

Although police cannot say that race was the reason for a stop, it is constitutional for them to say it was based on some other reason. Consequently, many police use race—Blackness—as an indicator of criminal propensities.[50] The fact that police stop a disproportionate number of Black motorists because a small number of them are criminals means that skin color, not behavior, is used as evidence of wrongdoing. As a result, Blackness is criminalized and every member of this racial group is viewed by law enforcement as a potential suspect.[51]

Not only do officers rely on various cues to define a so-called suspicious person; evidence suggests that they may also apply a similar perceptual framework around geographic space. That is, police define areas of concentrated disadvantage with large minority populations as "bad areas" that comprise a large number of suspicious people and activity.[52] To underscore this point, sociologists Carl Werthman and Irving Piliavin suggested that "past experience leads [officers] to conclude that more crimes are committed in the poorer sections of town than in the wealthier areas, that [Blacks] are more likely to cause public disturbances than Whites, and that adolescents in certain areas are a greater source of trouble than other categories of the citizenry."[53] Werthman and Piliavin refer to this process as "ecological contamination," whereby police view residents of these impoverished neighborhoods with greater suspicion than residents of affluent communities. Essentially, the socioeconomic status of the neighborhood where the police encounter the suspect may be ascribed to the individual regardless of his or her personal character-istics or behavior. In fact, a suspect's mere presence in lower-class and high-crime areas increases the chance that the he or she will become the target of police surveillance, aggression, and arrests.[54] Since Blacks are more likely to reside in poor, high-crime neighborhoods, they have increased contact with the police, which intensifies the opportunity for conflict between police and citizens.[55]

Some suggest that both race and concentrated disadvantage are related to perceptions of dangerous places and that large urban Black commu-nities remain highly segregated and face extreme racial isolation.[56] Even with the passage of *Brown v. Board of Education* in 1954, when the Su-preme Court declared it unconstitutional to racially segregate Black and White students in public schools, US neighborhoods continue to be ra-cially segregated, and Blacks live in areas with the most concentrated dis-advantage.[57] The 2010 US Census reveals that the average Black civilian who lived in a metropolitan area resided in a neighborhood that was only 35 percent White and as much as 45 percent Black, while Whites lived in neighborhoods that were 75 percent White and only 8 percent Black.[58] Large urban Black communities remain highly segregated, and they face extreme racial isolation.[59] Additionally, nonmetropolitan areas are in-creasingly segregated.[60] In fact, noted race scholars Douglas Massey and Nancy Denton assert that Blacks often face conditions of hypersegregation in that they are more likely to experience unevenness (the degree to which Blacks reside across communities), isolation (the unlikelihood of Blacks sharing neighborhoods with Whites), clustering (the degree to which Blacks live adjacent to one another), concentration (the amount of physi-cal space inhabited by Blacks), and centralization (the degree to which Blacks reside in and around the urban center).[61] Interestingly, of the segre-gated metropolitan areas in the United States, St. Louis and Baltimore are two of the forty areas nationwide that are persistently hypersegregated—defined as when many Blacks live in poor, densely packed neighborhoods near the urban core and isolated from the larger society.[62]

Scholars such as Massey and Denton have argued that the urban ghetto—which has become an endemic intersection of race and class—replaced slavery and Jim Crow to suppress and control Black populations.[63] The ghetto emerged as a colonial space because racism coupled with the political economy resulted in the systematic marginalization of Blacks to poor, crime-ridden neighborhoods.[64] Unemployment, poverty, drugs, violence, and crime often characterize economically distressed neighborhoods.[65] Consequently, sociologist Robert Blauner asserted, "the establishment of the urban ghetto subsequently gave rise to conditions that justified the 'forced, involuntary entry' of the police into these spaces."[66]

Several studies have shown that concentrated disadvantage in the neighborhood is associated with diminished satisfaction with police and reduced perceptions of police legitimacy.[67] Such neighborhoods, which are characterized by high rates of poverty and joblessness, often lack institutional resources that are critical to produce social ties and protective mechanisms among residents, which results in increased levels of crime, particularly violent crime.[68] As a consequence of the social ills that many Blacks encounter, some young Black males residing in disadvantaged neighborhoods reject mainstream values and adopt an oppositional cultural attitude that is conducive to violence to protect their self-image and establish and maintain respect.[69]

Nevertheless, not everyone who resides in distressed areas where violence is common endorses the use or threat of violence.[70] Even though direct personal contact with law enforcement is often what shapes attitudes toward the police, research suggest that vicarious experiences also play a role. These indirect police contacts can be internalized and used as information about how police will interact with citizens during subsequent encounters.[71] To the extent that police encounters are negative, such information can erode the reputation and legitimacy of police.[72] For example, in their examination of the effects of direct and indirect police experiences on attitudes toward the police, policing scholar Dennis Rosenbaum and his colleagues found that the effects of negative vicarious interactions were greatest for Black participants and lowest for White participants.[73] They also found racial differences regarding how citizens obtained vicarious negative information. Asked about the source of their good and bad information about the police,

White residents reported learning about adverse vicarious information with the police primarily through the media; however, Blacks and Latinos were more apt to receive such reports from people in their immediate environment, such as family members and neighbors. These findings coincide with sociologists Ronald Wetizer and Steven Tuch's study on public perceptions of racial profiling, which showed that Blacks were more likely than Whites to report being profiled and having adverse interactions with police. Hence, Black individuals would be more likely to know someone who has been racially profiled than Whites, who would rely on media accounts of such profiling. It is the cumulative effect of negative police experiences that explain Blacks' less favorable attitudes toward the police.[74]

All of the research discussed so far suggest that there is a great deal of difference between Black and White citizens' perceptions of the legitimacy and fairness of police, and it has not changed over time. This book focuses on police-citizens relations in two distinct cities that were the sites of nationally profiled deadly police shootings. This book does the important work of highlighting how historical racial oppression connects to Black people's contemporary perceptions and experiences with police, which led to deep-seated grievances with law enforcement and ultimately motivated unprecedented protests that underscored the sharp racial divide in America. Maya Angelou wrote that "history, despite its wrenching pain, cannot be unlived, but if faced with courage, need not be lived again." These words underscore the power of justice and equality and remind us that if we are to ever make further progress as a nation, we need to understand history and the consequences of the decisions that were made so as not to repeat it. Connecting contemporary events to history allows us not only to understand their significance but also to recognize patterns of racist acts. Linking the past to the present shows which bodies have been considered dispensable in the past and which continue to be expendable through different legal, social, and cultural moments. In the aftermath of two high-profile cases in Ferguson and Baltimore, this book makes historical and contemporary linkages in order to better understand the racialized experiences of Black people in this country and how they are generally perceived and treated by individuals and institutions.

2

"Guilty Until Proven Innocent"

Life under Suspicion

> We were playing basketball and minding our business. [The
> police] came down the street—two of them in the car—of
> course [they were] White. . . . They said something or what-
> ever like, "Hey, get out of the street." And [my friend] just
> looked at them or whatever and I guess they felt some type
> of way about him just staring at them. . . . They did a U-
> turn and everything. They got out of the car, grabbed him,
> slammed him all over the hood, and said "What are you
> looking at?". . . . I'm like "Hey, what you all doing? You all
> being too rough". . . . The guy turned around, he said "Hey,
> you shut the F up."
> —Kevin (Black Ferguson resident)

Reports from the DOJ legitimized what Black residents have long
known to be true: that they were often systematically targeted in investigatory traffic stops. As part of an ongoing inquiry into the killing
of Michael Brown, the DOJ published a searing report documenting
racial bias by Ferguson law enforcement.[1] Based on its finding that
court fines and fees for traffic violations and petty offenses by primarily
poor, Black citizens served as a means of generating revenue to fund
the city government—a practice that was aggressively promoted by
city officials—the DOJ's Civil Rights Division argued that Ferguson's
Municipal Court's procedures:

> are constitutionally deficient and function to impede a person's ability
> to challenge or resolve a municipal charge, resulting in unnecessarily
> prolonged cases and an increased likelihood of running afoul of court
> requirements. At the same time, the court imposes severe penalties when

a defendant fails to meet court requirements, including added fines and fees and arrest warrants that are unnecessary and run counter to public safety.[2]

In 2013, the city harvested approximately $2.6 million in municipal court fines, accounting for 20 percent of Ferguson's operating revenue.[3] To ensure collection of these fees, Ferguson issued a high rate of arrest warrants—specifically, approximately 1,500 warrants per 1,000 individuals in 2013, which was four times the rate for the city of St. Louis.[4] Studies show that, after being stopped in Ferguson, Black motorists were nearly two times as likely as Whites to be searched (12.1 percent vs. 6.9 percent) and twice as likely to be arrested (10.4 percent vs. 5.2 percent).[5] Moreover, these findings contradict the notion that searches of Black individuals in particular produce contraband; in fact, they resulted in the discovery of contraband 21.7 percent of the time, while similar searches of Whites resulted in the discovery of contraband 34 percent of the time.[6]

Similarly, the DOJ found that for years the BPD engaged in a pattern of conduct that violates the Constitution and federal anti-discrimination law.[7] The DOJ's blistering report revealed that from January 2010 to May 2015 BPD officers recorded 300,000 pedestrian stops. These stops, which were concentrated in Black neighborhoods, often lacked a rationale, as only 3.7 percent of the stops resulted in officers issuing a citation or making an arrest. The report also revealed that unjustifiable arrests were not uncommon. Local prosecutors rejected eleven thousand charges during this period because they either lacked probable cause or did not merit prosecution.[8] Just as disturbing is recent body camera evidence that suggests that officers from the BPD have planted drugs.[9] Although BPD activation policy requires that cameras be turned on during investigative stops, examination of the footage has revealed clear violations of this policy.[10]

In this chapter, I turn my attention to the accounts of Black and White residents of Ferguson and Baltimore and examine both their adverse and favorable interactions with and perceptions of police.[11] Not only did study participants draw from their own personal experiences in their appraisals, but those of their family, friends, and neighbors.[12] Throughout the chapter, I pay special attention to how these residents interpret and make sense of their complex relationships with police. We will see, in later chapters, how their encounters with police have motivated protest participation.

Residents' Experiences with and Perceptions of Local Police

This chapter analyzes 218 personal and vicarious police incident descriptions.[13] Table 2.1 provides an account of these experiences among residents, across race, in both cities. Negative police interactions were reported much more frequently than positive interactions. During the interview, I asked study participants what experiences they had with police and whether they would classify them as negative or positive. Of the people who had experiences with police, 148 negative police incidents were described, followed by 68 positive interactions, and 2 neutral accounts.[14] Just over half of the personal police incidents in Ferguson and Baltimore were negative.[15] Vicarious accounts were all negative in nature except for one incident reported in Ferguson and a handful in Baltimore. When race is taken into account, we see that incidents reported by Black participants were more than six times as likely to be negative personal encounters with police compared to incidents reported by Whites in Ferguson, and incidents reported by Black participants were slightly more likely to be negative in Baltimore.[16] However,

TABLE 2.1. Personal and Vicarious Experiences among Black and White Residents

| | Ferguson | | | Baltimore | | | |
	Black	White	Other	Black	White	Other	Total
Personal							
Positive	13	7	0	25	16	2	63
Neutral	0	0	0	0	2	0	2
Negative	40	1	0	37	12	2	92
Vicarious							
Positive	1	0	0	2	2	0	5
Neutral	0	0	0	0	0	0	0
Negative	25	2	0	22	5	2	56

TABLE 2.2. Negative Experiences with and Perceptions of Police Officers among Ferguson and Baltimore Residents

	Ferguson			Baltimore		
	Black	White	Other	Black	White	Other
Racial Profiling	31	0	0	14	2	1
Police Discourtesy	10	0	0	14	4	1
Aggressive Policing	19	1	0	22	3	0
Police Are Dismissive	0	0	0	1	5	1
Police Escalate Situations	0	0	0	2	1	0
Police Misconduct	2	1	1	0	0	0
Police Are Distrustful	1	0	0	1	1	0
Arrested after Calling Police	3	0	0	0	0	0
Slow Response	0	0	0	2	0	0
Wrongly Accused	0	0	0	1	0	1

incidents described by Whites were more than three times as likely as those described by Blacks to involve positive police encounters in Ferguson and incidents described by Whites were somewhat more likely to be seen as positive than those described by Blacks in Baltimore. While I report on the kinds of patterns that the study uncovered, it is important to note that my findings are not generalizable beyond the sample. Nonetheless, the strength of the patterns is suggestive of meaningful differences across racial groups and sites.[17]

As table 2.2 shows, residents reported a number of negative incidents with their local police agency. Common themes included aggressive policing, the widespread use of stop-and-frisks among Black males, discourteous officers, and unfavorable treatment of Black women. Study participants detailed accounts of direct and indirect experiences with heavy-handed policing practices, which undermined police legitimacy in the eyes of neighborhood residents.

Negative Police Encounters

AGGRESSIVE POLICING
In this study, 30 percent of negative police interactions were described as being overly aggressive and/or physically violent. Of those who reported

such police interaction, forty-one were Black and four were White. Julius, a Black Baltimorean, asserted that the police are "real aggressive for no real reason." Others described police acting aggressively toward male residents in high-crime neighborhoods. For example, Arnold, a White resident from Baltimore, complained that, because he lived in an area known for drug use, the police assume that "you're a druggie. They come up and just start at 10 instead of asking you, what you doing here calmly. They're screaming right out—they come out right with the aggression first." And Tray, a Black Ferguson resident, recalled:

> [The police] walk[ed] right into my house before and we weren't even the ones that gave them the call. They just came into our house with guns armed and everything. My daughter answered the door. . . . Ferguson had got a call; they thought it was at our apartment building. They came to the house with guns armed drawn on my daughter and basically they found out that we weren't the ones that made the call and I guess they rushed to the next apartment over.

Likewise, Rasheed, a Black Baltimorean, also recollected:

> [The police] bang[ed] on the door at three in the morning and I'm like, "What the hell is going on?" And they'd be like, "Hey is so and so here?" And we're like, "Who are you talking about?". . . . [L]ong story short they went to the wrong address. . . . The [officer] I actually spoke to was super aggressive . . . it was like, its three a.m. and you're knocking on my door and you're like telling me to go back inside the house or whatever.

Though officers are not immune from making mistakes, neither Tray nor Rasheed reported that the police apologized for their blunder, which contributed to their negative perceptions of police.

In addition, twenty study participants, eighteen of whom were Black, also made allegations of physical abuse by police. Some reported accusations or threats of physical abuse, even though they were not involved in criminal activity. For instance, while walking in a high-crime neighborhood with a male friend and his wife, "the police just pulled up . . . on the opposite side of the street . . . [and said] 'Get on the ground,'" stated Justin, a Black Baltimorean. He explained:

JUSTIN: So my buddy had an empty beer can in a bag, crushed. He's walking down the street, and I heard the police again say, "Get on the ground." And I'm looking back, and saying, "He's not really talking to me is he?" And so I stopped. He said, "If I tell you to get on the ground again, I'm going to shoot you in the back." A White policeman. I said, "Okay, he's talking to me." So I stopped. I've never been through this. So he's like "Get on the ground". . . . I got on my knees and . . . he says, "No, get on the ground." So I'm like, "What do you mean?" He said, "Get on the ground." It's like, it came to me. Get. On. The ground.

INTERVIEWER: Yeah, okay. So you initially went on the ground with your knees?

JUSTIN: Yes.

INTERVIEWER: And then he kept yelling, get on the ground—meaning lay on the ground.

JUSTIN: [The officer said] "If I tell you again, I'm going to shoot you in your back." So I got on the ground, completely. Stretched out, it was cold, it was wintertime, I'll never forget. And I laid face down . . . And next thing I know, a paddy wagon was pulling up—which is the van. . . . And he tells my buddy, "I'm locking you three up for drinking beer in public." He's like, "We're not drinking beer in public." He says, "This is an empty beer can." He said, "I was going to throw it in that trash can, which was across the street." He's not that type to just throw it on the ground. . . . I'm standing there handcuffed, so— I'm mad at this point, and I did the worse thing I could've [done]. I talked back. Now I said, "Why would you want to lock up a man for drinking? I didn't know the law here in Baltimore [said] that you can't walk down the street with a beer." I said, "I don't drink first of all, but why would you want to lock him up for having a beer?" [The police officer] said "Shut up, you just think you're a smart-ass". . . . Long and short, I think that's why they locked me up, because I was talking back, trying to find out.

Despite the fact that Justin and his friends reported not drinking, they were arrested and sent to jail; however, thirty-six hours later, they were released. Justin later learned from an officer that they were stopped because they were in a high-crime neighborhood. And Oscar, a Black male, stated that Baltimore police tend to "get a little carried away because of the power that they have on the community. I don' seen people get slammed on the head with handcuffs tied behind they back for no reason."

Also, according to Maurice, when Ferguson police were looking for his brother they "grabbed me by the neck and threw me down . . . [and] were hitting my face." Likewise, Montel, a Black male, noted that the BPD "stopped me with a quote unquote 'something's wrong with the tags.' One thing led to another, and I'm getting body slammed on my face" by the police. Though Montel was charged with disorderly conduct, resisting arrest, and attempted evading and eluding a police officer, he said the charges were "bullsh*t" and the "case [was] dismissed." Nevertheless, the incident of physical assault from the police left a permanent scar on the side of his face. For residents of Baltimore and Ferguson, a law-abiding status did not protect them from physical abuse by law enforcement. Aggressive crime control strategies were particularly salient among Black males in both communities. As a result, it was not hard for many Ferguson and Baltimore residents to believe that Brown's and Gray's deaths were the result of aggressive policing tactics.

While some residents described having been the victim of physical assault when they were abiding by the law, study participants also experienced police abuse when they were caught engaging in illicit activities. Some acknowledged that police typically resorted to violence to gain compliance; however, they complained, that force was still excessive. For example, Julius, a Black Baltimore resident, described a serious beating he took after running from officers who suspected he was selling drugs: "I was, you know, hustling, selling drugs. . . . I was walking and they jumped out. . . . I ran . . . And they caught me in an alley, and was kicking me and stuff like that. And [they were] looking for drugs . . . and they hit me with the flashlight after I was handcuffed." And Darnell, a Black resident from Ferguson, described how he and his friend were beaten by officers when they were fifteen years old:

I used to play basketball at the park down there . . . it was about to be after hours at the park. . . . [The police officer] pulled up and they like, "Y'all guys got to go." We're like, "All right, all right". . . . So he pulls off. . . . [But] we [had] just started a whole new game [and decided] we'll leave after this game. . . . [The officer] comes back. [He says] "Didn't I tell you motherf*ckers," you know, cussing at us and stuff, "Get the f*ck out, you guys need to leave". . . . [My friend] throw[s] the rock at his car, he comes back, calls another squad car, there's about six of us and they just whooped on all of us. . . . They hit me in my face once, my ribs twice saying you all need to get on. . . . That's the only time they ever really you know, roughed me up real bad like that.

And, after learning he had a warrant, Jaquann, a Black Baltimorean, turned himself in at the police station at 2:30 a.m.:

[The police] walked me all the way to the back where the booking place [is] . . . where they hold you at, without no handcuffs on. And once I got back there, they asked me to turn around. I turned around, they tried to put some handcuffs on me, I was like, "Why you putting handcuffs on me? I thought you were just going to put me in a holding cell, and send me on by my way." They slapped me down to the ground, and two other officers came in, and they was kicking me and all that type of stuff. They still hit me with resisting arrest, and a third-degree assault on a police, and I didn't even touch the police.

Although Jaquann did not specify why police had a warrant out for his arrest, unserved warrants often originate from traffic or civil cases, violations of probation or parole, or other, noncriminal infractions such as local ordinance violations.

Darryl, a Black male, described a more serious beating that took place at the Ferguson police station:

I mean, I got locked [up] by them before where they beat me up, man, when I had a seizure. Wrapped my face up and when I woke up out of the seizure I had a spit bag [device intended to prevent someone from spitting] on my face. . . . When they released me to the hospital I still had active warrants. . . . [When] I came back to file a complaint they locked me up again . . . and I got assaulted again. . . . I had knots on my head when I got out of there.

Although four Black residents in the study who were physically abused while engaging in criminal behavior admitted their guilt, they also indicated the inappropriate behavior of the arresting officers. In particular, participants expressed that, despite their participation in illegal activities, they expected officers would perform their tasks within the boundaries of the law. While the vast majority of accounts of police encounters were experienced in contexts that did not involve crime, those residents who were engaged in illicit activity appeared to face even more severe forms of police assault. These accounts coincide with reports from the DOJ in both Ferguson and Baltimore that revealed a pattern of excessive force used disproportionately against Black residents and in violation of the Fourth Amendment.[18]

A few Black women reported having experienced police aggression. Rosalind, a Ferguson resident, explained an incident with an officer: "I called a police [officer] one time. I had a dispute with a neighbor and [the police] just came to fight, they didn't come to ask questions. . . . Knocked at my door, just grabbed me out the house . . . and beat [me] up." Police aggression was more likely to occur when women defied gender norms. For instance, Helen, a Baltimorean resident, recalled a case involving police brutality that she learned about when serving for jury duty: "It was a Black woman and it was a White police officer. . . . She was very small. She was 4'11, 100 pounds and he was just rough with her . . . [after] she was cursing and she was getting loud. . . . [So] he [the officer] snapped, broke her arm at the elbow." Young girls were also not necessarily exempt from experiencing police violence. Shaquira from Baltimore explained "after I was in a fight at school . . . [in] 6th or 7th grade," police were called. She explained what happened when she was not permitted to call her aunt, who was her primary guardian:

> They didn't let me call them and then I called on my phone and then they took it from me. Well they tried, and I was holding it, and I'm on the phone with her and she hear[s] them yelling at me [and] all that and they threw me against the glass window in the school and had busted my lip and stuff.

Oscar, a Black Baltimorean, recalled having witnessed "one girl get jumped on by two officers . . . in a bar." While he was not certain what led to the incident, he explained that "four or five officers block[ed] the door so nobody could come in and out the bar while they [were] in the corner beating the girl up." Though fewer Black women reported being the recipient of physical abuse from officers compared to Black males, it is worth noting that no White participants in the study reported having any such encounters. Research shows that Black women in particular are treated more harshly than White women because they are less likely to display traditional gender behavior when they encounter a mostly White, male police force.[19] While Black women's experiences with the police remain distinct from that of Black males, "the forms of police violence against Black women are invisible within the current focus on police killings and excessive force."[20]

WIDESPREAD USE OF STOP-AND-FRISK AMONG BLACK MALES

Among the 148 negative direct and indirect police encounters reported in the study, 48 (32 percent of) interactions were described as racial profiling. Participants expressed frustration when they were stopped when they believed there was no basis for suspicion. For example, Eddie, a Black Baltimore resident, described sitting in his car in a Walmart parking lot, waiting to pick up some friends, when a Baltimore officer began "running my tags." He explained:

> I think he was only doing that because I was Black, and I probably looked suspicious to him, sitting out there, you know. Getting in and out of my car, you know, smoking and something, I don't know. He never did tell me the reasons why he did it. . . . All the ladies came out and they got in the car. And as soon as I got ready to pull off, I heard a siren, "Whoop," you know. And he's on the speaker . . . he even called my name. You know, "Pull over," you know. I'm like, "What's this all about?". . . . He said it was failure to show him my insurance card. That's what he charged me with.

When asked why he was stopped in the first place, Eddie responded, "He never told me why, you know. I guess I must've looked suspicious to him . . . I got a $100 fine." Though Eddie was stopped without reason, this was not an isolated incident, as many Black participants reported such encounters. Regarding Ferguson police, Raymond, a Black male, explained that on one particular day "I was at a stop light, and they just, you know, just decided just to pull me over. They seen I was a Black guy in the car." When Raymond asked the officer why he'd been stopped, the officer responded, "'It's just one of those situations'. . . . He said, 'Any time they have a feeling they can just run your plates.'" Research shows that many officers believe stopping Black motorists will result in greater "hits"—that is, that their in-car computers (called Mobile Data Terminals, or MDT) will return information indicating legal problems with vehicles or drivers.[21] In their analysis of racial profiling among Black motorists, sociologists Albert Meehan and Michael Ponder found that while most officers queried Blacks at a higher rate than Whites, officers who relied heavily on MDT technology disproportionately surveilled and stopped Black drivers.

Study participants often emphasized the arbitrary nature of officers' decisions to stop and question young Black males before the deaths of Brown and Gray. Nekeisha, a Black Ferguson resident, noted that "my brother and my boyfriend, because they're African American males, they already assume that they're up to no good just because of their appearance, the type of car they have and just the day to day basic stereotypes that African American males today face." Isabelle, a Black Ferguson resident, lamented, "My oldest son is 22. When he was in . . . middle school at the time . . . he and his friend would walk down the street. The police will pull them over just to ask them for ID, and they're just walking down the street." Similarly, Junior, a Black Baltimorean, reported:

[My doctor] . . . has a BMW and depending where he is, you know, he'll experience racial profiling. [Police will ask] "What are you doing in this car?" [Or he will be] pulled over, you know for—like saying he didn't have a seatbelt on or something like that and then ultimately letting you go after they checked your car to see whatever was up.

Ferguson and Baltimore residents believed that police targeted their communities because officers assumed that the young Black men who resided there were involved in crime. Similar to the current study, criminologists Rod Brunson and Jody Miller found that young men living in distressed neighborhoods in St. Louis were subject to heavy-handed policing practices *regardless* of their involvement in delinquent behavior, due to the confounding influence of race and place.[22]

Participants in the study were aware that heightened police suspicion of young Black men had to do with extralegal issues. Legal reasons for being stopped include faulty headlights or taillights, speeding, erratic driving, etc.; extralegal reasons for involuntary police contact tend to be shaped by race, ethnicity, gender, and personal characteristics such as clothing, hairstyle, and tattoos. Young Black citizens believed that they were frequently targeted by police for these reasons. For example, Daniella, a mixed-race Baltimorean female, said, "I've had friends where I may have been with them and we got pulled over in the car . . . [and the police were] taking [them] through a bunch of changes when they really didn't have to. They could have just wrote a ticket saying you were speeding too much." Asked if those who were stopped were people of color, Daniella responded, "Yeah, people of color, and [they] had the saggy pants [and] gold teeth. So I think they already have like a profile of this person is on drugs or selling drugs." Likewise, Tyrone, a Ferguson resident, complained that "if you've got tattoos and you're young, you a target. I could just be walking down the street minding my business. I can have my shirt off and the police just pull up on me. 'What are you doing? Where are you going?' Start asking me questions like they my parent." Carlos, a Black Ferguson resident, asserted that since the age of fourteen "I have been harassed [by police] . . . for walking in the street because I had dreads. . . . They thought I was a gangster or something but they didn't know I had a GPA of 4.0." Davina, a Baltimorean, described an incident that she witnessed while waiting for the bus:

> [O]ne morning I was waiting for the number 3 to go to Union Memorial . . . and these four guys they were just standing there talking, just laughing, and . . . [they were] just standing there with me . . . just waiting for the bus. . . . The next thing the lights [sirens] came on, came around [and] the police car was on top of the pavement. . . . [The police officer] said, "Come here." So they stood there and looked at him and the guy said, "Come here for what? Sir, we ain't bothering nobody." And he said, "I said come the f*ck here". . . . [B]ut they weren't bothering nobody. Just standing there waiting, trying to get to [location] I guess [for] a job [interview] or whatever. [The police officer] say, "Come the f*ck here." So the other one said, "Man just go and see what he want". . . . [The police officer said] "You all look suspicious 'cause they say four guys had just robbed somebody."

He said, "Sir, we been standing here waiting for the bus and it wasn't us." And [the police office] say, "Well, [that's what I] was told and the way you dress young man, you got on a hoodie." He said, "Sir, it's chilly out here, that's why I got a hoodie on you know". . . . [H]e asked them for ID and he told them, "Don't step up on the bus, don't get on the bus."

Davina was so dismayed by the officer's behavior and concerned for the young men that she chose not to get on the bus when it arrived just "to see what [the police officer] was going to do . . . I said [to the officer] 'they on their way to a job interview'. . . . But then when all four of them showed their ID, he let them go." As illustrated in these accounts, some Black men in Ferguson and Baltimore believed that police stopped them for illegitimate reasons, which reinforced perceptions that officers viewed them as criminals because they were Black and lived in disadvantaged communities.

Symbols of affluence were also cause for police suspicion and involuntary contact. Terrell, a Black Ferguson resident, stated that "my mother and father, they have good cars and my dad got a 2010 Cadillac and stuff like that so they flag them [pull them over]. They see a Black man driving a nice car, well, maybe he's a drug dealer, maybe—you know, it's just a lot of stereotyping." Likewise, Ebony, a Black resident of Ferguson, expressed:

I have a brother who I guess probably in the last two years he's been pulled over—stopped probably, I would say, twenty-four times . . . and that's when he's coming to visit me. He doesn't live in the neighborhood. He's a professional. He drives a very nice vehicle. But every time he's being harassed, "Are you a drug dealer? Where did you get your money?" Slamming him down on the streets for no apparent reason. [He's] not breaking the law [and he committed] no infractions. Just you're driving while Black.

Despite the fact that they were engaged in lawful behavior, it was not uncommon for Black men to be viewed with suspicion by law enforcement prior to Brown's and Gray's deaths. Aliyah, a Black Ferguson resident, said that over the years she has seen "young men getting stopped three and four in a car, four and five in a truck, windows tinted. . . . I've driven by and seen this. Everybody sitting on the curb in handcuffs, everybody going to jail." As a result, she advised her twenty-three-year-old son to "always make sure there's no more than two or three people in your car." Because Black parents were well aware that police stops could lead to physical, potentially deadly altercations, they commonly offered their children strategies for how to avoid the police and how to behave when they are stopped.[23] Though study participants acknowledged the reality of having to take extra precautions to avoid being viewed as suspicious, some expressed frustration and concern that they were targeted specifically and harassed because of their race. They were well aware that police regarded young Black males as "symbolic assailants," which, in turn, led to overpolicing.

Such police practices left Black males perplexed, especially when they were engaged in lawful activity. Thus, a few Black residents who were engaged in non-criminal activity questioned officers as to why they were being stopped. However, at times, this resulted in the threat or actual use of force and/or arrest. For example, Alonzo, a Baltimore resident, explained that while driving home after celebrating his thirtieth birthday with some friends, the Baltimore police pulled them over: "We wasn't inebriated, wasn't belligerent, the police officers, which were White, became very argumentative." When Alonzo's cousin asked the officer why they were stopped, "the officer felt as though he was trying to become a smart aleck, so to speak. And they put handcuffs on my cousin." When Alonzo's best friend asked why his cousin was being placed in handcuffs, he too was arrested, as was Alonzo, even though he reported having "said nothing." Though all three were charged with resisting arrest, they were released six hours later and the case never made it to court. And consider DeShawn's account regarding Ferguson police:

> They immediately ask[ed] for license [and] registration. [They asked] can you step out of the vehicle?. . . . [A]n officer never came to my vehicle and started the conversation—if you would like to call it a conversation—but started the conversation with, "Okay, sir, this is why I'm pulling you over." They always came with "License and registration." If I asked, "Why you pulling me over?" [they say] "Can you step out of the vehicle? Why are you being aggressive? Calm down," know what I'm saying? "Calm down before I taze you."

Because the majority of residents who believed they were targeted could not understand why the police would view them with suspicion when they were engaged in lawful activities, a few defied police commands. For instance, Reuben, a Ferguson resident, noted:

> One time they followed me d*mn near two miles and then they finally pulled me over and I went, "What you pulling me over for? Why didn't you pull me back over there? Why you following me that long?"

He continued, "In Ferguson, they would always . . . they would try to follow you and then flag you and then pull you over . . . [it] was more like they were actually trying to get you." Tyrone's account is illustrative:

> I did not have a good experience with no Ferguson police officer ever. I've been stopped more than I can count on my hands . . . One morning, I was walking to work. I was walking to the bus stop to go to work taking public transportation. The police pulled up on me. He was asking me like, "Where you going?" I'm like, "Why?" Like "Why are you asking me where I'm going? It's early in the morning. Obviously, I'm going to work or I'm going to school. Like leave me alone." Then, [the police officer] was like, "Get down on the ground." I'm like, "For what? I'm not getting down on the ground. I'm waiting on the bus. Leave me alone." So he got out of the car and put me in handcuffs. He told me it was a failure to cooperate with an officer. I got locked up right then and there.

In this account, Tyrone clearly took offense to having been randomly questioned by the officer and challenged the fairness of his suspicion. The lack of deference that Tyrone and other Black drivers displayed toward police is tied to the fact that they resented being stopped without any legal justification. Thus, they challenged the basic fairness of these intrusions. Black males, however, did not fare well with such challenges. Studies show that when suspects refuse to defer to the authority of law enforcement, they are more likely to be sanctioned through arrest, citations, or the use of force.[24] Tyrone's direct challenge may seem questionable, especially since the officer asked what appeared to be an innocuous question: "Where are you going?" However, Tyrone, like many Black men in the study, was routinely viewed with suspicion for being "out of place" when he had traveled to White and middle-class spaces. Moreover, Tyrone, along with countless others from Ferguson and Baltimore, were predisposed to mistreatment from their local police officers simply because of where they lived. Entire neighborhoods were criminalized regardless of criminal involvement, leading many Black residents in both cities to view police as "restrictive and discriminative enforcers and protectors of the dominant way of life."[25]

Moreover, the question "Where are you going?" has an onerous history. Prior to the Civil War, slave patrollers constantly questioned the activities of slaves. In an attempt to control their movement, authorities enacted criminal statutes barring slaves from leaving their master's property without a proper pass.[26] Some Black residents in Ferguson and Baltimore regarded officers' aggressive policing practices as an explicit attempt to restrict their movements. These contemporary accounts also illustrate attempts by police to regulate the movement of young Black men, exemplifying how the legacy of race and place continues to play a vital role in discussions of police-citizen relations. Because most Black individuals are well aware that they are viewed with suspicion, they generally perceive racially charged incidents as cases in which police acted in a biased manner. Most Blacks in the study believed police targeted Brown and Gray, because, like these two young men, they too had experienced differential treatment from law enforcement.

In addition to being randomly stopped and questioned by police, young Black men in the study reported having been subject to "stop-and-frisk" searches. In *Terry v. Ohio*, the US Supreme Court ruled that police officers are permitted to interrogate and frisk suspicious individuals without probable cause for an arrest, providing that the officer can articulate a reasonable basis for the stop and frisk. The court set a precedent giving police formal authority to stop citizens on the street based on a standard of proof less than probable cause and conduct "pat-down" searches of those citizens they stop.[27] Stop-and-frisk has remained a common police practice, designed to target minor violations with the justification of thwarting serious crimes. However, this policy places people of color under disproportionate scrutiny, as a number of studies have documented that Black civilians bear the brunt of stop-and-frisk.[28] The DOJ has reported that while Blacks comprised 63 percent of Ferguson's driving age population, they made up 86 percent of drivers who received a citation following a traffic stop by Ferguson police from 2012 to 2014; by comparison, Whites comprised 29 percent of the population in Ferguson, yet only 12.7 percent of vehicle stops.[29] In the city of Baltimore, officers made 520 stops for every 1,000 Black residents, compared to 180 stops for every 1,000 White Baltimorean residents from 2010 to 2015.[30] Even if stop-and-frisks do not lead to arrest and incarceration, these intrusions "are significant and emotionally meaningful violations of one's dignity."[31] Consider the account of Jerry, a Black Baltimorean, of having been stopped by the police:

> I had a tag light out. . . . [The police took] my license, [ran] my license and at the time it was a misunderstand[ing] with the motor vehicles. . . . I had something on my motor vehicle record . . . a flag on my license. An administrative flag. . . . But [it was a] very minor offense. It was not, I don't believe was an arrestable offense. But he took me into custody, patted me down [and] searched my car. . . . I was in jail with handcuffs and . . . my feet shackled.

Although Jerry was told by the officer that he was stopped for having a broken taillight, Jerry claimed, "I have still to this day never seen the taillight out." Further, Black males felt that, when they were together in a group, their numbers heightened police suspicion. Desmond, a Ferguson resident, provided a detailed account of an encounter he had with an officer:

> I was going out one weekend and I wasn't even speeding and he said he pulled me over for speeding. I wasn't even—I was probably going five miles over the speed limit. It was me and two of my friends in the car. And I asked him, "Why are you pulling me over?" He was just like, "I wanted to ask you the speed" and stuff like that. I was like, "Okay." He went back to his car, he came back, asked me and my friends to get out of the car and then he searched us and stuff like that. Then he just let us go on about our business. . . . I mean he didn't find nothing on us so he told us to get back in the car and go on about our business.

Despite being stopped for speeding, the stop was clearly investigatory. Yet, even though they were free to go, Desmond and his friends experienced a repeated pattern of being pulled over by the Ferguson police. He lamented: "They used to always harass us for no reason. . . . We'd be driving, going out on the weekend and something, and get pulled over, harassing us for no reason, searching us when they have no reason to search us." Junior, a Baltimore resident, described an encounter with police:

> [The police] thought I was smoking weed. And they pulled me over and they made me take off everything. It was winter time too. There was snow and everything; they made me take off my boots [and] my pants. Even if I was smoking weed, which I wasn't, it would've just been a little joint. And if I tossed it, is it worth somebody taking off their whole outfit and everything like that? So I felt like they took it a bit too far, but they end up letting me leave. But they called backup and everything.

Junior resented being subject to a physically intrusive search in public, especially since he reported having done nothing wrong to warrant suspicion. As a result of the demeaning search, Junior surmised that even though one is supposed to be "'innocent until proven guilty' . . . [with] Black people you're definitely guilty until proven innocent." Junior's assessment that the police engage in racial profiling is not without merit, as the term "stop-and-frisk" in many places has been synonymous with racial profiling.[32] Many Blacks in the study expressed feelings of frustration, anger, and resentment at the indignities they experienced at the hands of police in the name of public safety.

POLICE DISCOURTESY

While residents objected to being profiled by police, participants from both locations especially disliked the way officers spoke to them. One-fifth of negative police encounters were characterized as disrespectful. While most participants who reported the discourteous manner of police were Black, five incidents were from non-Black Baltimore residents. In these cases, non-Black participants admitted to having violated the law. For example, Brian, a White Baltimorean, said that, when pulled over for running a red light, the officer asked him, "'what's your driving record like?' [and] I said, 'I have a clean record.'" When the officer found out that he had a seatbelt violation, he "yelled at me . . . and got very belligerent with me." And after being charged with "stealing a $2,500 dog," Jody, a White female, complained that the officer who charged her was "just being rude." Socioeconomic status also appears to affect the treatment of White civilians. For instance, Anne, a White homeless woman from Baltimore, said that after her friend, who was also homeless, called the police, the officer responded, "'You interrupted us from our dinner,' talking about how, 'Oh you homeless bit*hes in here always calling on us like you can't take care of yourself.' [They were] being jackasses, honestly." Anne also reported that another time while walking toward city hall with a friend, "A police officer [was] walking to his car and he gave us the finger." Though such incidents are not as frequent as those reported by Black residents, as a poor White woman, Anne received her share of discourteous treatment by Baltimore police.

Complaints of verbal mistreatment by officers were particularly common among Black residents. When asked how the police treated her when stopped for a driving violation, Ebony, a Ferguson resident, responded "not with dignity . . . very disrespectful." Julius, a resident of Baltimore, agreed, stating that the Baltimore police are "disrespectful . . . [They] curse you [and are] real aggressive for no real reason." Likewise, Nina, a resident of Ferguson, stated that when she and her friend were in the park after hours, an officer approached them, and though they told the officer they were unaware that it was after hours, Nina asserted that the officer was "real rude and started cursing at us."

Some Black residents also reported that officers hurled racial slurs at them and made other derogatory remarks. Recall how Jerry, a Baltimore resident, was stopped for having a broken taillight on his vehicle and an administrative flag on his license. Jerry reported that the officer's remarks had racial undertones, as the officer stated, "'We got us a big one'. . . . 'Got me a big one, look at him. Look at his feet.' [He was] talking to his partner [saying], 'Boy, you're a big boy.'" Because of the officer's apparent racial animus, Jerry said, "I felt like I was in the 1950s or '60s or something." Recall Maurice, a Black Ferguson resident, who described how police barged into his house looking for his brother. He explained how officers threw racial epithets his way:

I'm being totally honest, my personal experience was a couple years ago, and they were actually looking for my younger brother. And [they had] no warrant. [I]t was Ferguson and St. Louis County [police]. They bust through my door, you know, looking for [name], my brother. . . . Didn't ask who I was, just illegally grabbed me by the neck and threw me down. . . . Busted through the door of the house, grabbed me down, looking, "Where is he? Where is he? Where is he?" And I'm acting like, "What are you talking about? I have no clue." "Where is he? Where is he? Where is he?" followed by finally putting the handcuffs on me, sitting me down at my kitchen table and whatever they were looking for, they didn't find it. "Yes nig*er, if we don't find this, you might as well tell us where it is."

Marcel from Baltimore explained that after "riding with a friend . . . [who] was speeding a little bit . . . we were taken out of the car, we were called names." When asked what he was called, Marcel responded that the officer "called me a faggot. And then when his backup came he got even more belligerent."

Other Black residents were also troubled by the offensive manner in which officers spoke to them during vehicle stops. When Aliyah, a resident of Ferguson, was stopped for swerving by police while heading to work, she tried to explain that she had a disability which "affects my muscles in my body at certain points in times." But the officer barked, "[M]a'am, just shut up and be quiet." Similarly, in the case of Edith, in Baltimore, when an officer came to her house because of a domestic dispute with her daughter and her daughter's boyfriend, she said that the officer "told me to shut up and let him talk. It was mean. I didn't know how to respond." Elderly individuals were not exempt from experiencing such disrespectful behavior. Joy, a Baltimore resident, described an incident when officers came to her house looking for her son:

> I told him, either you find a better way to talk to me or you leave my home now. Because I'm not the person that you're looking for. This is my home, I don't care if [my son] uses this address, he's not here, and you're not going to disrespect my home. [The officer said] "Yeah alright, I'm gone, but I will be back."

She objected, "You're here to protect and serve, and not to disrespect. And you can look at me and see I'm well over your age. I probably could be your grandmother, you know?" Similarly, Julius, a Baltimorean, acknowledged that after being "locked up for a drug charge," the police went to his parents' house to search it. Julius claimed that after "my mother and father [who] are 70-something years old . . . asked them about the warrant . . . [they] was cussing my mother . . . [they] put plastic cuffs around my mother and father." When asked if the police had a warrant, Julius responded: "They never had a warrant either but [when] my parents was asking them about the warrant they was real aggressive towards them." Research has demonstrated the lasting effects of degrading treatment by police on young Black males, who have experienced systematic alienation from institutions, such as schools and the job market.[33] Consequently, many often feel devalued and rejected with little to no stake in the daily functioning of the larger society.[34] Thus, verbal abuse and discourteous behavior from police can add to their feelings of isolation. We will see, however, that such treatment, along with police stops, was not just relegated to Black men but inclusive of Black women as well.

RESIDENTS' PERCEPTIONS OF HOW WOMEN ARE TREATED BY THE POLICE

In 8 percent of these incidents, Black residents reported that women were also targets of racial profiling. A few believed that the poor treatment they received was tied to the neighborhood where they lived. Jamia, a Baltimore resident, said that when her landlord "came to pick the rent money up one particular day, I hand[ed] him the money out of my hand [and] the police jumped [and said] 'get on the ground, get on the ground' . . . [thinking it was] a drug transaction." She explained, "Where we live at . . . is a Black community . . . [and] every time the police always come around grabbing people, every day." Likewise, Lorraine, a Baltimorean, said, "Me and a girlfriend of mine was walking down the street . . . around a crime area where they be selling different types of drugs. . . . Two White police they stopped me. . . . I had to show my ID . . . and they told me to go home." Though she was ordered to go home after she showed proper identification and responded to their questions as to where she lived, she questioned their reasons for stopping her because "I wasn't selling drugs, I don't even do drugs." Susanna claimed that while driving one night in her car with tinted windows an officer "pulled me over for no reason. He wanted to lie and say, 'Oh, your plates showed up two years expired.' I'm [like] 'no it don't. You run the plates again.'" She was certain that the officer just "wanted to see who was behind these tints."

Though fewer residents reported this, studies show an identical pattern of racial disparities in police stops for women.[35] One year prior to the death of Michael Brown, Black women residing in Ferguson were stopped by police for traffic violations more frequently than any other category of motorists. Additionally, Black women reported comparable experiences of being targeted and harassed just as Black men.[36] Latoya, for example, recalled a time "in Ferguson [where] they [the police] pulled me over . . . [because] I missed the screw in my drivers [license plate]. He pulled up that close to me to see that I was missing a screw in my license plate." Though she was given a warning, the petty nature of the stop left her feeling "nervous . . . [with] a little knot in [her] stomach" when she comes across the police. Since it was well known that the police often stopped Black residents in both communities for minor pretexts, some residents in the study explained that family and friends were unwilling to visit them. Devanta said:

> If I tell a family member, tell one of my cousins [or] tell one of my uncles [to] come over they'll say, "Ain't you in Ferguson? Naw, I can't mess with Ferguson." Then I hear all these rumors about Ferguson [police] beating people in jail or always stopping people for no reason, always trying to find a reason to pull somebody over. . . . [My family members say] "I know if Ferguson [police] pull me over I'm going to jail" and they know that so they feel like I'm not gonna test Ferguson.

In this case, Devanta's family members feared the police because they had been stopped before by officers with little to no legal justification. Consequently, to avoid being questioned and searched, they chose instead to avoid driving through their family's neighborhood altogether. In this sense, police succeeded in restricting the movement of Black citizens in public spaces.

Most residents spoke of having been stopped by male officers. This is not surprising, as the FPD had only 4 female officers out of 54 sworn personnel (7.3 percent) at the time of Brown's death.[37] In 2016, this number declined to just 2 female officers. There were, however, more women on the police force in Baltimore. In 2015, there were 403 female officers out of 2,646 sworn police officers, representing 15.2 percent of the BPD.[38] This number remained unchanged, as women accounted for 15.8 percent of officers in Baltimore in 2016.[39] According to the National Center for Women and Policing, women comprise 13 percent of the police force.[40] Although the BPD has a slightly larger percentage of women on the police force than the national average, Ferguson is well below. While much attention has been paid to disparate racial diversity within police departments, the FPD, as with many police agencies, lacks gender diversity. We will see in chapter 4 that, similar to men, the adverse personal and vicarious treatment that women experienced at the hands of police drove them to participate in street protests denouncing police mistreatment.

Positive Police Encounters

Although many Black residents accented the negative in recounting their experiences with police, many did acknowledge having positive police interactions as well. Specifically, among the 218 personal and vicarious police incident descriptions, 68 (31 percent) of these interactions were reported as favorable. There were, however, some differences between residents' experiences in Ferguson and Baltimore. Among those who had favorable police encounters, 21 (31 percent) were from Ferguson and 47 (69 percent) were from Baltimore. In addition, a fairly even distribution of both Black and White residents reported voluntary and involuntary encounters with police that were positive in nature. While citizens initiate voluntary police contact, the police initiate involuntary contact. We will see below that there were qualitative differences in responses based on the nature of the stops.

In particular, residents reported 19 positive police incidents as voluntary in nature and 25 as involuntary.[41] More of these voluntary experiences occurred among Baltimore residents than Ferguson residents (15 Baltimore residents compared to 4 Ferguson residents). In terms of voluntary police encounters, 11 women (58 percent) and 8 men (42 percent) reported instances in which they contacted police. Likewise, 11 Black (3 Ferguson residents compared with 8 Baltimore residents) and 8 White residents (1 Ferguson resident and 7 Baltimore residents) reported voluntary experiences with police. In Baltimore specifically, residents called on the police when they were victims of burglary and often noted the quick response time. When asked to describe a positive interaction with local police, Jerry, a Black participant, said, "I've been [a] victim of a burglary, so in terms of handling that you know, the response time . . . was fast. . . . [The officer] was very, I believe you know, he was concerned." In a similar manner, Fatima, a Black Baltimorean, noted that "somebody had tried to break into my home and I called the police you know, to report it. And they came out and I think they was there within 5 to 10 minutes, which was a good response time to me." Others Baltimoreans reported having been victims of car theft and that police followed through. Jim, a White resident from Baltimore, noted that he called the police after "my tires were vandalized in front of my apartment. . . . They came and took a report and . . . everything was all right." And Chris, a White Baltimorean, explained that while working at a car rental place, he often "would have to call [the police] and file a police report for any vehicles that have been stolen." Though sometimes there was not much the police could do, Chris recalled one incident when officers "went out for hours and hours to look for the vehicle . . . and they would follow up with me day by day. That was awesome." Overall, Black and White residents were more likely to seek contact with police when they were victims of car theft and burglary, in which cases they expressed being pleased with the responsiveness and behavior of the police.

In addition to initiating police contact, it was not uncommon for residents to experience involuntary police stops. Among incidents reported as positive in nature, 11 Ferguson residents and 14 Baltimore residents reported police-initiated stops. More men (16, or 64 percent) and Black residents (17, or 68 percent) recounted such contacts. Interestingly enough, though Blacks reported two times as many involuntary vehicle and pedestrian police-initiated encounters than Whites, a few reported such encounters as positive in nature only because the interaction was free of police violence. For example, Stanford, a Black resident of Baltimore, reported numerous times in which "I have been stopped walking through certain areas. They may ask where was I coming from, can I see some ID, and that type of thing. I have been frisked and asked for ID." He continued:

The relationship during that time—during each one of those times . . . [it] has been somewhat of a pleasant one. I personally have never been harassed, or had a stick drawn, or clubbed, or punched, or anything of that nature.

Stanford characterizes these police encounters as "pleasant" since "all of us [the Black community] are vulnerable," though he admitted that "the experiences that I have had [with the police] were almost like unnecessary" since he was not engaging in any criminal or suspicious behavior. Likewise, Julius, a Black Baltimorean, reported that, while standing on a street corner one day with some friends, the police "got out of the car and said, 'Man look, I don't want no trouble or nothing. I just ask you to take a walk. I'm just trying to do my job.'" When asked why the officers told them to leave, Julius responded that the officers said "we wasn't supposed to be on the corner." Although Julius evaluated the stop more positively because it did not result in physical or verbal assault, which he had experienced in the past, demands that Black men "take a walk" or "move along" are rooted in the legacy of slavery. They are a reminder of statutes in cities such as Savannah, Georgia, and Charleston, South Carolina, that restricted slaves from congregating, in order to prevent an uprising, indicating how the United States' racialized past still shapes the way Blacks are treated.[42]

Overall, Black participants believed they were presumed guilty by officers. Consider the account of Dennis, a Baltimorean:

I was walking through I think it's the Fulton Hill area, and they get some burglaries as far as people breaking into people's cars. And I was stopped and asked you know for my ID to be shown. Once I gave the ID to the police officer, who was a lady, it was a police woman. . . . When the results came back, she seemed to have a happy attitude that I didn't have any previous violation. And since I was fifty-three years old she was kind of surprised that in all that time I didn't have any criminal records. So that was a positive experience for me.

Although Dennis recalled that the officers' attitude toward him was very positive, there is something to be said about the fact that the officer expressed astonishment that Dennis did not have a criminal record. It is well established that Americans racially typify crime, as most of them strongly associate criminal activity with race and race with criminal activity. That is, the public generally characterizes Blacks as dangerous, hostile, and criminal, including police.[43]

While not as frequent, some Whites also reported involuntary police contact in traffic safety stops, and they perceived such interactions as fair. Amy, a resident of Ferguson, recalled, "I think one time I was speeding down the road, and I shouldn't have been. [I] got pulled over. And I didn't get a ticket. He [the police officer] did say, 'You need to slow down.'" Although she acknowledged "I have really not [had] no incidents with police," she was relieved to get off with a warning for getting caught speeding. Dylan, a Ferguson resident, explained that, after purchasing a car from a family friend, while waiting for the title he failed to register his tags. As a result, he received "two tickets . . . one was for expired plates and one was for . . . insurance." Another time he was stopped for the same violations and received three tickets, including one for failing to register with the Department of Motor Vehicles. Though he attempted to explain the situation to police, Dylan acknowledged that they "were doing their job. I understand why I was pulled over." Despite receiving an unfavorable outcome, Dylan accepted legitimacy of the stop. Overall, Whites reported having been stopped for legitimate traffic violations; thus, they regarded their encounters with the police as relatively favorable. Blacks, on the other hand, only considered involuntary contact to be favorable in those cases when the encounters did not lead to police violence; nevertheless, Blacks were well aware that police stops were usually investigatory in nature.

A few White residents also reported involuntary police contact when they were actually engaged in criminal activity. Brian from Baltimore admitted, "I had two experiences with DWIs, and both times the police officers came and I cooperated and they locked me up and they treated me fine." Similarly, Jody, a female resident of Baltimore, related:

> When I was nineteen, I was drinking and smoking pot. . . . It was like right on Baltimore city, Dundalk border. We had gotten arrested, we were underage. . . . When they arrested me I was terrified. . . . [I got] in the police car, they put handcuffs on me, they put me in the paddy wagon, took me to a [women's prison]. I was very compliant, whatever they told me to

do, I was very compliant. . . . One of the police officers said to the other police officer to take the handcuff off from me, that I was not a threat. They didn't see me running away [and] they didn't think that I needed [to be handcuffed].

As illustrated in Jody's account, Whites are generally viewed as "innocent" and as "less threatening" than Blacks.[44] The effect of these disparate views was that the police appeared to protect the interests of Whites, amounting to less harassment and more respectful treatment.

In sum, Whites whom I interviewed were primarily afforded respect and given the benefit of the doubt by police, while Blacks, in general, were viewed with suspicion and presumed guilty of wrongdoing. Many Blacks bear the brunt of unwelcome contact with police that is characterized by heavy-handed and unwarranted police tactics. Some reported being subject to suspicious inquiries without any particular justification. Others felt like they were treated as criminals or as subjects of surveillance. These experiences all contribute to many Black civilians' hostility toward police. In fact, the current study reveals that the cumulative impact of negative police encounters by Ferguson and Baltimore Black residents set the stage for reactions to the Brown and Gray killings. We will see in chapter 4 how deep-seated frustrations and grievances with police, the criminal justice system, and the state at large led to unprecedented protests across the nation in the wake of Michael Brown's and Freddie Gray's deaths in Ferguson and Baltimore.

3

"It's a Blue Thing"

Race and Black Police Officers

This may sound crazy [but] . . . Black police officers are more
harsh on Blacks than the White officers are.
—Justin (Black Baltimore resident)

When modern policing began in the first decades of the nineteenth century in the United States, there were no Black officers. Only after Radical
Reconstruction, which started in 1867, were Black Americans able to
move from enslavement and segregation to working in historically
White institutions, such as police departments.[1] From Reconstruction to
the 1940s, there were few Black officers. These few generally worked in
plainclothes—so as not to offend the sensibilities of racist Whites—and
were assigned to patrol Black neighborhoods.[2] During the segregation
era (1890s–1960s), the South rarely hired Blacks for their police forces,
and in the North people of color also remained underrepresented.[3] In
an attempt to appease Whites, many police departments did not allow
Blacks to arrest Whites or to work with White officers.[4]

However, the 1960s and 1970s marked a central change in American policing. Police and Black protesters visibly clashed in riots and
civil rights demonstrations. Powerful images of officers turning dogs
and fire hoses on Black protesters struck a public chord and provoked
strong criticism of the police. The Watts riots of 1965—triggered by police brutality in a racially segregated neighborhood near Los Angeles,
California[5]—prompted a vocal outcry that something had to be done
to improve community relations between police and citizens. Racial
representation in police departments came to be viewed as necessary,
eventually leading to the employment of more Blacks as law enforcement officers. In 1960, approximately 3.6 percent of sworn urban officers
were Black; by 2007, the number had increased to 12 percent.[6] While this

figure is nearly equivalent to Black representation in America's population, most Black officers are geographically concentrated in urban areas across a few states.[7] The integration of Blacks into historically White agencies has generally been viewed as a way to reduce racial tensions.[8] But is this the case? If so, it is possible that having more Black officers on the police force would not only have affected the volume of people who took to the streets to protest police violence but it could have changed the tenure and outcome of protest events following Michael Brown's and Freddie Gray's deaths.

Community Accountability or Minority Threat?

In Ferguson, approximately 94 percent of the police force is White, and in Baltimore, 47 percent of the police department is Black. The President's Task Force on Twenty-First Century Policing recommended increasing the diversity of law enforcement agencies to help develop trust between police officers and the communities they are sworn to protect and serve.[9] Recently the US Department of Justice's Civil Rights Division and the US Equal Employment Opportunity Commission (EEOC) joined together to launch an interagency research initiative, called Advancing Diversity in Law Enforcement, designed to help police departments recruit, hire, retain, and promote officers that reflect the diversity of the neighborhoods they serve.[10]

Assuming a relationship between race and police behavior, many academics and commentators put forth the theory of "community accountability," which means police agencies would be answerable to the communities that they are designated to protect and serve.[11] This theory holds that one way to reduce conflict between the police and Black citizens is to hire more Black officers and assign them to Black neighborhoods.[12] The belief is that greater diversity in the police force will foster more impartial law enforcement and bolster police-citizen relationships. Some academics, commissioners, and reformers argue that promoting the diversification of law enforcement personnel may enhance the legitimacy of police agencies from the point of view of residents and improve the quality of police-minority relations.[13] Others assert that hiring more Black officers is necessary because they bring different perspectives and predispositions to the work force—for example, they may have a greater understanding of Black communities and display less prejudice toward Black citizens than their White counterparts.[14]

The theory of "minority threat" offers an alternative viewpoint. Grounded in the conflict theory of law, the minority threat theory maintains that racial and ethnic minorities are perceived as threatening to dominant groups and that both White civilians and officers may associate the perceived threat of minorities with the threat of crime.[15] Since law enforcement may share these perceptions, they might respond to racial minorities with increased crime control.[16] However, Black officers may not be exempt from viewing poor Black Americans as a threat to their well-being, either. Some may be pressured to use coercive crime control strategies against Blacks because of peer expectations within the police department, while others may perceive Black citizens as challenging their authority.[17] For example, sociologists Kenneth Bolton and Joe Feagin have found that more experienced Black officers noted the pressure White officers put on younger Black male police officers to engage in abusive behavior toward Black civilians in an effort to prove that they are "real" officers.[18] Consequently, some fall under the influence of mistreating people of color in order to be considered part of the "good old boys" network, with hopes that this would lead to career advancement.

This chapter turns attention to Ferguson and Baltimore residents' views of Black officers prior to the deaths of Brown and Gray.[19] I examine residents' experiences with and perceptions of Black police in comparison to White officers. In particular, I consider how residents' race structures their attitudes toward Black officers and pay specific attention to how residents interpret and make sense of them. Such an examination is necessary, given that many communities of color have called for police departments to recruit more people of color to reduce police violence against them. It is also possible that the presence of Black police could ease the racial tension in protest events where demonstrators stand up against police violence.

Perceptions and Experiences with Black Officers

During each interview, residents were asked a series of questions about their experiences with and perceptions of police. One question that drew a mixed response was whether there were differences between how

TABLE 3.1. Experiences with and Perceptions of Black Police Officers among Ferguson and Baltimore Residents

	Ferguson			Baltimore		
	Black	White	Other	Black	White	Other
Black Police Are Aggressive	3	0	0	12	1	0
Black Police Courteous/ Understanding	9	0	0	4	2	1
Black Police Engage in Occupational Socialization	14	0	0	12	0	2
Black Police Do Their Job	3	1	0	0	0	0
Black Police Engage in Misconduct	0	0	0	1	0	0

Black and White officers policed civilians of different races. I found a fairly even distribution of responses to this question, but regardless of whether residents believed Black officers policed differently than White officers, most responses drew from racial-specific perceptions of the nature of policing.

Among the 152 residents from Ferguson and Baltimore, sixty-five police incident descriptions and perceptions of Black police were documented. In particular, thirty incidents/perceptions of Black officers were made in Ferguson and thirty-five in Baltimore. Of the sixty-five incidents/perceptions that were reported, forty-five incidents were assessments of Black officers, followed by seventeen direct personal encounters, and three vicarious experiences with Black police officers.[20] As table 3.1 shows, among those who reported their encounters and views of the police, three sometimes contradictory themes came up repeatedly: Black officers were viewed as courteous and understanding; Black police were depicted as aggressive in nature; and Black law enforcement was described as facing occupational socialization on the job.

Courteous and Understanding

Among police incidents and perceptions of Black officers, 16 (25 percent) were viewed in a favorable light. Specifically, both Ferguson and Baltimore residents perceived that Black officers enforced the law more fairly than Whites and were courteous and respectful when they policed.[21] Interestingly, such perceptions were particularly common among women. When men did make such assertions, they came either from White males or from Black men who did not report prior direct interactions with Black officers. For the most part, Black participants felt that Black officers could relate to Blacks in ways that White officers could not. Rachel, a Ferguson resident, asserted, "I think as a Black police officer, he understands and sees a situation better than a White police officer would understand and see it . . . because he identifies with us." Similarly, Erica, from Baltimore, stated, "a Black officer would understand a young Black male more than a White officer would. I guess it's more about perception and knowing the background I guess which is linked to race." And Daniella, a Baltimorean resident, explained what she perceived to be the difference between Black and White officers:

> I feel like [if] you have a White officer and he may be patrolling a Black neighborhood or just patrolling around the city, he already has in his head a stereotype. If he sees a bunch of young boys on the corner, [then he thinks] they're probably up to no good, they're probably dealing drugs and so forth. Where a Black police officer he may think that way, but one of those boys could be maybe his nephew, his cousin, a relation or something. And they may be taken back and not so much already to assume they're going to do something bad.

Given the shared racial background, some Black residents from Ferguson said that Black police were better able to understand the Black community and culture than their White counterparts. Deja mentioned, "I think a lot of African American officers better understand our community, our race, our heritage." In a similar vein, Mike said, "Black cops usually know about the neighborhood more . . . And they rarely view us as bad, bad people, especially young Black men." Rachel recommended "that in order to police an area, you should be at least from that area or know something about the people that you're policing because then you'll be able to give them a fair shake." Some residents believed that when social distance between officers and citizens is minimized, police are more likely to exhibit friendly behavior. This view is supported by research that shows that Black officers demonstrate greater understanding of Black culture due to their greater knowledge of the community and its norms, which can help alleviate mistrust.[22]

Such views, however, were not just attributed specifically to Black officers. Most residents accepted that police officers, in general, are better able to identify with their own racial/ethnic group. Brian, a White Baltimorean resident, said: "[With] a lot of Hispanic police officers . . . maybe they relate a little bit more with the Hispanic community; just like Blacks can." As Brian spoke to the interviewer—a Black female—he admitted that "with your experience, you know being Black, you can relate on some level that, with me being a Caucasian, I'm not exposed to. You know I didn't live in that area, so you see what I'm saying, it can only help." While the interviewer herself had never resided in a Black inner-city neighborhood, Brian assumed that shared racial background improves relationships. Likewise, Elisabeth, a White woman from Baltimore, explained:

> I think that if you're a Black police officer, you have a little more understanding of your own race, Hispanic the same thing and Whites—if you're a White male you don't hardly understand much of [the] opposite races really. So I think it would depend highly on the officer's own race. So, that's not saying that every White officer is racist, but I just think that there is an element of when you've never walked a mile in someone else's shoes you can't truly understand.

Tied to officers' ability to better identify with people of their own race was the perception that Black officers were less likely to appear racially biased and more likely to appear legitimate, especially among Black residents. This belief was connected, in turn, to the perception that Black police officers were less punitive. For instance, Charlene, a Black Baltimore resident, believed that "a Black police officer, he might let the Black person go if they were doing something minor." Others based similar views on the experiences they had with Black officers. Isabelle, a Black resident of Ferguson, explained an incident in which she got pulled over in the city of St. Louis for speeding: "[P]olice officer pulled me over, but he was Black. And he just told me, he says, 'slow down, there are kids here.' And I told him, 'I apologize' . . . and he let me get off." Likewise, Devanta, a Black Ferguson resident, explained that while she has indeed received a traffic ticket from a Black officer, some Black police will tell her "go on [a]head my sister, just slow down. . . . I'm a give you a warning this time."

Such comments must be put into perspective. Studies of police demonstrate that when citizens come into contact with officers and behave poorly (i.e., showing disrespect, being rude), they have a higher likelihood of getting arrested than those who behave positively.[23] Since Black citizens are more likely to perceive the behavior of White police as racially biased or illegitimate, some may display defiant behavior, especially if they believe they were stopped for no good reason. However, hostility toward police increases the odds of being ticketed and arrested.[24] Thus, many Black residents in the study simply believed that encounters with Black officers would result in an outcome of receiving neither a citation nor an arrest.

In sum, Black and White residents who favorably evaluated law enforcement emphasized their ability to both connect to Black citizens and their communities as well as their perceptions that Black police would be less punitive after stopping Black citizens. While these accounts suggest that hiring more Black officers may be a viable option for improving police-minority relations, thus supporting the community accountability theory, recall that such views were more common among women and less common among Black men who had reported direct encounters with Black officers. In fact, we will see that, while a number of study participants had favorable perceptions of Black officers, others believed that they responded *more* harshly toward Black civilians.

Black Police Are Aggressive

In their accounts of Black officers, it was not uncommon for residents to contend that they operate rather aggressively when they encounter Black civilians. Among police incidents and perceptions of Black officers, 16 (25 percent) reported such aggression, the vast majority of these reports coming from Baltimoreans. Such perceptions were particularly common among women; the men making these assertions were either White, or Black men who did not report prior direct interactions with Black officers. Black Baltimoreans stated that Black police were generally aggressive in their policing tactics. Chaundrise acknowledged that in addition to White officers, "Black officers are also using excessive force." Oddly enough, some reported that Black police were *more* aggressive than their White counterparts. Jamia claimed, "The Black [officers] are sometimes worse than White ones. . . . They like get louder and [more] violent." In her discussion of how Black police treat Black civilians, Bree-ann responded point blank, "I think sometimes worse than they would with someone else." And Davina complained:

> But with Black police in the White neighborhood and whatever it look like to me they be just as humble and you know they don't, you know they don't talk as nasty with [an] attitude like they do towards the Black guy. You know they curse the Black guy out and whatever, sling them around 'cause I've seen them sling my son around. Sling him around; throw him up against the wall, just like Freddie Gray.

Davina's views of Black officers were tied to having observed the differential treatment they displayed toward men, including the harsh treatment of her son. As a result of her vicarious experience, she viewed police officers, both Black and White, in an unfavorable light. Others also experienced negative encounters with Black law enforcement. Consider the dialogue in which Donald recounted a negative personal encounter he had with a Black officer:

> DONALD: I give up plasma too, right. And Black and White police officers—the police officer down there actually called me "a poor a*s nig*er" and did like this, you know [put his hand on the butt of his gun].
> INTERVIEWER: So you're giving plasma and there was a police officer there?
> DONALD: Yes, he's the one that secure; you know security line.
> INTERVIEWER: Okay, was it a White Officer?
> DONALD: No, Black Officer.
> INTERVIEWER: And he called you a—
> DONALD: A poor a*s nig*er.

It is worth noting that, according to Donald, the Black officer's comments were made in the presence of a White officer. Donald, however, was not the only one to remark on the harsher treatment Black civilians faced when Black police officers were partnered with a White cop. Fatima noted hearing of a "situation where you may have a White officer and a Black officer respond and the White officer is kind of like the more peaceful person, but the Black officer is just talking to them, you know, just real nasty and just being mean. It makes people feel like, 'why you talk down to me?'" For some residents, having Black officers talk down to them remained rather unsettling. Alex detailed an incident in which two officers came to his door to handle a domestic disturbance:

> ALEX: So two officers pulled up, they knocked on my door, I open the door, it was a Black officer and a White officer and the White female officer police she was polite and she was nice. . . . She was White, but the other officer was Black and he just immediately looked at me and said, "What's the problem?" I said, "No problem I never called the police." And then he said, "Can I see your wife?" I said, "See my wife? She never called the police either." So I called and said, "Sweetheart, can you come down here? This officer wants to see you." She said, "What's wrong?" I said, "I don't know." I mean he was standing there and he just kept going on. It was like he was picking a fight.
>
> INTERVIEWER: What was he saying?
>
> ALEX: He was saying okay, well, he asked me a question and I said, "Officer I didn't call you." He said, "I didn't ask you if you called me." I said, "Well what's the problem?" And then I asked this female [officer], I said "What's wrong with your fellow officer here?" She said— she had to tell him to calm down. I mean he was wanting to fight me because . . . I told him, I did not call him. That was all. That was it.
>
> INTERVIEWER: And what was he saying?
>
> ALEX: He said, "Somebody from here called us." I said, "No it hadn't been here." I didn't want to pinpoint the fact that I heard noise next door, so then somebody came down the street and said, "No officer it's the house next to them." He never apologized or nothing he just walked away and I think he said, "Get your story right." I said, "I never called you." . . . And he kept looking at me and—I don't know he just wanted—he wanted to go further with it, when there wasn't anything to go further about.

Alex's negative encounter with the Black officer left him to conclude that some Black officers are more aggressive toward Black residents compared to White officers. These findings are consistent with reports from the 1960s in which poor Black citizens contended that Black officers engaged in aggressive tactics and were just as harsh (or harsher) and physically abusive as their White counterparts.[25]

Other Black Baltimoreans that I interviewed believed that mistreatment at the hands of Black police was the result of the newfound power that comes with being a police officer. For example, Emarald lamented that Black officers "have threatened [Black] people just [to] make them do what you want them to do." This is consistent with the work of scholar Nicholas Alex, who found that some Black officers were "hardliners," acting more aggressively toward Blacks in an attempt to elicit respect from their colleagues and maintain their authority.[26] Criminologists Joshua Cochran and Patricia Warren also found that Black officers are viewed negatively when a stop is perceived as discretionary and less than justified.[27]

Such evidence is not surprising and is tied to history. During the time of slavery, landowners who owned more than one hundred slaves would rely on overseers to run their plantations. While the overseer was usually a White male, occasionally an enslaved Black male would serve in the position of overseer and was tasked with supervising the labor of slaves, protecting his master's property, and ensuring that his interests were not threatened.[28] While the average slave overseer served as an intermediary between the master and the slave community, some ruled as petty tyrants, whipping other slaves unmercifully.[29] Since some overseers traded the well-being of other slaves for power and prestige, they were not trusted among many slaves.[30]

However, some participants in the current study believed negative treatment of Black law enforcement toward Black civilians was the result of unconscious racial bias. Racial prejudice pervades American society and police are no exception.[31] One of the most prevailing stereotypes is the association of Blackness with criminality or dangerousness. Such perceptions are then filtered through the stereotype, which is reinforced through an v villusory correlation" process.[32] This leads to the formation of cognitive scripts—complexes of beliefs, attitudes, and behavioral predispositions—that are automatically triggered and guide behavior in certain situations.[33] Thus, anyone's views, regardless of their race, toward black and brown bodies can ultimately be tainted and result in treating people of color prejudicially.

Consistent with prior research, the current findings, as we have seen in this section, reveal that Black residents, specifically from Baltimore, reported personal and vicarious experiences of being treated harshly by Black officers.[34] Clearly, having more Black officers does not necessarily equate to better treatment of Blacks. Thus, evidence suggests that the diversification of police departments in and of itself is insufficient to improving police-minority relationships.

Occupational Socialization

But what of police departments? In an effort to improve police-citizen relations, there has been a push to diversify them. When the demographic composition—race, gender, class, income—of a police organization reflects the composition of the population it serves, this is known as passive representation.[35] However, simply adopting diversification strategies to improve relationships between police and minority communities may not prove effective unless active representation occurs. In contrast to passive representation, active representation is concerned with how diverse representation affects policy-making.[36] While it is common to assume that passive representation would lead to active representation in police organizations, high levels of organizational socialization may preclude this from occurring.

Police forces are well known for their use of socialization to change the attitudes and behaviors of their employees. It is not uncommon for organizational administrators to instill a common set of assumptions within their employees and inculcate a world view that values organizational loyalty above personal beliefs.[37] According to political scientist Harlan Hahn, the degree of cohesion and solidarity among officers has been noted as a conspicuous yet unusual component of the police profession and has been described as a "blue-wall."[38] As such, this profession reflects fraternal support and emphasizes adherence to the norms of a police subculture—a distinct set of values and beliefs that shape officers' behaviors.

Residents certainly had much to say about their perceptions of their local police departments. In all, 14 accounts (22 percent) from Ferguson and 14 accounts (22 percent) from Baltimore emphasized in their assessment of police subculture the challenges Black officers faced on the job. Specifically, Black residents in both cities believed that Black police officers often attempted to conform to the informal norms of the occupational culture within police departments. Marcel, a Ferguson resident, asserted that, upon joining the police force, "what the Black officer is trying to do is trying to fit in . . . [because] he belongs to a club." In a similar vein, when speaking of Black police, Ebony, from Ferguson, acknowledged that while some officers treat Black citizens respectfully, she admitted that "some of them are just trying to fit in and they don't think about what's right and what's wrong." Marcel and Ebony's comments suggest that Black officers seek acceptance in the police organization and that career advancement is tied to adopting the standards of police culture. The theme of proving oneself was common, as residents believed that officers tried to demonstrate to their colleagues that the color of their uniform trumped their racial identity. Consider the response of Baltimorean resident Abelina:

> [Black police] got to let [White officers] know they still with them. But [Black officers] seem like they turning against [Black people], to prove a point to [White officers]. . . . They got to really actually prove something to them, to their White counterpart, you know. . . . When you do the job, like we're told, "You do it, or you don't do it at all. You do it my way or the highway." And then so that way it looks like [Black officers] come in so much more forceful then the White ones and you say, "Dang, you didn't have to do that." You know, and sometimes they don't. But they go out of their way and they just like to prove a point 'cause the White man is standing right there.

As indicated from these accounts, some residents viewed officers more monolithically. That is, residents were convinced that both Black and White officers behaved similarly at work, which entailed negative treatment toward Blacks. Lorraine, a resident of Baltimore, asserted that there are "crooked cops out there," both Black and White. Cliff, a resident of Ferguson, bemoaned that once a Black officer "gets around the White cop, they want to be all so big and tough and start beating everybody up." Likewise, Terrell, who lived in Ferguson, articulated that he perceived that Black officers are "trying to prove a point, you know? Like they run around—they wanna do what the White [officer] do basically.

That's how I feel. The White [officer] flags [stops] a Black guy, then [Black officers] wanna flag [stop] a Black guy."

Not only did these participants see no difference in treatment between officers of different races, some believed that Black officers "have been tainted by their occupational association with [W]hite officers."[39] A considerable body of research shows that White officers generally perceive and treat Black civilians negatively.[40] Reflecting the dominant attitudes of the majority population toward people of color in the United States, White police officers often negatively stereotype Black American as criminals. Residents who were interviewed perceived that rather than defy or challenge such stereotypes, some Black police were more apt to conform to occupational roles, which entailed stereotyping people of color. In the case of police, all officers are dealing with enormous systemic and cultural forces that build racial bias against minority groups, especially Blacks. Consequently, Alonzo, a Baltimorean resident, concluded that "it's not a Black or White thing, it's a blue thing." The "blue cops" position referred to by Alonzo is the idea that the color of the uniform—not one's skin color—is the only color that really matters.

Many scholars have asserted that Black officers are simply "blue." The occupational nature of policing entails working odd hours under stressful conditions, which generally results in officers developing strong loyalty to one another while being insulated from the civilian population that they serve.[41] The literature shows that within law enforcement agencies there are strong informal groups with a distinctive police subculture where there are strong pressures to conform.[42] Officers of color are not exempt from conforming to the informal norms of the culture within the department. They may feel obliged to adopt the values of the police force to maintain a positive self-image of being a good officer or to advance their careers, either because they feel pressure to do so or because they agree with the organizational view.[43]

Faced with the pressure or desire to conform to informal rules, Black officers may remain silent even after witnessing injustice. In fact, many Black residents here believed that the "code of silence," which shields officers from scrutiny, was often at play. Ferguson resident Maurice, for instance, described an incident in which Ferguson and St. Louis County police barged into his house looking for his brother. Maurice described having been verbally and physically assaulted by six policemen in his house even though he responded to their questions and did not resist. He noted that officers "were calling me the 'N' word and stuff like that. And [the Black officer] didn't say nothing. I don't know if it was because he was at work, or you know what I mean?" What remained particularly disconcerting for Maurice was that the Black officer on duty remained silent while other White officers hurled racial slurs at Maurice. Marcus, also from Ferguson, recounted a similar incident:

> I remember about three months ago, I was going to visit my grandmother about nine o'clock in the morning, and this was the last thing I had. I had my cell phone charger on me. I went to the corner store to buy some chips and a soda, come outside, eat my chips, drinking my soda, walking to my grandmother's house. The police swooped down on me undercover. There is a Black one and a White one. [They] tell me they've seen me with a gun. I knew they were lying, but they said they had seen me with a gun. Basically, it was a cell phone charger. I had a metro traffic warrant. They locked me up for it. The Black police officer didn't want to lock me up because he had seen it was bogus. He was just joining the force and the White guy, he has been on the force longer so he had to listen to him. They took me in and gave me resisting arrest. I didn't resist. I just asked them, "What are you locking me up for?" and they called that resist.

Though Marcus did not specify how he became aware of the Black officers' reluctance to book him, Marcus perceived that the officer had to take his partner's lead since he had seniority. Consequently, the Black officer remained silent even though, Marcus claimed, "it was bogus." Likewise, Cassandra recounted an incident in which a Baltimore officer thought she was eating pizza in a subway station: "[T]his one Caucasian police officer came up to me and started yelling at me, threatened to lock me up, which I don't know why."[44] Cassandra, who was a minor at the time, noted that "he was one Caucasian in a group of Black . . . police officers [but] the Black police officers didn't say anything." Research shows that the police code of silence not only exists but can breed, support, and cultivate other forms of unethical behavior in the police force.[45] In some cases, the insularity of the police subculture not only buttresses informal norms about police violence or mistreatment but diminishes police accountability to the civilians they are to protect and serve.[46]

Although there was certainly frustration on the part of participants that some Black officers held their racial identity as less important than their occupational identity, others speculated as to why this was the case. Regarding officers in Ferguson, Arlene, a Black resident of Ferguson, remarked:

> There are not even enough Black officers to band together and say, "We're not going to let this keep happening. We're sitting here in the locker room, we're hearing how they're talking about us." There's not enough for them to stand back because they don't have any backing. They don't have any backing, so they have to back each other.

Arlene suggests that the inadequate representation of Black police officers in Ferguson undermines their ability to meet the needs of local Black citizens. In other words, the institutional context of the police organization may inhibit Black officers from providing active representation. Others were cognizant of what was on the line for Black officers who went against the police subculture. Abryann, a resident of Baltimore, stated, "[Black officers] might feel more persuaded to act a certain way or act accordingly." She continued:

> [N]o one wants to work in a hostile environment. . . . From the stories I was able to read through different news outlets for those that did work differently, they were reprimanded, they were fired, they lost any access to their pensions, they were blackballed, so I don't know. I think maybe it just might be a matter of survival . . . maybe these are the circumstances they find themselves in.

Failure to conform may not only result in ostracism or lack of career advancement, as Abryann noted, but potentially become fatal. Edith, a resident of Baltimore said, "Black officers are outnumbered by White officers and they have to be able to get along with and also show that they have the White officers' back so they can be protected as well." Likewise, Arlene, from Ferguson, said that Black police "fall right in there because that's their work environment [and they don't want] no hostility between them. Somebody's got to protect them. . . . That's who protects their back." Some believed that Black officers may be reluctant to get involved in accusations of police violence for fear of retaliation and exclusion within the department. Given that police have a dangerous job, looking out for and defending one another is common among officers. Ultimately, the strong culture of policing, which emphasizes conformity to prevailing norms, can overwhelm individual racial differences such that officers are officers first and foremost, regardless of their race.

Political scientist Elaine Sharp has found that while racial representation in elected positions has decreased the amount of racial bias in order maintenance arrests, increased representation in the police force does not reduce, and may even be positively associated with, bias.[47] Likewise, public administration and policy scholars Vickie Wilkins and Brian Williams have not found a link between Black representation among police officers and a decline in racial disparities in vehicular stops.[48] Surprisingly, they found that, with increased Black police representation, Black motorists are more likely to be racially profiled. Wilkins and Williams explained such findings as the result of occupational socialization in police agencies that discourage minority police from advocating for the interests of minorities. Black officers were more likely than White officers to use coercive actions in resolving conflict, which would be consistent with the "blue cop" identity. However, the authors also found that Black officers made decisions to engage in supportive activities in Black neighborhoods out of concern for the community. In addition, Ivan Sun and Brian Payne found that Black officers were more coercive than White officers in handling disputes among civilians.[49] As a result, they concluded that Black officers' identities cannot be solely referred to as "blue cop" or "Black cop."

Black participants, however, seemed to be aware of the bind that some Black officers found themselves in. That is, they exist in a state of dual loyalty. On the one hand, as Black people, they may relate to and be committed to the Black community. Their awareness of previous police violence and the likelihood that many officers live in or near the community that they police suggests that they would be empathetic to Black citizens. Yet, on the other hand, they remain committed to a contrasting set of occupational values and obligations. In his discussion of Black police, Raymond, a resident of Ferguson, asserted, "because they're [a] minority in their own police station or where they may be, they may

have to go along with certain things they probably wouldn't [want to]."
And Trevon, who lived in Ferguson, claimed that officers "don't got no
choice but to do exactly what their chief is telling them to do." Similarly,
Jason from Baltimore asserted that Black officers can "become institutionalized within that system and now you're following orders." Hence,
Baltimorean resident Junior concluded, "It's not about the race of the
cops, it's about racism of the actual system that they protect and serve."

The result of police socialization is "an ideology and shared culture
that breeds unprecedented conformity to the traditional police norms
and values."[50] The socialization of an officer can be formal (e.g., police
training) or informal (e.g., learning norms and acceptable behavior
from other officers). Civilians, including the participants in this study,
are certainly not privy to the ins and outs of the occupational culture of
policing. But the very perception that officers, including Black officers,
are socialized to police people of color in disadvantaged communities
more aggressively than Whites or those residing in more affluent neighborhoods has negative implications. Racial minorities' perceptions that
police forces as a whole treat people of color unfairly and disrespectfully
only serve to undermine their trust and cooperation with the police.[51]

So would having a higher percentage of Black police officers in Ferguson or Baltimore have changed how the protests unfolded? It's possible, but probably not. The research I did for this book indicates that
some residents, especially those in Baltimore, believe that simply hiring
a higher proportion of Black officers in the police force does not indicate that the department will function better. If Black officers are hired
and placed in occupational settings that socialize them to embrace the
stereotypes of Black civilians as threatening, then it is illogical to expect
police-community relationships to improve.

Some studies conclude that when Black officers are represented in
high enough numbers—more than 40 percent—they are more likely to
represent the interests of Black civilians, as they will be less likely to fear
consequences from their department or derision from their peers.[52] In
particular, criminologists Sean Nicholson-Crotty and his colleagues asserted that "[t]here is an inflection point at which Black officers may
become less likely to discriminate against Black citizens and more inclined to assume a minority advocacy role or to become neutral enforcers of the law"—thus, engaging in active representation.[53] However, the

current research shows that, even in Baltimore, where nearly half of the police force is Black, residents encounter discrimination and mistreatment even from Black officers. This is likely because police-minority interactions are embedded in an ecological context, which is rooted in historical racial tensions and geographical concentrations of socioeconomic disorder. In the United States, Blacks disproportionately reside in socially disorganized neighborhoods that are burdened with high rates of unemployment, poverty, and decay.[54] As discussed earlier, Ferguson, the St. Louis metropolitan area, and the city of Baltimore have long histories of racial isolation and disadvantage. Research shows that high rates of poverty, disorder, and crime affect the type and quality of policing that civilians receive, with low-income residents often becoming the targets of police surveillance and violence.[55] Consequently, distrust and animosity characterize police-minority relationships.

Thus, it is unrealistic to assume that high proportions of Black officers within a force will improve citizens' views toward the police without addressing the structural problems in poor neighborhoods. While increasing the racial diversity of law enforcement agencies has intuitive appeal, it is a simple solution to a much more complex problem. What we will see in the next chapter is that people's adverse experiences with police—Black or White—spurred their decisions to take to the streets and protest against police violence.

4

"We Stand United"

Why Protesters Marched

It is our duty. This is our duty, I believe that if someone—if you, for instance, committed a crime, and I saw it and did nothing I am worse than you. Because I watched the wrong-doing happen and I allowed it to continue and did nothing of it. I believe that we all have power within ourselves. We are all powerful with our words and with our different talents and I believe it's everyone's civic duty when they see something wrong to stand up to say something . . . . It's my civic duty as a human being and as a United States constituent [to protest] . . . and stand up [against] injustice.
—Tremaine (Black Baltimore protester)

Some witnesses of the Ferguson, Missouri, shooting claimed that Michael Brown had his hands up in a gesture of surrender when Officer Darren Wilson shot him, while other observers alleged that, earlier in the incident, Brown was the aggressor, reaching into the police vehicle and fighting for Wilson's gun. After sorting through conflicting witness accounts, on November 24, 2014, the St. Louis County prosecuting attorney, Robert McCullough, announced that the grand jury declined to prosecute Wilson for Brown's shooting. The pronouncement triggered civil unrest in Ferguson and mobilized protests throughout the nation against police brutality that were documented across social media platforms.

Within five months after the St. Louis County grand jury's decision, Freddie Gray, a Black resident in Baltimore, Maryland, was arrested by the BPD. While in police custody, Gray sustained injuries to his spinal cord and subsequently died on April 19, 2015. Gray's death sparked outrage that erupted into protests and looting in Baltimore, which was also covered in detail on social media.

The deaths of Michael Brown and Freddie Gray at the hands of police not only rocked the cities of Ferguson and Baltimore but sparked civil unrest across the nation. The killings gave rise to the Black Lives Matter movement, initiated in 2013 following the death of Trayvon Martin, to protest systemic racism. In fact, what gets referred to as "the Black Lives Matter movement" is the collective labor of a wide range of Black liberation organizations, including groups like the Black Youth Project 100, the Dream Defenders, the Alliance for a Just Society, the St. Louis Action council, Millennial Activists United, and the Organization for Black Struggle, to name just a few.

The depth of anger and frustration among protesters was palpable, as they roused a sleeping nation and urged it to come to terms with the many, largely Black civilians who are murdered by police. Recognizing that such incidents are not isolated, activists demanded equal justice in America.

The question of why individuals participate in protest movements often surfaces among researchers. They suggest that initial participation in social movements is connected to social psychological factors (e.g., conceptualization of grievances), biographical factors (e.g., time constraints), and social ties and networks.[1] Individuals with biographical availability—who are relatively free from life responsibilities such as full-time employment and familial obligation—are the most likely to participate: specifically, young adults and individuals of advanced middle age. Personal turning points in one's life also can facilitate initial contact with social movements because they represent periods during which individuals are both biographically and emotionally available.[2] Social networks have also been shown to increase individuals' likelihood to become involved. There is a dynamic element to this process: while people often get involved in specific movements through their preexisting interpersonal relationships, their very participation also establishes new bonds, which can affect subsequent developments in their activism.

Participants in the current study provided detailed accounts of why they participated in protest movements. Many of these explanations support the findings of previous work on this topic, including grievances, increased efficacy, and collective identity. Grievances arise when a person or group experiencing inequality and feelings of relative deprivation has been the victim of injustice or has a sense of moral indignation about some state of affairs.[3] Social movements and protests are more likely to occur when there is a poor fit between a group's interest and the capacity of political institutions to address its concerns.[4] When citizens perceive that they have been unjustly deprived compared to other groups, protest behavior becomes likely.[5] The literature further distinguishes between relative deprivation based on personal (i.e., individual) and group comparisons.[6] Research shows that individuals who experience both personal *and* group relative deprivation are particularly motivated to take to the streets.[7] As discussed in chapter 2, many Black Ferguson and Baltimore residents experienced an erosion of their dignity due to routine, unwarranted police stops. Later in this chapter I will show that residents' negative experiences with police, both direct and indirect, spurred their participation in protests.

Along with grievances, efficacy—or an individual's expectation that it is possible to change conditions or policies through protests—is a strong indicator of the likelihood of protest involvement.[8] This phenomenon has several different components. Individual efficacy refers to beliefs that individual actions have the potential to shape, and thus alter, the social structure.[9] However, according to social movement scholars Jacquelien Van Stekelenburg and Bert Klandermans, in order "for the perceptions of the possibility of change to take hold people need to perceive the group to be able to unite and fight for the issue *and* they must perceive the political context as receptive to the claims made by their group."[10] The belief that collective protest efforts will shape the outcome of a problem is referred to as group efficacy.[11] Bert Klandermans shows that people are more likely to participate in protest movements when they perceive that it will assist them in redressing their grievances at affordable costs.[12] That is, the more effective an individual believes collective action participation to be, the more likely the person is to participate.

Collective identity is also important, as it is often tied to grievances and reinforces distinctions that exacerbate feelings of relative deprivation.[13] Identity is our understanding of who we are, who other people are, and other people's understanding of themselves or others.[14] Collective identity reflects a sense of "we-ness" or "one-ness" based on shared characteristics or experiences among group members and can serve as the basis of engagement in collective action.[15] When these identities become politicized, they not only lead to shared grievances but also link feelings of inequality and unfairness with an external enemy.[16] When such identities are salient, the ability to identify and cooperate with out-groups makes normative modes of negotiation less likely.[17] Several studies reveal that when people identify with a group membership (i.e., race/ethnicity, gender, age, etc.), they are more inclined to protest on behalf of that group.[18]

This chapter examines protesters' accounts of what drove them to engage in collective action (i.e., protests, marches, rallies, demonstrations) and how they mobilized. The chapter also considers the role of the media in mobilizing protest movements, especially among young people, who were at the forefront of the movement. We will see that adverse experiences with police, as illustrated in chapters 2 and 3, drove many Black civilians to the streets to protest the police brutality against Black individuals for which Ferguson and Baltimore have a troubling record.

Why Protest?

Of the 115 protesters I interviewed who were engaged in collective action, 78 were from Ferguson and 37 were from Baltimore. Table 4.1 illustrates a host of reasons that protesters gave for engaging in activism efforts.[19] The top four reasons reported were the idea that Brown and Gray were victims of injustice; the belief that the deaths of both young men were not isolated events; feelings of a moral and ethical responsibility to get involved; and the desire to affect change.[20]

TABLE 4.1. Reasons for Engaging in Collective Action

	Ferguson	Baltimore
Victims of Injustice	13	5
Not Isolated	20	4
Moral Responsibility	13	10
Potential for Change	30	9
Information	2	4
History in Making	4	2
Curiosity	4	1
Support Young People	4	1

Victims of Injustice

Asked what led to their engagement in protests, activists frequently articulated that grievances, or feelings of injustice, initiated their participation. Among the protesters that I interviewed, 18 activists (16 percent)—89 percent of whom were Black and two-thirds were women—identified both Michael Brown and Freddie Gray as victims of police violence. With regard to Brown's death, the number of shots fired by former Officer Wilson outraged some. Derrell, a Black male, boldly announced that the "reason why I started protesting [was] because I thought that they did Michael Brown wrong by shooting him so many times." And Tyrone, a Black male, claimed that Brown was "killed like an animal. It's unjustified like, 'no, this [is] not right.' So like that's what actually brought me out to protest because it hurt me so much." Within a day after Brown's fatal shooting, crowds amassed at three locations: Canfield Drive by the vigil area, West Florissant Avenue near Original Red's BBQ, and South Florissant Road in front of Ferguson Police Department headquarters.[21]

More commonly reported by protesters than the number of shots fired was the shock of observing or learning that Brown's dead body lay on the street for four hours. Although Brown was killed around noon on August 9, 2014, his body was not removed until approximately 4 p.m., at which time his body was transported to the St. Louis County Medical Examiner.[22] St. Louis County Police Chief Jon Belmar asserted that processing the crime scene thoroughly was of the utmost importance.[23] The DOJ also contended that, in accord with police practices, the crime scene detectives processed the scene with Brown's body present in order to "accurately measure distances, precisely document body position, and note injury and other markings relative to other aspects of the crime scene that photographs may not capture."[24] In fact, some forensic professionals claim that, while four hours is a long time on a public street, at times bodies remain at crime scenes even longer than Brown's did.[25] Investigative procedures of this type prescribe leaving the scene untouched until evidence is collected.[26] Police reports of Brown's death claimed that investigative procedures, coupled with a chaotic scene that threatened the safety of investigators, explain the delay in processing the crime scene.[27]

Despite attempts to maintain the integrity of the scene, the sight of Brown's body lying in the street for more than four hours made little sense to Ferguson protesters. Some, especially Black women, perceived it as indicative of police disrespect of Black bodies. Monique stated that "the main reason we started protesting was how the fact [they] left him out there . . . for four and half hours in a hundred degree weather." Rachel concurred, stating that "the way that they did the investigation, the crime scene was enough to let people know that we had to take to the streets because it took them four and a half hours to get him up off the ground. And that in itself was a spit in the face." Rosalind described the scene:

> I saw him laying there. . . . [He] was laying there like he was a dead dog. This boy just laying in the street bleeding, just blood running. Then when the ambulance did come, they didn't come and lift him up; they came and blocked the scene because they had taped everything off. They just had everybody stand back. They came and they blocked him with the ambulance and they lifted him into a SUV.

Protesters expressed anger and distress at the indignity of Brown's body lying on the street for hours in the hot sun. According to the DOJ report, it took approximately twenty minutes for police to cover Brown's body with several sheets.[28] While Brown's body remained uncovered, some residents took pictures of his corpse with their phones and posted them on social media[29] When crime scene detectives and the medicolegal investigator completed the processing of Brown's body, he was placed in an unmarked vehicle from the St. Louis Livery Services, a private contractor for the St. Louis County Medical Examiner's Office.[30]

The image of Brown's corpse lying on the street fueled local residents' anger and tension even after the body was removed.[31] It was this image that proved to be galvanizing, along with shared outrage over Brown's violent death. For some activists, Brown's death was arguably akin to a lynching—a racialized, state-sanctioned form of violence without due process that occurred with regularity during the nineteenth and twentieth centuries.[32] Lynchings were brutally violent and entailed torture, burning, mutilation, and castration. From Reconstruction until World War II, thousands of Black men, women, and children were lynched due to fears of interracial sex, perceptions of casual social transgressions, and allegations of serious violent crime.[33] Used as a tactic to maintain racial control, lynchings not only targeted the entire Black community but were carried out with impunity, as public spectacles.[34] Similarly, many argue that Brown's killing was unwarranted, though it appeared to be lawful; his corpse was left on the street corner for hours in the same way that Black bodies were left hanging from trees, his killer was not held liable, and his character was attacked as a form of justification for the killing.[35] While Brown was a high school graduate a week shy of starting college, in the weeks following his murder an investigative journalist alleged that he had committed crimes as serious as murder and was part of a gang—claims that proved to be false. Two media outlets, the *St. Louis Post-Dispatch* and an online California journalist, petitioned the St. Louis Court for access to any existing records for Michael Brown prior to his turning eighteen.[36] In addition, a writer for the *New York Times* stated that Michael Brown was "no angel."[37]

Other residents were distraught because of their belief that, at the time of the shooting, Brown's hands were up in surrender. This viewpoint was particularly common among the Black women who have been at the forefront of the protest movements. Rebecca reported, "If [Brown] did have his hands up, then he surrendered and [the police] still killed him. That was dirty." Isabelle said, "I don't believe that the boy rustled and tussled with that cop. That cop shot that boy while his hands were up, while that boy was surrendering." And the following conversation reveals Monique's eyewitness account of the moments before Brown's death:

> MONIQUE: I was out there across the street the day [Darren Wilson] shot [Michael Brown]. People were outside saying he shot him. When I look around, I was just one of the people that saw the boy laying there. And it was like a hundred degree weather. And he just shot him like he was mounted up here. And [the] boy, did have his hands up.
>
> INTERVIEWER: You mean—how do you know?
>
> MONIQUE: I was there. I was there. They were trying to interview me and stuff for a while. . . . I was across the street at an apartment and when we looked out there. . . . The boy had his hands up. We just heard the pop pop, looking through the garage and we ran out there. . . . Then all of a sudden they told us to get back.

INTERVIEWER: So, did you see Michael Brown when he was alive? I mean, you saw when he had his hands up? Is that what you said?

MONIQUE: I was actually—I was in the house and a lady said, "They look like they finna[38] shoot a boy," and they said, "No he has his hands up". . . . I didn't wanna tell too many people this because I don't want anybody asking me too many questions. I was at a house with a lady in Canfield Apartments and they saw—the lady said, "There's a boy out there, looks like the police finna shoot him," and they shot him. When we ran out there, the police were there and they told us to get back.

Although Monique, along with several witnesses, asserted that Brown had his hands up, other witnesses said the teenager attacked the officer and attempted to take his gun.[39] In declining to indict Wilson on any criminal charges on November 24, 2014, grand jurors deferred to Wilson's account that he feared for his life before killing Brown. In describing to the grand jury why he killed Brown, Wilson explained, "It looks like a demon," asserting that Brown had the "most intense aggressive face." Despite being six feet four inches tall and weighing 210 pounds, Wilson said that, when he grabbed six-foot-four, 294-pound Brown, "I felt like a 5-year-old holding onto Hulk Hogan. . . . that's how big he felt and how small I felt just from grasping his arm."[40] Wilson ultimately depicted Brown as a villain with supernatural powers who had to be terminated.

Descriptors of Black males as demonized monsters are not new. Racial classifications have been used throughout US history to justify the enslavement of Black people, who were commonly portrayed as animalistic, violent brutes who needed to be tamed.[41] Following the Civil War, many Whites argued that the institution of slavery kept Black men subdued and thus was necessary for public safety.[42] During the 1970s and 1980s, in the context of the war on drugs and the war on crime, young Black males were stereotyped as the poster child for violence; consequently, they became the enemy.[43] Clergy leaders Jamie Hawley and Staycie Flint assert that throughout American history "Black men are the *invisibly visible*—caught in a paradox of being devoid of participation in socioeconomic and political structures but always visible enough to incite public fear."[44] Black people's skin color makes them visible. When

Blackness is coupled with a tall and heavy physique, Blacks become hypervisible. However, hypervisibility simultaneously renders Blacks invisible, erasing who they are as distinct individuals. Hawley and Flint argue that when Black men are ascribed supernatural powers it "deprives them of a real presence in the world, of bodies that have spirits that exist *apart from and independent* of Whiteness, the White gaze, and White expectation." As a result, it is perhaps not surprising to learn that the grand jury chose not to indict Wilson for Brown's death.

The grand jury findings aside, the DOJ conducted its own investigation and concluded that Wilson was not the aggressor, based on physical and forensic evidence, as well as eyewitnesses statements, which changed upon further investigation.[45] Thus, Wilson was ultimately cleared of criminal violations of federal civil rights laws. Even though the St. Louis County grand jury and the DOJ declined to prosecute Wilson, Michael Brown's family was awarded a $1.5 million settlement in a wrongful death lawsuit against the city.[46] Settlements for civil claims are not uncommon; the ten US cities with the largest police departments collectively paid out more than $1 billion from 2010 to 2014 to settle police misconduct cases.[47]

The initial shock of Brown's violent death turned into disbelief and seething rage. Not only did many perceive that a deep sense of injustice had taken place but, as discussed in chapters 2 and 3, they also found themselves the recipients of unjustifiable police contact. This sparked demonstrations in Ferguson, as well as civil disorder in cities across the nation.[48] The perceived injustice of Michael Brown's death led to group-based anger, and the link between perceived injustice and group-based anger was amplified by direct and indirect negative experiences with the police. Among the Ferguson protesters that I interviewed, 63 percent reported personal and 76 percent reported vicarious experiences with police that were negative in nature prior to Brown's death. Of those who reported these experiences, all were Black with the exception of two Whites. Even participants that did not have personal encounters with law enforcement had heard about or knew someone who had experienced direct negative interactions with police. In their examination of personal and vicarious experiences with police among Black, White, and Latino residents of Chicago, criminologist Dennis Rosenbaum and his colleagues found that their adverse effect on attitudes toward police was greatest for Blacks, most likely because they discussed incidents of police mistreatment with others.[49] In this way, the relationship between perceived injustice and group-based anger, further strengthened by individual and shared grievances, energized protest participation.

With regard to Gray, some Baltimoreans were also aggrieved by what they perceived to be injustice. First, a video shot by a bystander revealed Gray, unable to walk, shouting out in pain as officers dragged him to a police van, where they placed him without securing him with a seatbelt.[50] Second, though he requested an inhaler multiple times because of his difficulty breathing, he did not receive one, nor any medical attention.[51] What remained most troubling to these Baltimore residents was that Gray, upon arrival at the police station, was alive yet unresponsive due to a severe neck injury. Gray was treated for three broken vertebrae and a crushed voice box—akin to injuries suffered in a car accident.[52] His injuries proved fatal, and he died one week after his arrest.[53] Joy, a Black woman, said, "I thought it was senseless and useless for the [way] Freddie died." Jessie, a Black man, reported having engaged in protest movements because "the whole situation didn't seem right to me . . . [from] the whole beginning they said [one thing] happened and then when you watched the video something [else] had to happen prior to that."

The circumstances surrounding Gray's death triggered outrage among civilians. Karis, a Black woman, noted, "my people are angry and sore and in pain over that boy's death." Emma, a White woman, explained:

> [Freddie Gray] was arrested and physically harmed. He was arrested but with no probable cause—like no apparent reason. [He was] physically harmed and still not sent to a healthcare facility right away. And then later died when he was in the hospital. . . . I mean the city was obviously really angry about his death.

Similar to protesters in Ferguson, the indecent way in which police treated Gray evoked strong feelings; Gray's broken spine coupled with officers' lack of deference to his inability to breathe and to walk stoked their anger. Activists that I interviewed viewed Gray's death as unjust, which led many of them to take collective action. Like the Ferguson protesters, most reported negative encounters with police. Specifically,

among the Baltimorean activists in the sample—all of whom were
Black, with the exception of two White, two mixed-race, and one Asian
activist— 51 percent reported having personal and 57 percent vicarious
police encounters that were negative in nature. The relationship between
their perceptions of injustice and group-based anger, further strengthened by these experiences, led to protest participation. Within six days
of Gray's arrest, hundreds of people demonstrated outside the Western
District Police Station.[54] Protests continued to unfold at the police headquarters and City Hall after Gray died on April 19, 2015, and a statement
was released that Gray's spine had been 80 percent severed.[55]

Because of previous incidents of Black individuals being injured or
killed at the hands of police, many of the activists I interviewed did
not expect to see any charges levied against the officers. Ania, a Black
woman, said: "I hope that there's justice but . . . [a]nytime any charges
has ever been brought upon Baltimore City Police, the most that officers
got was 'suspended with pay.' No one never was fired, or anything due to
any incidents that they have ever done." Consider the following dialogue
when Ania was asked what would need to happen in order for justice to
prevail:

> ANIA: For them [the police] to pay for their actions. Because they were
> wrong.
> INTERVIEWER: Okay. What would "pay for their actions" entail?
> ANIA: Just as well as if me or you was to commit a crime that big—we
> would have 25 [years] to life. Why can't they get the same numbers
> that me and you get? You human, too. [The police] just [have] a
> badge.
> INTERVIEWER: Yeah. Face the same punishment?
> ANIA: Yes.
> INTERVIEWER: Or potentially face the same punishment.
> ANIA: Same punishment.
> INTERVIEWER: As any other person who killed any other person?
> ANIA: Exactly. That's what's best. A murder is a murder. It's all the same.
> Would it have been different if . . . his life would had been took by
> one of his peers? They would have been—they would have had no
> bail. And if any person outside without a badge gets locked up for
> murder, you have no bail. You're going to sit until you're proven

innocent or guilty. These officers got arrested, turned themselves in one day, and all their bails was paid by that next morning. There's no justice in that at all.

Despite Ania's hope, none of the six officers charged in the arrest and death of Freddie Gray were convicted. Nevertheless, the City of Baltimore agreed to pay Gray's family $6.4 million to settle a civil suit in September 2015.[56] Though the city accepted all civil liability in the arrest and death of Gray, it did not acknowledge any wrongdoing by police.[57]

Police are rarely found liable for criminal charges and generally enjoy immunity for their actions, a tendency that has its roots in slave laws. For instance, the 1705 Virginia Slave Act declared:

If any slave resist his master, or owner, or other person, by his or her order, correcting such slave, and shall happen to be killed in such correction, it shall not be accounted [a] felony; but the master, owner, and every such other person so giving correction, shall be free and acquit of all punishment and accusation for the same, as if such incident had never happened.[58]

The homicide of a slave was considered justifiable when a slave "forcibly" resisted arrest, such that attempts to make an arrest "cause[d] reasonable fear of loss of life, or of great bodily harm."[59] Today White officers who kill Black "suspects" need only declare that they feared for their lives and they will be let off the hook. Parallels between the language of the slave codes and arrest laws in some states should cause citizens to pause and consider if American laws support homicides that are structurally rooted in injustice and grounded in racial hostility.[60]

Not Isolated Events

It would be a mistake to conclude that protests in Ferguson and Baltimore were solely about Michael Brown and Freddie Gray, although their tragic deaths outraged the nation. In the study, 24 activists (21 percent) took to the streets to protest the pattern of criminalization they had directly or indirectly observed. In other words, they saw themselves as

aggrieved victims. All were Black with the exception of two White protesters, and 12 were men and 12 were women. As mentioned in chapter 2,
the DOJ reported a pattern of excessive use of police force against Black
residents in both Ferguson and Baltimore. Participants also observed
that police brutality is not rare.

In his discussion of police shootings, Clayton, a Black Ferguson protester, objected that "this has to stop and I feel like it hasn't stopped. This
can't keep happening. Black men or anybody like that, the police can't
keep doing this. They've been doing it for a while and I feel like they
can't keep doing it. This has to stop." Likewise, Jamia, a Black Ferguson
activist, asserted, "This is not the first case that this has happened. It's
just that we getting tired of it." Garret, a White Baltimorean, said, "I
have seen [my friends] be treated horribly. Because of assumptions that
people are making based on the color of their skin or their poverty or
what part of town they live in."

The report that Brown's and Gray's deaths were not isolated events
are not surprising. Several Black protesters from Ferguson cited a
string of highly publicized incidents of questionable use of force by
police over the past few years. Carlos, for example, stated: "What got
me out the chair was we got plenty of people out here getting killed.
Trayvon Martin got killed. Eric Garner got killed, and Kajieme Powell
got killed by a police. So it's too many police murders going on, and
they [the police] keep on getting away with it. That's what got me out
my chair is they keep on getting away with it. Free murder." And Tray
recounted that "this lady that was choked out in whatever town she
was in and then it was another lady beaten on the highway. A guy was
choked out he said he couldn't breathe." Both Carlos and Tray spoke
of Black individuals who have been the recipients of violence, including 17-year-old Trayvon Martin, who was fatally shot by a member of
a civilian neighborhood patrol in Sanford, Florida, in 2012; Eric Garner, who died in July 2014 after a New York City police officer placed
him in a chokehold for selling untaxed cigarettes; Marlene Pinnock, a
great-grandmother, who was beaten by a California Highway Patrol-
man on the highway in July 2014; and Kajieme Powell, a mentally ill
man shot by St. Louis police officers as he was approaching them with
a knife in August 2014. Protesters in the sample were well aware of
these cases, along with those of many other people of color who were

victims of police brutality, and the need to air their grievances regarding the integrity of Black lives fueled their decision to engage in street demonstrations.

Although protesters were familiar with a string of high-profile cases of police violence and misconduct toward Black civilians, the reality is that many incidents do not receive media attention. Several male activists that I interviewed reported having been the victim of police brutality themselves or having family members who were mistreated by law enforcement. Javon, a Black Ferguson activist, admitted he got involved in street protests because "I been a part of police brutality, I have friends that have been a part of police brutality, and I could have been Michael Brown." In a similar vein, Steevie, a Black Ferguson protester, provided a detailed account of his family members having been abused by police:

> The same way that officer accosted Michael Brown walking down the street, my son has been accosted for walking down the street for doing nothing other than walking down the street. My nephews have been accosted walking down the street by the police for doing nothing. I've driven in front of police cars, and I've seen my nephew walk down the street. I've seen police cars drive past, turn around, come back, and I've driven my car in front of the police car to block the police from my nephew. I've seen my son come down the street, I've seen police cars drive past and turn around. My son is twenty-two. This started when he was sixteen. My son is six foot three inches. They can't tell the difference whether he's a boy or a man. He is a boy, but they still accosted my son.

Based on their experience of police, these Black men perceived that they could end up like Michael Brown or Freddie Gray, which compelled them to take to the streets.

Black women also felt obliged to take part in protest events for these reasons. Dyshelle from Ferguson recounted, "It just felt like enough was enough. It was an urge in me when I, you know, saw the kid's blood . . . on the ground. . . . It could be my little brother. That could be me." And Latoya from Ferguson said, "I want to get out the fact that we are all capable in this time to be a Mike Brown or a Trayvon Martin. . . . It could happen to anyone and we need to keep it from happening to anyone." As we saw in chapters 2 and 3, many Black civilians did not experience law enforcement as defenders of peace but rather as an occupying force that was more likely to violate their civil rights, not unlike slave patrols.[61] In his book *Chokehold: Policing Black Men*, law professor Paul Butler contended:

> There has never, not for one minute in American history, been peace between black people and the police. And nothing since slavery—not Jim Crow segregation, not lynching, not restrictive covenants in housing, not being shut out of New Deal programs like social security and the GI bill, not massive white resistance to school desegregation, not the ceaseless efforts to prevent blacks from voting—nothing has sparked the level of outrage among African Americans as when they have felt under violent attack by the police.[62]

For Black women and men, the fear that they or their loved ones could be the victims of police violence fueled their decision to engage in collective action.

However, there is a lack of reliable national data on the number of people who are actually shot and killed by the police. Ironically, it was only after the death of Michael Brown in August 2014 that then FBI Director James Comey became aware that his agency does not collect this data.[63] The FBI reports that 444 people were shot and killed by police in 2014.[64] But police departments are not required to submit data on police shootings; thus, the FBI's data underestimates the number of civilian deaths at the hands of police. In fact, after this lack of national statistics became evident, the *Washington Post* tried to collect it themselves, using all possible sources (i.e., local news, media reports, public records, internet sources), and found that 986 people were shot and killed by police in 2015—more than two times what the FBI reported the previous year.[65] Moreover, Blacks were found to be three times as likely to be shot and killed as Whites and represented 40 percent of all unarmed individuals killed by the police.[66] Correspondingly, the *Guardian* undertook a similar count of police shootings and reported that 1,134 people were shot and killed by police in 2015.[67] They also found that Black people were more likely than Whites, Latinos, and Native Americans to be shot and killed by the police.[68]

While data on police use of force remains inadequate, a recent study by Harvard professor Roland Fryer examined both fatal and nonfatal shootings by ten major police departments in Texas, Florida, and California between 2000 and 2015.[69] Surprisingly, he found that, while racial bias exists in police use of force, there was no evidence of bias in police shootings specifically. Fryer discovered that Blacks and Latinos were more likely to be recipients of nonlethal forms of force, such as being slapped, grabbed, pushed, handcuffed, or pepper-sprayed by an officer. However, the study found no evidence of racial discrimination in officer-involved shootings. Despite these contradictory findings, evidence still shows that Blacks are more likely to be recipients of police use of force. Consequently, the combination of police brutality and patterns of injustice led many Black citizens to conclude that they were perceived as enemies of the state. The belief that they are often viewed as an arbitrary menace led many Blacks to say enough is enough and to stand up for their rights against repression.

Desire to Affect Change

Among the activists that I interviewed, the desire to achieve change was a central factor in their protest participation. Consistent with the role of efficacy, 39 protesters (34 percent)—specifically, 34 Black, 3 White, and 2 other races/ethnicities, 18 of whom were men and 21 were women—expressed a desire to affect change. Waiting for others to bring it about was not an option; many protesters considered themselves responsible for demanding reform. Tray, a Black protester from Ferguson, said that "I believe our voices . . . [need to be] heard, you know what I'm saying, for some things to be done. Because nobody is going to go in the Oval Office. Nobody is going to come down here and say we are going to do something about it." Kristina, a Black Baltimorean, said that what motivated her to get involved was "I don't want police to keep going around killing young Black men." Likewise, Jaquann, a Black Ferguson activist, responded what got him out of his chair was "trying to stop these cops—police killing young kids—Black kids. That'd get me out of my chair, to get out there and put myself on the line for it and be committed to it."

Out of this strong desire to eradicate police brutality developed many grassroots organizations. For example, Vanished Expressions originated after ten young Black people from Ferguson came together to demand the arrest of Officer Wilson.[70] In an attempt to be heard and to keep pressure on the local and state government, they chose to sleep outside in tents for months. In explaining how this group originated, Tyrone admitted that, on the first day of protests, he chose to stop working at a bar and grill and an auto body shop because "I figured that would be effective at the time." As a result, he said,

> I slept on my book bag. Then, the next day, I slept on a cardboard box. The next day after that, I got a tent. People just started supporting me from then on. It's like a group. We all just started coming out and sleeping out[side]. . . . We had about ten people that were sleeping outside [by the third or fourth night of protesting].

However, what led Tyrone to decide to sleep outside was the state-ordered curfew put into effect from midnight to 5 a.m. by then Missouri Governor Jay Nixon, on Saturday, August 16, 2014, after the eruption of violence and looting.[71] Finding Tyrone outside of Ferguson city limits at 1:00 a.m., the youth was told by officers, he said, to "'go stand over there.' I was like, 'can I stay here all night?' They was like, 'yeah.' So I slept outside." Though the curfew was lifted two days later, Tyrone and many members of Vanished Expressions continued to camp outside in a vacant parking lot. Darius acknowledged that prior to the demonstrations in Ferguson "we didn't know each other . . . [however] one day one of our [current] group members had said, 'I'm fixing to stay.'" This led others to make the decision to "stay outside [all night]." Asia explained: "[After] we just recognized each other's faces in the marches, [we] came together when we had our first night of the free assembly [and] slept outside. It was not planned. . . . We were literally outside for the past at least 55 days." In fact, demonstrators continued to protest well into the winter months.

Members of Vanished Expressions marched every evening *and* camped outside during the summer months to ensure their collective voices were heard. Devanta, a Black woman, explained:

> We've been out there ever since Mike Brown got killed. [Vanished Expressions] was formed in the midst of that. In the midst of when people started leaving that's when [Vanished Expressions] said we not leaving,

we gon' sleep out here on the ground until justice [is served]. And they slept out in the tents, slept out on the ground and did what they said. . . . At the end of the week [when] people started going home saying, I'm wasting my time like when people start losing hope that's when [Vanished Expressions] was formed. That's when [Vanished Expressions] said we not gon' give up. We gon' sleep out here on these grounds. We gon' watch every night. Some people gon' hear us. It's some people out there who gon' pull over and march with us. It's some people out there who gon' listen to us. That's how we felt.

What initially began as the outrage of a group of individuals grappling with the broader social and structural issues that revealed themselves in the wake of a police shooting materialized as a highly resilient assembly of young people, determined to protest institutional racism, thus launching a new generation of activists petitioning for police reform and social justice while rallying that "Black Lives Matter." The Black Lives Matter movement emerged in the wake of George Zimmerman's acquittal of the killing of Trayvon Martin, an unarmed Black teenager, in Florida in 2012. In response to this decision, three Black women activists (Alicia Garza, Patrice Cullors, and Opal Tometi) coined the social media hashtag #BlackLivesMatter and created a contemporary movement against systemic oppression that expanded following the Ferguson incident and is now international in scope, with 37 chapters. According to its website, Black Lives Matter is working to transform policies that place Blacks under disproportionate police scrutiny and lead to disadvantages in the criminal justice system, including mass incarceration. Racial minorities—specifically young Black and Latino men—are considerably more likely than Whites to serve a prison sentence. In 2016, Blacks made up 13 percent of the US population yet comprised 33.3 percent of the state and federal prison population.[72] Latinos were 17 percent of the US population but 23.2 percent of those incarcerated.[73] In contrast, Whites made up 63 percent of the total population but only 30.1 percent of the prison population.[74]

Some argue that mass incarceration is a system of racial and social control with severe consequences. In her book *The New Jim Crow*, civil rights advocate, litigator, and law professor Michelle Alexander argued that mass incarceration is a well-disguised system analogous to Jim

Crow.[75] Alexander makes the case that systematic mass incarceration of poor people of color amounts to a new caste system tailored toward the political, social, and economic circumstances of our time. Similar to Jim Crow, it is legal to discriminate against individuals with a felony record in nearly the same way it was once legal to discriminate against Blacks. Once labeled a felon, the old forms of discrimination apply, as this country "authorizes discrimination against them in voting, employment, housing, education, public benefits, and jury service."[76] Consequently, an individual with a felony record becomes a member of a stigmatized caste who is condemned to a lifetime of second-class citizenship.

As a result, the Black Lives Matter network advocates for cultural dignity, respect, and social justice for *all* people, including oppressed groups. By stating that "Black lives matter," activists are not invalidating the lives of non-Blacks, as some believe. Rather, the movement draws attention to the systemic violence and oppression that Black people face on an ongoing basis.[77] As Garza, one of the co-founders of the Black Lives Movement, stated, "Given the disproportionate impact state violence has on Black lives, we understand that when Black people in this country get free, the benefits will be wide reaching and transformative for society as a whole."[78] Although cries of "Black Lives Matter" have been met with responses that "All Lives Matter," as if they are at odds with each other, the Black Lives Matter movement has been trying to say just that: all lives matter equally. However, as it relates to the criminal justice system, there is undeniable evidence that Black lives matter *less* than White lives. As we saw in chapter 2, Black participants in the current study are more likely to be stopped by the police and they are more likely to be recipients of police violence. They are also more likely to be incarcerated at disproportionate rates. In principle, all lives do matter; however, the reality is that America has not abided by that principle. Since White individuals' lives have been more greatly valued throughout American history, the movement asserts that the fate of Black people, Black rights, and Black lives are fundamental to the liberation, rights, and lives of the entire nation. In other words, when Black lives matter, all lives matter.

Recognizing that police violence is one manifestation of state violence and oppression, activists in both Ferguson and Baltimore called for change beyond the criminal justice system to ensure racial equality.

Asia, a Black Ferguson protester, asserted that the change that needs to occur is "creating a [different] government system." She explained:

> Right now we have a system that was not created for us. So I want us, the people, to take back our nation and build us a system that's made to work for us and not [en]slave us so we have to work three jobs and still cannot afford to get a pair of shoes that we want. It's just crazy.

Similarly, Allonte, a Black Baltimorean, complained that "it's a whole lot that needs to be changed, you know. First, [Black people] need jobs, you know. They need job training you know. You need housing, you know affordable housing. Some of them vacant buildings down there need to be torn down." Some Ferguson protesters and Baltimorean activists spoke out against entrenched poverty, substandard housing, and lack of economic opportunity. Jason, a mixed-race activist from Baltimore, believed the source of the problem is "the institutionalized and systematic oppression of people of color."

In response to this widespread oppression, more than fifteen racial justice organizations formed after Ferguson, including the Movement for Black Lives, Organization for Black Struggle, Black Youth Project 100, Hands Up United, and Say Her Name, to name a few. These organizations assert that state violence can take many forms, such as mass imprisonment, inadequate school systems, predatory state and corporate practices, and deinvestments in communities of color. They propose solutions that include ending the war on Black people (i.e., the criminalization of Blacks, the use of bail and capital punishment, the reliance on imprisonment to deal with social and economic problems); reparations for generational oppression (i.e., slavery, redlining, mass imprisonment, surveillance); investments in the education, safety, and health of Black people; economic justice; community control; and political power.

Although the Blacks Lives Matter movement has been criticized for being too decentralized, with no obvious leaders, unlike in the 1960s, the reality is that hundreds and thousands of leaders across the county have spoken for the movement and expressed their concerns in their own cities and regions.[79] Such a "leader-full" movement prizes collaboration over having one central figure deciding for everyone else what tactics to prioritize over others.[80] As a result, racially conscious organizations such as Black Lives Matter have garnered public awareness and government response in addressing racial and gender inequality and have also succeeded in humanizing the victims of police brutality, including Eric Garner, Tamir Rice, Sandra Bland, Philando Castile, Alton Sterling, and many others. Also, since its inception, the Black Lives Matter network has remained vocal about the removal of Confederate symbols and monuments in an effort to end White supremacy in the United States. After the fatal shooting of nine Black parishioners at Emanuel Africa Methodist Episcopal Church in Charleston, South Carolina, by twenty-one-year-old neo-Nazi Dylann Roof, activists fought for the removal of the Confederate flag from the State Capitol.[81] After then-South Carolina Governor Nikki Haley signed into law a measure to remove the flag, activists filed petitions and demanded the removal of the flag from other public spaces as well. In addition, student protests reached new heights in colleges across the nation. The protests led by Black student activists at the University of Missouri and Yale University, who rallied together to protest the discrimination and racial insensitivity that they asserted had plagued their campuses for years, led to resignations at both schools.[82]

This global movement also impacted political conversations, forcing 2016 presidential candidates to reckon with a legacy of racism. In 2015, Black Lives Matter leaders met with Democratic presidential candidates Hillary Clinton and Bernie Sanders to discuss policing reform and racial injustice.[83] In 2016, President Obama met with Black Lives Matter civil rights activists in the Oval Office to discuss police-community relations, criminal justice reform, and systemic educational inequities.[84] In response to the national police crisis, President Obama appointed a national task force to identify best practices for improving policing in general and, in particular, improving relations with communities of color.[85] Obama also called for the end of federal transfers of certain types of military-style equipment to local police departments.[86] In December of 2016, the FBI announced a new effort to track the number of people killed by police each year in the United States.[87] As former Attorney General Roberta Lynch stated, the lack of data has made it "very hard to determine the causes of police shootings, or even whether there was an increase in such episodes or simply more publicity about them."[88]

Moreover, the DOJ conducted investigations of Ferguson and Baltimore, just as it had done with other cities where incidents sparked concern about the use of force among law enforcement.[89] As discussed earlier, the DOJ issued a scathing report that detailed unconstitutional police practices in both cities, all of which exacerbated racial bias.[90] Despite public acknowledgement of these issues, the protection and liberation of all oppressed individuals remains a goal that many activists look forward to achieving.

Moral Duty to Get Involved

20 percent of protesters emphasized a moral obligation to demonstrate against police brutality and institutional racism. Of the nine men and thirteen women, all were Black with the exception of one White protester and one of another race. Alonzo, a Black Baltimorean, clearly articulated his civic responsibility: "Someone was killed and you want to show solidarity. . . . I felt it was my civic duty as a Black male, you know, to show that, you know, we stand united and that all Blacks are not thugs, drug dealers, robbers, hoodlums." Correspondingly, in her response as to what motivated her to demonstrate, Marie, a Latina Ferguson protester, responded:

> It's my human duty [to protest] . . . And to not answer that call is a disgrace to my humanity. . . . You see a child drowning in a river, and you don't jump in to save them, are you complicit in that? I say yes, and I say that there are thousands—thousands—of people, young people, primarily Black and brown, dying in the river. And to not act, to not critique off of Facebook, to pretend that it doesn't impact me, is a slight on my humanity.

Activists mentioned the moral responsibility of getting involved time and time again. After observing several weeks of protests, Brittany, a Black Ferguson activist, proclaimed:

> I had called up a friend and I said, "Let's go." It was something in my heart that told me, "You have to go out there with your people. These are your people. These are the streets that you have grown up in. This is it. You have to go out there. Your voice has to be heard."

Protesters' accounts underscore a moral duty to fight for what's right. Some protesters felt a compelling need to get involved because the aftermath of Brown's and Gray's deaths affected their neighborhoods. Craig, a Black Ferguson activist, stated that what got him out of his seat and into the streets was that "I seen mostly just something bigger than me. It was like in the spirit, 'Hey get out your seat [and] do this. Go down there and see what's going on. . . . I live here so I should see what's going on in my city." Likewise, Dyshelle, a Black protester from Ferguson, said, "I've never experienced a protest. I just felt the sense to be there, like I was needed." She explained that she felt a need to "be with people who are tired of police brutality and were tired of racism, to stand up finally." In fact, the urge to get involved was so compelling that Luke, a White male from Arkansas, returned to Ferguson, his hometown. He explained:

> I've been born and raised in Ferguson . . . until I was twenty-three or twenty-four. So Friday—Friday the fifteenth, I jumped in my car, drove, was coming back to St. Louis. Car broke down. . . . State trooper gave me a ride to the gas station. I hitchhiked from the gas station to the bus station to Joplin, and I took a bus from Joplin to St. Louis. . . . I had to come home. Felt it so strong I couldn't fight [it].

Having lived in Ferguson for decades, Luke believed it was necessary to go home. After Brown died on Monday, Luke returned to Ferguson by the end of the work week to check on his family and friends and engage in the mass demonstrations.

The sense of obligation to get involved was also partly tied to protesters' group membership as racial minorities. Specifically, a few Black protesters from Ferguson identified themselves in terms of their collective racial identity ("us" or "we").[91] For example, Rhianna recalled thinking, "We should go out there and march with *our* people." Likewise, Keston articulated that "it makes me feel good as a Black man to know that *we* stood up for ourselves." According to psychologist John Turner, the redefinition from an "I" to a "we" makes people think, feel, and act as members of a group and transforms individuals into collectives.[92] Some protesters attached such strong emotional significance to their racial group membership that they redefined themselves in terms of their collective identity. Willie, for instance, boldly asserted that, upon deciding to get involved in street demonstrations, he observed "a sea of people. And it was great. It made me feel once again *proud to be Black*." Dyshelle asserted that, as a Black woman, "I just felt the sense to be there . . . to be with *my* people." Though every individual has a personal identity (by which I mean self-definition in terms of personal attributes) and several social identities (by which I mean self-definitions in terms of social category membership, such as nationality, ethnicity, gender, age, etc.), studies suggest that one is more likely to define their social identity in terms of what makes him or her similar to others when one's social identity becomes more salient than their personal identity.[93]

In sum, activists here noted several factors that motivated their engagement to participate in protest movements. Many protesters not only called attention to their perception of the ways that Brown and Gray were victims of police injustice; they explicitly tied their protest involvement to broader patterns of criminalization that have led to heightened police scrutiny of Black civilians. Many activists articulated a strong desire, as a result, to affect change and a moral obligation to fight for justice as their rationale for engaging in collective action.

The Role of Social Media in Mobilizing: Protest and Social Movements

While several factors influenced activists' participation, technology played an instrumental role in the ability of distressed communities like Ferguson and Baltimore to mobilize as a movement. The news of the death of Michael Brown first emerged on Twitter, a popular microblogging service, before it was reported in the national news.[94] During the three weeks surrounding the November 24 announcement of the grand jury's decision not to indict Wilson, social media activity increased dramatically, with the hashtag indicator #Ferguson appearing in over six million tweets on Twitter.[95] As the accounts of the case proliferated on mainstream and social media platforms like Twitter, Instagram, YouTube, and Facebook, the discourse expanded to include police brutality against people of color, as well as systematic racism and inequity in America.

With 56 percent of the US population carrying video-enabled smartphones, the increased use and availability of these technologies not only played a key role in prompting public outcry but created a sense of urgency and immediacy, which galvanized thousands to mobilize against police violence.[96] Specifically, 44 (39 percent of) protesters that I interviewed discussed the role that social media played in their activism efforts. For some, it was a critical tool in facilitating and coordinating offline collective action. For instance, some participants reported publicizing information about ongoing events. Darius, a Black Ferguson activist, acknowledged that "I have an Instagram [account] and I post things on there. I have Twitter and I post things on there also. Facebook. Just to keep everybody informed of what's going [on]." Carie Anne, a White activist from Baltimore, said that, during the height of the unrest in Baltimore, she sent "articles and posting events and information of things that are going on in Baltimore." Social media also proved to be a valuable tool to garner information about the actual location and timing of protest events. Chaundrise, a Black Baltimorean protester, said, "[I was] learning about different protests and a lot of organizing [that] has been happening via social media." Keston, a Black protester from Ferguson, said, "When I see people post things on social media about meetings or events that are going on, I also share that information with my friends of the social media in case it didn't get to them and they feel that they wanted to be a part of that." Many people relied on social media to serve as an educational tool for those outside the movement and to quickly exchange information about real-life protest actions, which served as a medium to attract other activists.

Online participation in cyberspace that is divorced from offline participation has remained a contentious issue. Exclusively online participation is referred to as "slacktivism," which entails low-risk, low-cost activities via social media. Slacktivism critics argue that exclusive online involvement lacks participation engagement and commitment, yet proponents contend that online participation provides otherwise disengaged youth with a medium to develop and apply civic and participatory knowledge and skills.[97] However, numerous participants were engaged in traditional modes of off-line participation (i.e. protest, marches, rallies) with many relying on social medial as a tool to motivate conversations around pressing social issues.

In addition to helping activists organize, social media was also used to share information about protest events that was not filtered by mainstream media. Many activists in Ferguson stated frequently that local and national news chose to cover riots and violent acts of protests while ignoring countless peaceful demonstrations. Luke, a White Ferguson activist, asserted that the media is deliberately "putting out misinformation." Asked what the media failed to accurately portray, Luke responded:

> In my opinion, the protesters were predominantly peaceful. What's not being portrayed is that, you know, there's been a community working together in a lot of ways. Whether it was from where people were trying to run up in stores and loot, to the actual community standing in front of the stores not allowing that to happen, to community people donating just water and food. . . . The narrative's been that the protests have been not peaceful or unruly or rowdy or there have been arrests, you know. [The media is] portraying [protests] as unruly, not peaceful, when largely it's peaceful.

Luke was not alone in his assertions; several protesters underscored that demonstrations were in fact peaceful. Diamond, a Black Ferguson protester, stated that the media generally portrayed "the fighting and the looting . . . [but] a lot of protests are very peaceful . . . you didn't always see that in the media that it was peaceful. . . . That people were hugging and talking and laughing." Similarly, Latoya, a Black protester from Ferguson, said, "When you're involved and you're in the community actions and you're at the vigils and you're at the protests, you don't see what they say on the media. You don't see violent rioters. You don't see that. You see people who want justice, people that are hurt. You get a whole different side of the story." And Dwan, a Black Ferguson protester, admitted that there "was one day of looting . . . [but] the next day after that it's all been peaceful." When asked why the media focused on the violence, he responded: "Do the news people want to see 100 people not making any noise, just peacefully being at a protest? Or do the news want to show scattered chaos? So the news present it however they want . . . because that's what makes good news." Such findings are not surprising and confirm other studies showing that the mass media tends to emphasize both the violent and sensational aspects of protests, because such coverage is newsworthy.[98] Most participants in the study, however, would agree that without the uprising, the issues of race, justice, and police violence would have easily slipped forgotten into the news media.

Admittedly, the deaths of Michael Brown and Freddie Gray did lead to large-scale disorder in Ferguson and Baltimore. This included massive destruction of property, looting, vandalism, and the burning of a QuikTrip in Ferguson and a CVS in Baltimore. The intensity of the uprising prompted the mayor of Baltimore to declare a state of emergency and deploy approximately five thousand National Guard troops throughout the city.[99] The Missouri governor also declared a state of emergency and imposed curfew in Ferguson after several nights of protests following Brown's death.[100] During and after these events, many commentators, including city officials, politicians, and the media denounced such violence and destruction of property as "senseless" and without justification.[101] Participants in the Ferguson and Baltimore uprising were often described as "thugs," "criminals," and "delinquent."[102] Here the problem is framed in terms of good/bad, right/wrong, lawful/unlawful, and the solution is presented as authorities' use of repressive actions, such as increased arrest rates and convictions, tougher sentencing for those engaged in offending behavior, and harsher legislation targeting criminal behavior.[103] Scholars Matthew Morgan and David Waddington argue that:

> Although framing the response to riots in terms of simply binary logic outlined above may be politically expedient—the appearance of quick and decisive action in times of crisis can translate into valuable political capital for a leader—it is also reductive, flawed, and even dangerous. Viewed through this lens, riots appear in monochrome and the nuances that colour our understanding of public disorder are lost.[104]

Although emotionally charged and volatile, riots are expressions of pent-up anger, as they are symptomatic of systemic social problems. Such outbreaks are a culmination of underlying issues ignited by a particular causal event—such as police shootings—or long-held anger (regarding broader police abuse, residential segregation, economic inequality, and racial tensions).[105] As historian Thomas Sugrue claims, "Almost all the several hundred riots that happened between 1963 and 1970 were sparked by confrontation between African Americans and the police."[106] This is not surprising, given the long history of injustice that precedes them—slave patrols, racial neighborhood segregation enforced by law enforcement, and the widespread tension and harassment directed at Blacks by the police, including the Ferguson and Baltimore residents whose experiences are detailed in chapters 2 and 3.[107]

Consequently, in the wake of riots in Ferguson and Baltimore, many Americans were left wondering why Black Americans looted, burned down businesses in their own community, and failed to adhere to Martin Luther King Jr.'s message of peaceful protests.[108] The reality was, however, that protesters did peacefully protest. After the initial looting and rioting that occurred between August 10 and 21, 2014, and the second round of riots that erupted after the grand jury's decision not to indict Officer Wilson on November 25, members of the Ferguson and St. Louis community, along with Black Lives Matter demonstrators, held peaceful protests around Brown's memorial and outside the Ferguson Police Station for more than ninety days.[109] Similarly, following the looting that broke out after Freddie Gray died, the Baltimore uprising turned into celebration after Baltimore State's Attorney Marilyn Mosby announced criminal charges against the six police officers involved in Gray's death.[110] Yet mainstream media ignored these events, as well as the two-day block party in the streets of Penn North and the tens of thousands of people who marched from Baltimore City Hall to Penn North following Gray's death.[111]

Not surprisingly, protesters lamented that mainstream media failed to provide balanced coverage of protest events. In some cases, Black Ferguson protesters accused some mainstream news outlets of taking the accounts of what happened out of context. Aaliyah lamented that "there's a lot of distrust going on with the press. . . . They're doing a lot of spinning of words. . . . Instead of giving the full text when they interview people, they take little inserts, and they don't give the full detail." Jada concurred, stating that "a lot of media isn't our friends. You know, they're just in it to get what they can and so many times they've taken our words and misconstrued them to a point where I'm like, 'was that even me?' You know, like, that wasn't me. I didn't say anything like that." Asked to give an example, Jada explained:

This one time [a news network] asked to interview me and the first time it was okay. It was okay, they kind of took bits and pieces of it but it was nothing, you know, out of the ordinary. But the second time it was as if I said that "we're going to tear this city down" and that's not what I said. [The reporter] asked me, "What are you afraid of?" And what I said was, "I was afraid that the city was going to get torn down." What she put in was, "This city's going to be torn down."

Some protesters were frustrated and angry about the lack of balanced coverage and the media's distortion of their statements. However, activists have little control over the "stories" that mainstream media choose to cover or how the media represent the protesters' assertions.[112]

In an attempt to bypass the mainstream media and counter such messages with their own narrative, activists found it necessary to spread news about the events on the ground via social media. Darius, a Black activist, claimed that "the news portrayed everything in Ferguson as a lie . . . and gave out false information. So, on my side I try to give out the right information to each person." Because Black voices are generally marginalized in predominately White media and public spaces, most well-connected young protesters relied on social media to document and share protest events and police activity, unfiltered by institutionalized media. Here, they relied on social media exchanges to challenge the prevailing narrative and ensure their voices were heard while giving the public the opportunity to virtually connect and experience a repressive state system in Ferguson. This proved to be rather effective in rapidly diffusing communication and mobilization efforts, as there were more than 3.6 million tweets about the Ferguson incident within five days of Brown's death.[113] Similarly, 9,600 tweets about the Baltimore uprising occurred within 24 hours of Gray's death.[114]

The role of "word-of-mouth" media in bringing attention to social justice issues is not new. For instance, slave narratives that depicted the horrors of slavery before the Civil War were a common form of expression; these narratives, told by former slaves such as Olaudah Equiano, Frederick Douglas, and Harriet Tubman, rallied public opinion against slavery. From the 1850s to the 1930s, national debates about slavery, racism, and segregation also played out in photography, which provided proof of the brutality of these institutions.[115] In their book *Envisioning Emancipation: Black Americans and the End of Slavery*, Deborah Willis and Barbara Krauthamer argue that the use of photography served as "important historical sources that can inform the thinking of readers and scholars about the intertwined histories of slavery, freedom, and photography."[116] Arguably, the use of employing photographs as documentary evidence of racism allowed Blacks not just to fight against the crusade of slavery and segregation but also to convince Whites of their shared humanity through affirmative imagery of Blacks.[117]

In addition, the emerging Civil Rights Movement in the 1960s was galvanized by the murder of Emmett Till, a fourteen-year-old Black boy. A Chicago native who was visiting family in Money, Mississippi, Till was accused of whistling at or flirting with a White woman, which was forbidden for a Southern Black male during that period. Several days later, the woman's relatives brutally beat and killed Till before disposing of his body in the Tallahatchie River. Though Till's body was mutilated beyond recognition, his mother insisted on an open-casket funeral to shed light on the systemic violence inflicted on Southern Blacks. Graphic images of Till's disfigured body were circulated in two Black publications, *Jet* magazine and the *Chicago Defender*, which received worldwide attention. The photographs of Till awoke the world to racial hatred in the United States and ultimately galvanized the Civil Rights Movement.[118]

The struggle for civil rights came to a head during the advent of television in most American homes in the 1950s. Television news became a powerful catalyst for change, as it played a central role in shaping public opinion.[119] Televised images of police dogs and fire hoses turned on demonstrators in Birmingham, Alabama, as well as violence at the Pettus Bridge in Selma, served as turning points where Americans directly witnessed the violent repression of Blacks.[120] National newscasts recorded the movement, which helped to change Americans' thinking about segregation.[121]

Similar to the Civil Rights Movement, the recent social movements in Ferguson, Baltimore, and elsewhere attempted to bring about racial equality and put an end to police violence. While many activists saw themselves as continuing the struggle of the 1960s, this new generation of activists incorporated technology as a tool for organization and communication. The reliance on social media permitted ordinary citizens to share events on the ground in real time, or close to it, allowing them to avoid depending on mainstream media. Moreover, the use of social media radically facilitated information sharing and group coordination at a speed and scale that does not compare with any other media source.[122] While neither police brutality nor protests are new, the widespread dissemination of images of police violence struck an uneasy chord in the nation as the public bore witness to state-sponsored violence primarily against Black individuals. Social media served as a game changer because of its discursive ability to reach all domains of social life, allowing people to quickly share their experiences and offer alternative accounts of what happened both locally and globally.

Using social media as a catalyst, activists relied on connectivity and social networking to spread messages of their own about the inequalities they were protesting. Not only was social media used to capture public attention and attract activists, but to enhance the coordination of protests and to contest the failures of mainstream media to provide accurate accounts of events on the ground.

5

"I Will Be Out Here Every Day Strong!"

Repressive Policing and Future Activism

[The police] want us to shut up. They want us to go home.
They want us to stop protesting. I told them that I will not
stop protesting because it's my family, and if you want me
to stop protesting you have to put a bullet in my head to do
that because I will be out here every day strong. . . . [The po-
lice] tried to bribe me. They said if you go home we'll stop
arresting your people. So that kind of messed with me because you're not finna bribe me to stop protesting.
—Carlos (Black Ferguson protester)

Without a doubt, there are some risks to engaging in protests that confront the state, which has the authority to use repressive tactics. Such
risks include arrest, harassment, and violence, all of which can cause
physical, emotional, psychological, and financial harm. The anger and
frustration of any aggrieved group can motivate individuals to engage
in activism efforts, but these emotions do not always channel themselves into protests, due to lack of resources, fear of repression, and/or a
lack of confidence that the efficacy of collective organization will result
in change.[1] If collective action does take place, the motivation of individual participants often plays a critical role in channeling grievance
toward collective goals. At the same time, emotions also have the power
to demobilize a movement, especially when feelings of anger and despair
exacerbate fears of violence, isolation, and repercussions from powerful
institutions.[2]

As previously discussed, social movement scholars have debated for
decades why individuals choose to participate in protests.[3] Some have
explored the role that emotions play in fostering a collective social identity against an external enemy that leads to collective action. For others,

the intense emotions (mainly anger) of individuals who perceive the in-group to be strong are strongly correlated to their desire to partake in collective action compared to others who perceive the in-group as weak.[4] Protesters have varying degrees of motivation; while some are more driven to participate than others, most engage because they expect to achieve a positive outcome as a result of their actions, despite the considerable risks involved.[5]

However, protest involvement does not always have a positive outcome. While emotions, motivation, and identity are important factors that lead individuals to engage in protest movements, they are often tested when protesters come into contact with repressive tactics. Given that most high-risk protests involve actions against the state, the state often calls upon police forces to suppress protests, to act as a deterrent for subsequent protests, and to restore order.[6] However, the degree of repression used by the police (e.g., escalated force, negotiated management, strategic incapacitation) varies depending on the level of threat protesters pose to those in power.[7] For instance, protests that aim to seize or dismantle state power often meet with extremely repressive police action (i.e., the Arab Spring Protest in Egypt) compared to those that seek reforms within an existing sociopolitical order (i.e., protests against sexual assaults on campus). At times, extreme repression has been observed to provoke *greater* levels of protest,[8] as seen in the Civil Rights Movement in the 1960s, and can strengthen commitment among protesters and encourage radical action.[9] Moreover, the nature of police intervention can actually influence the direction of the movement: the tolerant and selective styles[10] of protest policing could facilitate the integration of the protest within a complex structure of political bargaining, while repressive protest police tactics may shift the objective of the protest itself to one that focuses on the issue of policing.[11]

Others argue that the effects of protest policing on social movements is contingent on when repression is applied. That is, the impact of repression during the initial stages of protests reinforces the resolve of individuals already engaged in the movement and motivates future protesters, while repression during later parts of demonstrations often hastens their decline.[12] Finally, the effect of protest policing on movements is contingent on the structure of the movement. Hierarchical and centralized protests tend to be more susceptible to repression (coercive force becomes more

Figure 5.1. Published by the Baltimore Sun Company, LLC ("TBS"). Used with permission.

effective once it unseats the few people in power), while leaderless, non-hierarchical protests tend to be more resilient, which was the case with Occupy Wall Street and recent demonstrations in India against rape.[13]

Although there is an abundance of scholarship on police protesting and its effect on social movement organizations, fewer studies focus on the micro-level effects of repression—that is, its impact on individual activists.[14] In her detailed discussion of the effects of repression, social movement scholar Jennifer Earl describes her finding that whether or not individual protesters are deterred by repression depends on the kind of repression and its (il)legitimacy.[15] Regarding the relationship between repression and escalation of protests, urban sociologist Eric Hirsch has found that participants with strong political solidarity may become radicalized when repressed.[16] Other researchers argue that individual protesters become radicalized only when the repression is viewed as unjustified and they are integrated into networks that encourage protests.[17] Beyond deterrence or escalation, literature on protest policing and individual protesters has not suggested other likely responses to repression.[18] It is also worth taking into account not just the generic

Figure 5.2. Photo by Wiley Price. Used with permission.

relationship between protest policing and protests but the fact that the protests were about policing and police violence to begin with.

Police Repression and Racism

The US police force has become increasingly militarized. During the height of the Civil Rights Movement, the Los Angeles Police Department (LAPD), in response to the Watts riots—in which Black and Latino communities rose up in protest after a controversial police stop of a Black civilian by a White officer—established the first prominent Special Weapons and Tactics (SWAT) team in 1965.[19] In the decades that followed, the use of SWAT teams expanded rapidly, as local police joined forces with the federal government in the "War on Drugs" and the "War on Terror."[20] Federal legislation (i.e., section 1208 of the 1990 National Defense Authorization Act and section 1033 of the 1997 National Defense Authorization Act) authorized the transfer of military-grade equipment (e.g., grenade launchers, fully automatic weapons, armored vehicles, and aircraft) to state and local law enforcement agencies.[21] Since 1990, more than $5 billion worth of military equipment has been given to local law enforcement agencies.[22]

Police militarization is linked disproportionately to disadvantaged racial/ethnic groups. An examination of thousands of SWAT deployments found that Black and Latino people were much more likely to be impacted than Whites and that the disparity was even greater in deployments conducted for the purpose of serving a drug-related search warrant.[23] Political economist Albert Hirschman offers an explanation as to why racial minorities may be disproportionately affected by police militarization.[24] When individuals find themselves in undesirable situations within an organization to which they belong, including the government, Hirschman argues, they can respond in a few different ways. First, individuals may "exit" or withdraw from the relationship; yet, given that Blacks are two to three times more likely to live in poverty than Whites, this option is not feasible for many.[25] Second, individuals may "voice" or express their grievances formally or informally to repair the problem. Research shows, however, that increases in segregation lead to decreases in Black civic efficacy.[26] Economists Elizabeth Ananat and Ebonya Washington note that politicians who represent relatively segregated Black communities typically do not vote for policies favored by Black constituents.[27] This is reflected in Ferguson, where 67 percent of residents are Black yet prior to Brown's death there were virtually no Black politicians. Additionally, in their examination of more than fifteen thousand US protest events between 1960 to 1990, social movement scholars Christian Davenport, Sarah Soule, and David Armstrong found that Black protesters were more likely than White protesters to draw a police presence and that police were more likely to take action at Black protest events.[28] In fact, they found that, before the early 1970s, police were more likely to make arrests and use force at Black protest events, evidencing a "Protesting While Black" phenomenon. Although the authors found that this phenomenon only occurred in some years when a subject's demeanor (i.e., what protesters actually do at events in terms of behavioral threats) was taken into account, they conclude that "in many years white protesters enjoyed a greater privilege of protest, and thus greater access to democratic institutions, than did African American citizen/protesters."[29] Consequently, racial minority groups are often the least able to avoid the unfavorable consequences of militarized police force.

In Ferguson, the response to police handling of protests received strong criticism by the public, as police relied on militarized tactics, including the use of canines, tear gas, and military weaponry.[30] In Baltimore, though police displayed initial force restraint at the onset of the peaceful protests, the police response became increasingly militarized as protests became violent.

Protester Perceptions on Repressive Protest Policing Tactics

Drawing on in-depth interviews with 102 Ferguson and Baltimore street protesters, I identified three distinct characteristics[31] of protesters depending on their commitment to the goals of protest—revolutionary, intermittent, or tourist. *Revolutionary protesters* were individuals who either participated in some form of collective action every day or every other day; have stopped working or going to school; slept outside on multiple occasions following protest events; or believed their purpose in life was to facilitate collective action. Overall, they expressed a deep level of commitment to the protest movement. *Intermittent protesters* were those who engaged in some form of collective action at least four or more times; went to work or school but still engaged in collective action efforts because they were committed to the cause; and, in general, held a middle-ground commitment to the movement. *Tourist protesters* were classified as people who took part in collective action less than three times or expressed more curiosity than commitment about the social movement. Overall, their level of commitment was characterized as being sporadic.

In all, protesters in the study reported having had both negative and positive experiences with police in Ferguson and Baltimore prior to the deaths of Michael Brown and Freddie Gray. Specifically, in Ferguson, eighteen revolutionary, thirteen intermittent, and seven tourist protesters experienced negative police encounters; in Baltimore, two revolutionary, eight intermittent, and nine tourist protesters reported such encounters. In Ferguson, six revolutionary, four intermittent, and three tourist protesters experienced positive police interactions, while, in Baltimore, three revolutionary, seven intermittent, and six tourist protesters described experiencing positive encounters with local police. Although most activists in the study reported unfavorable encounters with police, some acknowledged favorable police interactions.

Below I provide in-depth descriptions of the three most common themes regarding the handling of street protesters by officers: acts of intimidation (surveillance, perceived hostility, verbal assault, and arrest); escalated use of force and strategic incapacitation, including violent repressive tactics (use of tear gas, rubber bullets, gun threats, and physical force), which was most commonly reported among Ferguson protesters; and negotiated management strategies coupled with strategic incapacitation, which was common among Baltimore street protesters.[32]

Acts of Intimidation

SURVEILLANCE

Though it was not commonly employed, eight Ferguson protesters emphasized the risk of police surveillance during protest movements. In his discussion of confrontations between activists and police, Luke, a White revolutionary protester, questioned its wisdom: "[Do you think the police are] gonna forget that you threw bottles at them? That you got in their face? That you cursed them out? That you didn't listen to what they say? . . . [The police are] identifying people [and] profiling even protesters, and doing whatever type of surveillance." Luke's point is a valid one, as many Black revolutionary activists acknowledged that they were indeed surveilled by law enforcement as they engaged in public demonstrations. Asia, a Black activist, said, "If I'm leading a chant or something, they'll sit there and get their camera out and literally record me." Similarly, DeShawn, a Black demonstrator, stated that the FPD "take[s] picture[s] of everybody that's out there every single day. Every rally. Every protest. . . . They taking pictures of license plates. They following people to their homes. I've been followed to my home." Several other revolutionary protesters asserted that police followed them home. Tyrone, a Black activist, said that police were "sitting at my house, like sitting outside of my house one day in a black truck." Donte, a Black protester, recounted:

> DONTE: The sheriff went to my mom's house three times trying to find me.
> INTERVIEWER: Why is that?
> DONTE: I don't know. They won't tell her. . . . I mean the only reason I can think of is because I'm out here protesting and the cops are

trying to target who they feel is a threat to them. I'm not standing out
there saying, "F*ck you, I'm going to shoot you." But they feel like—
they got they cameras out, they got their cameras out . . . So they
know who's a threat to them [and] who's going to give them trouble if
this doesn't turn the other way. . . . [The police target me and] other
men and women that be out there.

Protesters who were vocal in challenging police violence against
unarmed men placed themselves at risk of being targeted for surveillance by police. While some protesters identified these tactics as the
state's attempt to suppress the social movement, we will see that for revolutionary activists such actions only served to intensify their resolve,
which further galvanized the resistance.[33]

PERCEIVED HOSTILITY

In addition, nine Ferguson protesters noted many hostile actions taken
by law enforcement. Rachel, a Black intermittent, recounted:

I had my two little girls. And everybody was talking about a peaceful
protest. This was the night that the riots broke out. And we were up there.
And we were—our protest was in the middle of the street. The police
came out across the street up near Ferguson [and] they had dogs. They
were in riot gear with the shields up and their sticks and their helmet on
and all that stuff. That just felt so intimidating because nobody had—
there weren't any fights, nothing was broken into. . . . And then somebody
had a soda—had bought it from QuikTrip or something, took the soda,
and threw it over the crowd and hit the police cars. When they did that,
the police launched the dogs. They didn't let them go, but they launched
it. And the crowd started running back. And there was a lot of people out
there. So my little girls, they're like this tall. I took them. I grabbed them.
I put them between my legs like this and I held them like this because I
didn't want them to get trampled and fall.

Alexus, a Black revolutionary activist, also recalled an incident when the
police "opened the door and let a dog out on them. Everybody started
running, and then after that is when everything started going crazy." The
use of canines against protesters and other repressive tactics led some

activists to perceive their movement as a continuation of the Civil Rights Movement of the 1960s. As a result, Tyrone, a Black revolutionary activist, concluded that such repressive policing strategies are "their modern way of spraying water and sicking dogs on you."

Others were perturbed by the racially insensitive nature of some officers. For instance, several protesters described the police smiling and laughing at them as they demonstrated. Susanna, a Black intermittent protester, stated that "people was crying and they was hurt and [the police] was thinking that it was funny and they was laughing." Others believed that some of these actions on the part of protest officers were intentional. Javon, a Black revolutionary protester, noted: "When I'm on the front lines, I said from day one, all I get is winks, smiles, kisses, and racial slurs. . . . Like 'we just waiting on the right moment' type sh*t. Like 'I got you' . . . it's to agitate." Similarly, Devanta, a Black revolutionary activist, reported an incident that occurred while she and others were protesting:

> After Michael Brown got shot . . . the first week I was out there protesting with them. . . . We [were] walking on the sidewalk and the police [were] driving by flicking us off [extending their middle finger] smiling. . . . I was literally walking down Shaw on the south side and I'm walking down the sidewalk and I see the policemen. They [were] riding in the middle of the street going back and forth with [their] tanks and they was smiling at us, flicking us off you know.

The perception that some officers were intentionally disrespectful, insensitive, and hostile further exacerbated tension between the two groups. For some protesters, the adverse response they received from law enforcement during protests was analogous to the unfavorable treatment they received from police more generally.

VERBAL ASSAULT

Another common theme regarding how police responded to protests after Brown's death was the use of racist language by police toward demonstrators, as reported by eleven Ferguson protesters, all of whom were Black. Such sentiments were more often reported among Black revolutionary activists who protested on the front lines; some officers, they stated, spoke to them in a belligerent manner, calling them names and using racial slurs. According to Donte, officers would yell "get the f*ck off the street, nig*er. B*tch move. F*ck you." Javon agreed, explaining that, when officers were arresting him and his friends during a protest, they were "calling us nig*ers, calling us stupid." Monique reported that "[they] called us monkeys and nig*ers." A video recording on YouTube shows a Ferguson officer saying to protesters "Bring it, all you f**king animals bring it."[34] This led Monique, along with many others, to conclude of Ferguson officers that "[t]hey're racist."

Demeaning police behavior could lead individuals to respond in kind.[35] A few activists acknowledged that they countered by verbally insulting officers. For example, Donte, a revolutionary protester, described being dragged out of his car by an officer after leaving a demonstration and the officer yelling, "Shut the f*ck up, nig*er." Donte admitted that after the officer "talked crazy to me," Donte retorted, "Who the f*ck you talking to?" The exchange of insults escalated, and the officer beat Donte with a weapon. Prior studies have shown that citizens' demeanor is often shaped by police officers' actions toward them;[36] thus, belligerent or demoralizing police behavior has the potential to exacerbate a situation and subject citizens to more serious kinds of mistreatment.

ARRESTS

Additionally, twenty-five activists—specifically, twenty-one protesters from Ferguson and four from Baltimore—identified either the threat of or actual arrest during protest events. Among Ferguson protesters, Derrell, a Black intermittent protester, stated that the police were "telling protesters to stay off the street or if they don't, they getting grabbed up and locked up." Leonetta, a Black revolutionary protester, acknowledged that "I'm normally to the back . . . I'm never on the front line [protesting] . . . [because] I, for one, am not willing to go to jail." Mike, a Black tourist demonstrator on parole, agreed, arguing that protesting is "not safe because I don't know what kind of attitude the cop might have that may stop me. . . . If they give me one of them charges, I'm gonna be done for."

Protesters in Baltimore also reported having witnessed the arrests of demonstrators. Mass arrests were said to occur after the looting and rioting on the evening of April 27, 2015, that resulted in the declaration of a state of emergency and the deployment of the National Guard by Governor Hogan.[37] Demarco, a Baltimore intermittent protester, stated that, during that period of time, "[j]ust being with a group of people meant you was going in cuffs." Others asserted that police arrested people who violated the curfew set by then Mayor Stephanie Rawlings-Blake from April 28 to May 3, 2015. The curfew, which was from 10 p.m. to 5 a.m., applied to everyone in the city with the exception of emergency workers, students traversing to and from school, and employees traveling to and from work.[38] Jason, a mixed-race revolutionary protester, asserted that activists "were nightly being berated and like shoved and pushed and people were being arrested and hit." However, some complained that the order by the mayor was enforced selectively, in certain areas of Baltimore. Jamia, a Black tourist, complained that "that curfew was phony 'cause it was only enforced through the city." While a curfew was set in the city of Baltimore, more than two hundred people were arrested for curfew violation.[39] This is considered strategic incapacitation, as it entails policing strategies that include the use of no-protest zones, including curfews.

Arrests were more common among those who protested on the front lines and engaged in confrontations with protest police. Eight protesters (seven from Ferguson and one from Baltimore), all of whom were revolutionary activists with the exception of one, reported having been arrested while protesting.[40] Carlos, a Black relative of Michael Brown, admitted, "I got arrested four times because I protested." Because Carlos and other fellow activists, most of whom were Black, were arrested on multiple occasions, Carlos claimed that "[police] tried to bribe me. They said if you go home we'll stop arresting *your people*" [emphasis added]. Despite the risk of subsequent arrest, Carlos refused to stop protesting. Likewise, Tyrone, a young Black activist, explained that, while protesting, he and other protesters "linked up and held arms together. [But] they [the police] singled me out. . . . They just caught me off guard while I was protesting. Grabbed me and like a couple of other people." Consequently, he was charged with failure to disperse. Admittedly, several revolutionary protesters acknowledged engaging in acts of civil disobedience or orchestrated takeovers of public spaces, thus facing greater repression.[41] Other revolutionary activists on the front lines, like Tyrone, were recipients of strategic incapacitation, or targeted policing, for attempting to disrupt the social order.

The incidents described in this section—surveillance, perceived hostility, verbal assault, and arrest—represent common practices of protest policing. Such tactics further undermined police legitimacy in the eyes of activists, especially revolutionary demonstrators. Moreover, such coercive police action eroded the legitimacy of governing authorities among tourist and intermittent protesters, as they observed how more vocal activists were treated and/or personally experienced repressive actions even amid peaceful demonstrations.

Violent Repressive Tactics

TEAR GAS AND RUBBER BULLETS

In this study, thirty-two Ferguson protesters reported that protest police deployed tear gas and shot rubber bullets during demonstrations.[42] Such accounts were common across race/ethnicity and protester type. Raymond, a Black intermittent protester, asserted that the police "were kind of handling it wrong by throwing tear gases and so forth. [It] didn't matter the circumstance, [they] came up in military form." And Clayton, a Black tourist, claimed that "once you [start] throwing like tear gas and having the SWAT out there with the little tank things they was in, you're not coming to be peaceful." He continued to describe the effect of authorities throwing tear gas into a crowd of protesters:

> That tear gas burned and they was just throwing it, just riding down the street throwing it at everything and they blocked both sides so you can't run anywhere. You can't just go anywhere. And the tear gas hurt and they just, you know, was throwing the tear gas for no reason. That was the only time where I felt like, "Okay they don't care, they don't care who they hurting, they don't care if its kids or they don't care if you out here to protest in a positive way".... So during that day, yeah I feel like nah, they didn't care; they against us they want to hurt us and things like that.... That day, that was the worst I ever felt about the police. It was like, "Okay, this what you get." They was treating us like we're animals.

Clayton was clearly distraught that officers would use repressive tactics to control a crowd full of children and adults. According to the after-action report in Ferguson, while some law enforcement representatives stated that the use of tear gas and pepper spray by the police was an attempt to control dissident protesters and disperse demonstrators,[43] protesters found it troubling and believed that police were attempting to control them by violating their constitutional right to peacefully assemble. Such actions only reaffirmed the beliefs of some that the police are biased against Blacks. Yolanda, a Black tourist protester, said, "I thought this was a democracy. So we don't have a right to walk down the streets and protest peacefully?" Police officers' response to the demonstrations only served to undermine their legitimacy in the eyes of many protesters. This has policy implications, because if civilians who are policed perceive that they are treated as a military enemy, public trust is weakened.[44] Research has shown that trust is vital in maintaining public safety and controlling crime.[45] Senior Counsel for the Center for Justice at the American Civil Liberties Union, Kara Dansky, has reported that "when police respond with an unnecessary degree of force or a military appearance, they risk turning what might otherwise be a peaceful encounter into a violent attack."[46]

Many protesters asserted that, in the days following the looting and riots, protests were peaceful. Thus, the launching of tear gas and the shooting of rubber bullets into crowds to subdue demonstrators was considered extreme and inappropriate. As Trevon, a Black revolutionary protester, described, "The police started to shoot tear gas. . . . they shot so much of it . . . like 50 to 60 tear gas canisters . . . And plus I got shot by a rubber bullet [by the police]. . . . I'd say I passed out for about like 20 minutes." Trevon admitted that, afterwards, "I was basically scared to frigging go to sleep. . . . How they would just shoot at innocent people in a crowd. And now what if they were shooting live rounds? I could have been dead." Some protesters, like Trevon, were impacted by the physical and psychological trauma of not only being on the front line during street protests but simply being present during demonstrations.

Many protesters cited the use of tear gas and rubber bullets as evidence of police militarization. Such tactics were perceived as dangerous and unacceptable, as it placed demonstrators' safety at risk while inciting fear. Ashley, a Black tourist activist, admitted it took her awhile to engage in protest movements "because I was kind of scared. Because you had a lot of people throwing tear gases at the protesters. Some of the cops were throwing tear gas." While such repressive tactics from the police instilled fear in some demonstrators, they also fueled further anger and distress among other Black protesters, resulting in animosity toward police. Reuben, an intermittent protester, asserted that "it made people want to basically attack them [the police]. That's what their reaction was when people was throwing tear gas back at them." Willie, a tourist activist, agreed and explained, "I understand you have to maintain control, I understand that. But, I think that force against force never works. It's just gonna erupt. For every action there is an equally or better, greater reaction. And that's what I think is true here." Thus, the use of tear gas and rubber bullets were viewed by many demonstrators as a heavy-handed, aggressive, and unjust response that incited legitimate anger and animosity toward the state.

GUN THREATS

Twelve revolutionary, seven intermittent, and four tourist protesters from Ferguson mentioned the threat of gun use by police during demonstrations.[47] Crystal, a Black tourist, explained, "You don't know how the police are going to handle things from people being out protesting. . . . I'm scared of how [police are] going to react to the people protesting . . . They might say, 'Well, we seen somebody with a gun. That's why we shot.'" Evelyn, a Black tourist protester, stated that she chose to protest during the day because she knew police "wouldn't have the rifles pointed at you." Other revolutionary activists recalled having guns pointed at them while protesting in the evening. As Javon, a Black activist, recounts:

> They was saying that we had to leave . . . and as we was leaving they stood in front of the car, pulled out they AK-47, put it to my head, told me don't move, got me out the car, and said we had a Molotov bomb on us. . . . All of [the police] had they guns drawn. We had a pick-up truck, so we had people on the back of the truck and people on the inside. . . . I was on the passenger side, my cousin was driving. And [the officer] put his gun to me, was like, "Don't move, let me see your hands." But I already had my hands up though because its "hands up, don't shoot" anyway. . . . He told me to get out, gun still drawn to my head, and I'm like, "Why [do] you got the gun out for? I'm only peaceful protesting." And he put me in the [hand]cuff and . . . they had me to the ground for like two hours.

Similar to the use of rubber bullets and tear gas, protesters were enraged by the threat of gun violence by the police. Luke, a White revolutionary activist, lamented, "I just don't think when predominantly a peaceful protest with men, women, grandmothers, grandfathers [and] children [are] in the crowd, that they should be subject to loaded live M16s raised in their face." Here, Luke cites a controversial tactic used in the military—the use of "overwatch," a "technique intended to provide a layer of security for officers and citizens by having a sniper monitor armed threats from a higher position that provides the sniper a better view."[48] While such an approach is employed as an active-shooter defense tactic in mass gatherings, it has been deemed an ineffective and inappropriate strategy for crowd control.[49] Not only does such behavior instill fear and alarm among those peacefully protesting, but this approach further increases the perception among protesters that police are reacting in a militaristic manner.

PHYSICAL FORCE

In addition to the threat of gun use by police, fourteen activists from Ferguson reported having witnessed or endured physical assault from law enforcement. Revolutionary activists were more likely than the other types of protesters to make these reports,[50] as detailed in the accounts below. Donte, a Black protester, describes a personal encounter he had with an officer *after* protesting:

> I'm assuming [the officer] had to be watching me because when I left [the demonstration], he flagged me over [pulled me over]. Flagged me over. He walked up to my car. He dragged me out of the car and he threw me on the ground. He searched my car. He threw all my clothes and the poster outside the car or whatever. . . . And then he threw me on the ground. So I ask[ed] him "Why? What's the cause for?" He told me, "Shut the f*ck up, nig*er." So you know, as a man—Me, as a man Donte [last name], as a man, I'm not going to lie to nobody. He talked crazy to me so I said something to him. . . . [I said] "Who the f*ck you talking to?". . . . He took out his night club, stick or whatever and hit me with it. Now this is at eleven o'clock at night.

Black women protesters were not exempt from enduring police violence, either. Asia, a Black revolutionary activist, recalled that she and her daughter witnessed a young activist "get hog-tied. . . . [The police] choked her and hog-tied her." Darius, a Black protester, recounted the same incident, stating officers "knocked one of my organizational members . . . knocked her out. When she was conscious she didn't know she got knocked out. They hogtied her and everything." Several Ferguson demonstrators described the escalated force approach used by protest police; many complained that police responded to non-violent demonstrators with a dramatic show of force, pointing sniper rifles at peaceful protesters, flooding demonstrators with tear gas, shooting rubber bullets to disperse the crowd, and, at times, using excessive force.

Overall, protesters in all three categories described and complained about aggressive police force. However, revolutionary activists were more likely to report the repressive actions they witnessed or experienced multiple times firsthand. Perhaps this is not surprising, as revolutionary protesters on the front lines were more vocal about denouncing police brutality compared to other types of protesters and, thus, more likely to challenge the authority of law enforcement. For this group of activists, the negative interactions they had with police drove them to protest. However, at the same time that they decried the fact that too many Black men, women, and children are often killed by law enforcement with impunity, they continued to experience repressive policing.

Protesters' Perceptions on Negotiated Management Protest Policing Practices

While Ferguson protesters expressed feelings of fear and anger toward the repressive and militarized tactics of police, Baltimore protesters responded in very distinct ways. Recall that, during the onset of protests in Baltimore, the police department reacted with force restraint. In fact, when protests initially started, there was no deployment of lethal force and minimal to no deployment of nonlethal force.[51] As a result, seven Baltimore protesters reported having more favorable impressions of protest police than protesters in Ferguson. Jonathan, a Black tourist protestor, stated that, during one protest he attended, the "police was talking to [demonstrators] . . . and the police wasn't aggressive at all that day." Similarly, Helen, a Black tourist activist said that when "I participated in one of the protests . . . [the police] were quiet." Breeann, a Black intermittent demonstrator, agreed, asserting that "the police handled things very well. . . . they stood their ground but they were very peaceful." Even those who did not have generally favorable perceptions of the police admitted that, in this instance, protest police responded appropriately toward demonstrators. Deanna, a Black tourist activist, admitted, "I think they did alright. . . . I think probably [they did] alright [because] they could have done a lot of killing, which would have only made things worst." Deanna's statement is in line with a report prepared by the Johns Hopkins University Office of Critical Event Preparedness and Response, stating that "force restraint likely prevented further escalation of crowd activity and damage to community, as well as preventing longer-term damage to Baltimore Police Department (BPD)-community relationships."[52]

Nevertheless, the tactical strategies used by the BPD were not without problems, as the soft approach eventually became militarized. The city leadership in Baltimore suggested a "de facto strategy of negotiated management and mass demonstration force restraint."[53] This "soft approach" strategy required officers not to engage protesters, avoid arrests, and wear regular uniforms without helmets and gloves, to avoid provoking an incident.[54] Police initially used this approach during the onset of protests; however, the BPD did not operate with a formal plan to handle mass demonstrations.[55] In fact, the after-action analysis of Baltimore City's response to the unrest declared that the lack of a strategy to address mass demonstrations coupled with confusing and overlapping chains of command, as well as poor communication (both internally and with the public), created problems.[56]

Consequently, as protests turned violent, police took on a more militarized response. The soft approach turned aggressive when the BPD gathered intelligence that demonstrations would take place at the Mondawmin Mall, a major bus hub for students. When the BPD learned that some Baltimore Public School students called for a "purge" (a reference to *The Purge*, a 2013 movie about a twelve-hour-period in which any crime could be committed without punishment once a year), police confronted the students with riot gear, helmets, and shields. Some students responded angrily by throwing debris, bricks, and rocks, and a SWAT armored response vehicle deployed a chemical agent and smoke to disperse the crowd. As looting and rioting took place, the police response became more militarized. Police resorted to using armored response vehicles and pepper-spray balls to disperse crowds while wearing riot gear.[57] The initial strategy of force restraint quickly evolved into a militarized response from law enforcement akin to that of Ferguson.

Nevertheless, protesters in Baltimore had more favorable perceptions of how police handled events than Ferguson protesters. Perhaps the initial use of force restraint appeased protesters by giving them an opportunity to exercise their right to protest. But, with the increasing militarization of police tactics, such opinions quickly changed.

Future Community Action

Protesters were asked if they would participate in collective action three to six months from the time of the interview.[58] While past behavior is often indicative of future behavior, very few reported having engaged in protests before the Ferguson and Baltimore unrest. In particular, a total of five revolutionary, fourteen intermediate, and six tourist activists mentioned previous activism.[59] Despite limited previous experience, revolutionary activists remained wholly committed to continuing participation, as most were willing to sacrifice individual interests in favor of the collective cause. However, intermittent demonstrators were willing to engage in subsequent activism as long as it remained peaceful or to partake in other forms of community action. Tourists were less likely to report plans to engage in future demonstrations given the risks; however, they reported various ways they would continue to engage in community efforts. Table 5.1 summarizes the extent of negative protest policing for each group of protesters, and their responses to the questions on future participation.

Revolutionary Protesters and Future Activism

Overall, seventeen revolutionary activists reported commitment to engage in future protests. Revolutionary protesters insisted they would remain active in future protest movements despite having experienced violent repressive tactics and police intimidation. For example, even though he was locked up for protesting, Darius, a Black Ferguson

TABLE 5.1. Summary of Responses Related to Protest Policing and Participation in Future Activism or Community Action among Ferguson and Baltimore Protesters*

	Repressive Protest Policing Tactics						Future Participation in Protests		Future Participation in Community Action
	Rubber bullets and tear gas	Physical force	Arrests	Surveillance	Perceived hostility	Verbal assault	Yes	No	Yes
Revolutionary	11	13	11	8	4	6	17	0	4
Intermittent	15	7	8	0	3	2	16	0	16
Tourist	7	4	6	1	2	3	6	8	18
Total	33	24	25	9	9	11	40	8	37

* Respondents reported more than one subcategory of repressive policing tactics. What we have in table 5.1 is a summary of all responses to each subcategory. Thus the responses are not mutually exclusive.

demonstrator, declared that he would continue to engage in protest activity because "we want to see a change." Likewise, despite having been arrested while protesting and declaring Ferguson officers as "nasty and rude," Shandra, a Black Ferguson activist, resolved to continue her activism efforts because "I'm hoping for change. I've got a grandson . . . I will be one of them people that helps change it for real for him." Marie, a Latina Ferguson activist, vowed to continue "as long as it takes." She acknowledged that, after police were "throwing tear gas canisters . . . [and] pointing me out in a protest . . . [it] solidified that I would [continue to] be active." In fact, a few Ferguson protesters were adamant about effecting change, even if it cost them their lives. Despite being recorded by police while on the frontlines, Asia, a Black activist, asserted, "I'm doing this for a reason. [I would] rather die out of the outcome or I'm in a history book. You know? I'm doing it for a purpose."

While some revolutionary demonstrators were willing to die for the cause, others were reluctant to put their lives on the line, yet remained wholly committed to protest participation. When asked where she would be in three to six months as it relates to community action, Devanta, a Black revolutionary Ferguson demonstrator, acknowledged the risk of protesting, stating, "I don't want to see myself in jail or . . . dead or nothing like that [for protesting]." Nevertheless, Devanta had every intention of continuing to protest against police violence. Despite the personal costs of participation, some protesters responded to threats of repression by developing a greater resolve.[60] Sometimes extreme repression has been observed to provoke stronger levels of protests among the organizations and hasten the formation of social movement.[61] When repression is perceived as illegitimate, it is not uncommon for people to become more extreme in their approach.[62]

Four revolutionary demonstrators who were persons of color reported that, while they did not plan on continuing on with subsequent street protests, they intended to engage in various community efforts to effect change. Dyshelle, a Black Ferguson activist, stated that, in the next three to six months, "[I will be doing] less protesting but getting more into the community." She said she planned to work with different organizations "to be an advocate [against] police brutality." Consider Amber's strong commitment to bring about change in the city of Baltimore:

> I'm still here on the front line, I'm still doing the work. Like I said I'm working with the Downtown Cultural Art Center, we really are—we have some, some programs that are geared towards disadvantaged or disenfranchised young people. . . . I'm connected with a lot of different city leaders and stuff like that. . . . I have been doing the work prior to this, you know. I've been, you know, hanging in the hood and doing voter registration drives in 2010–2011, hosting back to school events and stuff like that. So I've been here doing the work and so I'm going to continue.

Amber planned to continue her community outreach endeavors. In addition, she emphasized the need to build political power for herself by voting. She was not alone in her efforts to foster political power. Jason, a mixed-race activist, also described his plans to work with politicians:

> I'm working with currently the house majority whip Dwayne Haynes. Delegate Dwayne Haynes, he's the house majority whip for Maryland and Antonio Hanes who's the delegate for my neighborhood and I can

see myself working on either one of their campaigns and whoever is running for mayor. I hope to work on one of their campaigns so that we can have someone inside of these positions of power somewhere that's going to work for the people. And I'm not just saying to go to your office and work for them but be active in the community. [We need] to be talking to people, hanging out, eating with people, having fun with people, working with people, getting things done and bringing the community back together because it's broken. So in three to six months I hope to be working with these people in leadership roles, forming active plans to reunite our city.

Ultimately, repression by authorities, particularly in Ferguson, created internal solidarity among the vast majority of revolutionary protest members to continue participation in protest movements or remain committed to engaging in community action efforts to bring about change.

Intermittent Protesters and Future Activism

Similar to revolutionary activists, many intermittent protesters indicated that they would continue to engage in future protest demonstrations. Specifically, sixteen intermittent demonstrators, all of whom were Black, reported plans to remain active. Brittany from Ferguson proclaimed, "I followed this the first day, the exact first day that it happened, and I have continued and I will continue." Allonte, a Baltimorean protester, said, "If they were goin' to protest again and have all the marches, yes I would support, you know. And like I said I live down in that community so I would have to support them, you know." Others, particularly Ferguson protesters, emphasized that they would continue to be involved in street protests under certain conditions. For example, Keston, a Black activist, stated, "I would love to participate in these peaceful protests." Rachel, a Black protester, explained that she would be involved "as long as [the protests are] peaceful. I'm not getting involved in anything that's going to threaten me to have to go to jail. I don't want to go to jail as a protester. When they're out with that tear gas and all of that I don't come out." Although intermittent protesters reported plans to engage in future protest, their involvement remained contingent on demonstrations being void of violence.

Sixteen intermittent demonstrators, across race/ethnicity, asserted that they would get more involved in the community.[63] Brown's and Gray's deaths shed light on problems such as unemployment, underemployment, poverty, and lack of resources. As a result, intermittent protesters chose to become more engaged in their neighborhoods. Several demonstrators anticipated taking a more hands-on approach to assist young people. Asked about her short-term plans with community action, Ebony, a Black Ferguson activist, asserted that "my number one thing is I'm volunteering [to] work with young people." Jack, a White Baltimore protester, noted that he planned to engage with a specific organization "that's youth-led. . . . The leadership is all youth-based." And Tremaine, a Black Baltimorean activist, stated, "I see myself educating more kids on what's really happening and what they can do today, even in elementary school, to fix it."

Others were committed to connecting with others in order to have difficult conversations about race. As a White Baltimore activist, Emma, said:

I guess just personally trying to, you know, outside of Freddie Gray's specifically trying to do my part . . . trying to undo racism. . . . But I think that like on a personal level I have been trying really hard to like connect with other people that are also working on this issue actively. . . . One group is not going to [do] it but I think like having these difficult conversions is a start. [We need to] really critically analyze how our institutions operate and how our society operates and what . . . organizing can do to change these systems for the better.

In general, contrary to revolutionary activists, intermittent demonstrators were not willing to endure the threat of arrest or personal safety to engage in collective street action; however, they were motivated to engage in other forms of action within the community.

Tourist Protesters and Future Activism

As we have seen, most revolutionary and intermittent protesters intended to engage in protest events in the short term. In contrast, eighteen tourists, regardless of race, planned to participate in some level of community action. In Ferguson, some sought to avoid protest events, given the risks. Kent, a White demonstrator who loathed the aggressive manner in which officers responded to Ferguson protesters, said that he was recently asked to "join a committee to archive people's narratives on their experiences of Ferguson and in St. Louis." Since he "thought that would be a good way to honor people's experiences," he planned to serve on this committee. Others, like intermittent demonstrators, anticipated that they would become more politically engaged. After noting that protest events were "too chaotic," Deja, a Black protester, admitted, "I don't have any plans to actively participate. What I do plan on [doing] is encouraging people during voting times to get out to the polls . . . [to get] people to elect some Black officials." While Helen, a Black demonstrator, reported that protest police in Baltimore were "quiet" when she protested, she wanted to "teach about the political process, the political system, just like basic stuff that people don't necessarily know." She planned to create a blog so that community residents "know who your politicians are and what they've done." As evidenced in these accounts, some chose to engage the community in creative ways.

Others were motivated to reach out to youths. Toby, a Black Ferguson demonstrator who attended a protest and rally, said as a pastor he "may not be marching . . . [but he would start] mentoring . . . and really focus[ing] on young people . . . to make sure our young people are well informed [so] they don't have to suffer." In a similar vein, Reginald, a Black Ferguson activist, said that despite the fact that police operated in a "very militaristic, threatening way" toward protesters, he saw himself "being more involved in some of the . . . community organizations for young people." A few women were committed to specifically mentoring young girls. While Abryann, a Black Baltimore demonstrator, said she would like to "mentor in some capacity and just be a positive role model," she desired "to target teenage girls." In a similar vein, Joy, a Black Baltimore demonstrator said she would like to "take two or three little girls, or young ladies, under my belt" and mentor them.

Overall, most Ferguson tourists were deterred from participating in the movement because of the coercive ways that authorities policed protest events in the wake of Brown's death. Thus, they were more inclined to engage the community in other ways. While Baltimore protesters did not report being deterred from Baltimore protests, some preferred to affect change by focusing their effort on engaging the community.

Nevertheless, six tourists, all of whom were Black, did report that they would engage in future protests, yet this was contingent on several factors. A couple surmised that they would get involved if their schedules permitted. Karis, a Black Baltimore activist, acknowledged that "I'm quite sure it will be some protest still going on in [Freddie Gray's] name. . . . I might participate [but] it depends on where it will be and what time you know." Similarly, when asked about subsequent activism efforts, Daniella, a Black Baltimore protester, stated she would participate "if it works around like my kids' schedule . . . [and] it doesn't interfere with anything I have to do being a mom." Others said they would engage in activism efforts if they felt strongly about an issue. Willie, a Black protester from Ferguson, said he would get involved in subsequent protests "if it's something I feel strongly about, if it's something I feel that needs to be addressed. I want to let my voice be heard because I think it's time."

However, eight tourist demonstrators said they would not continue with subsequent protests. The use of such repressive tactics by police, in particular, served to deter Ferguson demonstrators. Latoya, a Black demonstrator, admitted, "I don't see myself getting really involved. After my experiences and things that I've seen, I'm scared to get involved. I know that's a cowardly thing to say but it is the truth. I'm not afraid to admit that I'm a little scared to get involved." Crystal, a Black tourist, had similar sentiments, asserting, "I'm scared of how the [police are] going to react to the people protesting, or saying certain things." And Isabelle expressed that, after police were "throwing tear gas bombs . . . [and some] started looting I backed down . . . I was scared you know, because I don't want to get killed." For these reasons, several made a conscious decision to avoid participating in subsequent demonstrations, as they felt officers' actions engendered fear.[64] Several Baltimore tourist demonstrators also remained noncommittal about engaging in subsequent protest events or community action. Jonathan, a Black activist, stated that, rather than get involved, he anticipated that he would be "observing and seeing how they are going forward."

So what do the above findings imply about the impact on repressive tactics on protesters' motivation? I found limited evidence on the impact of protest policing on the de-escalation or deterrence of protests. On the contrary, individuals who were already very committed to the movement continued to be actively engaged. While protest policing had some influence on tourist protesters' participation, these protesters adapted different ways of engaging in the overall ideological goals of the Black Lives Matter movement through community action. In other words, while some groups of protesters may have felt intimidated by the repressive tactics they directly experienced, their motivation to become involved in changing the racially biased institutions and policies of society at large was not impacted, reaffirming their commitment to the overall ideological goals of the protests.

6

Public Disorder

Why did massive uprising take place in Ferguson and Baltimore? Protests in these two cities were the most devastating moments of disorder since the Los Angeles riots of 1992. What was so unique about Ferguson and Baltimore that explains the weeks of explosive race-based unrest that erupted there and garnered national attention? In this chapter, I turn my attention to explaining the causes of the disorder in Ferguson and Baltimore in order to lay the groundwork for understanding the conditions that can lead to future uprisings in other places.

I begin by exploring the Flashpoints Model of Public Disorder because it incorporates several elements acknowledged as having an underlying role in the initiation of disorder into a general framework of analysis. The central basis of the model is that public disorder cannot be explained by a single factor but is best understood by considering broad features of social context and specific patterns of direct interaction. The Flashpoints Model of Public Disorder is a multivariate framework that explains why some disorderly incidents flare up ("flashpoints"), triggering a volatile reaction, while others fail to ignite.[1] David Waddington and his colleagues developed the Flashpoints Model during the 1980s, when they undertook an examination of case studies of violent and nonviolent episodes of crowd behavior in England and Wales.[2] This model was originally comprised of six integrated levels of analysis—structural, political/ideological, cultural, contextual, situational, and interactional—and later revised to include a seventh level: institutional/organizational.[3] The following briefly outlines these seven levels.

The *structural level* focuses on relevant macrosociological factors pertaining to the relative distribution of power and resources. This level is concerned with the sources of collective societal grievances tied to feelings of subjective deprivation and inequality (i.e., joblessness, poor housing stock, underfunded schools, etc.), political powerlessness, and social exclusion that underlie collective societal grievances.[4] This model maintains that conflict is more likely to arise if disadvantaged groups are inhibited from improving their position, if the state remains unresponsive or opposed to such grievances, and whether police reaction is viewed as repressive.[5]

Directly connected to the structural level is the *political/ideological* level of analysis, which examines how central political and ideological agencies (i.e., government, prominent politicians, the media, senior police, etc.) wield several forms of influence on police attitudes and behavior toward the injured segments of society.[6] In some cases, this pressure is explicitly exercised, as in the case of government pronouncement on police decisions; in other cases, this pressure is subtle, where police take their cues from the ideological climate of opinion produced by local politicians, community representatives, and the mass media.[7] Politicians and commentators will generally use the media to represent the dissenting group in a more or less favorable light. The process of vilification may compound the sense of injustice felt by members of the dissenting group, who are often marginal to the political mainstream or are defined as problematic. Consequently, this may increase their willingness to resort to the use of violence to promote their demands, resulting in harsher treatment by the police.

The *cultural* level of analysis deals with the ways in which people understand the social structure and their place within it, how they define themselves and other social groups, and their definitions of the rules informing their behavior in particular situations.[8] Concerned with the values, norms, and patterns of thought developed in distinct sections of society, the model's cultural level involves the contrasting ways of life, belief systems, and codes of conduct of the relevant parties that increase the potential for conflict.[9] Conflicts are more likely to occur when actors fail to communicate with one another. For example, the risk of problematic situations is greater in circumstances in which officers come from outside departments, are not sufficiently attuned to political cultures, and remain unconcerned with preserving healthy police-community relations.[10] It is also necessary to note that subsections of protesters and police may endorse differing values and beliefs regarding appropriate behavior and the legitimate rights of individuals and groups. For instance, distinctions must be made between paramilitary police and more conventional police units, and between demonstrators committed to peaceful protests compared to those willing to resort to physical use of force if needed.[11]

The cultural level has a great deal of overlap with the *institutional/organization* level, which focuses on factors such as traditions and philosophies of policing, formal systems of accountability, training regimes, operating principles, and mission statements.[12] In general, policing institutions tend to be centralized, have a tradition of deference to local and national government, inadequate police training in public order management, a philosophy of "hard" policing (i.e., zero tolerance), weak or nonexistent systems of accountability, and disorganized or malfunctioning operating procedures for dealing with public disorder.[13]

The *contextual* level focuses specifically on the dynamic setting in which public disorder arises. Generally, disorderly events have a specific history prior to erupting into public consciousness.[14] Communication processes are salient, as they can stoke up or suppress the potential for disorder.[15] This may include a negative history of interactions between the police and community members, which can become highly charged,[16] as well as the arousing effect of rumors, media sensationalism, and threatening statements from one or both parties.[17] In the absence of dialogue between demonstrators and representatives of the police, police will likely resort to surveillance and intelligence-gathering.[18] However, if police attempt to insure themselves against the "worst case scenario" by accruing large numbers of personnel and "less lethal" weaponry, they risk creating a self-fulfilling prophecy.[19]

The *situational* level takes into account the spatial setting pertaining to the relevant social interaction. However, the spatial context is mediated by social and cultural settings.[20] This can include the extent to which a specific location lends itself to surveillance by the police or permits officers to disperse the crowd in a manner that does not appear arbitrary.[21] For instance, a certain location may hold "cultural and/or symbolic significance, representing 'turf' to be defended by civilians, or a 'no-go area' to be retaken by the police."[22] The prospect of disorder is likely if the dissenting groups are within close proximity to one another and police perceive that they have a legal and political duty to defend target locations.[23] If one side interprets the course of action taken by the rival party as reprehensible, it only increases the possibility of misunderstanding and heightened conflict. Under this model, opposing parties interpret each side as committed to a repugnant course of action. Regardless of whether one side or the other is actually committed to a sinister act, what matters is that these situational cues are interpreted as such by the opposition.[24] Unclear lines of communication between police units, police commanders, and the crowd only increase the likelihood of misunderstandings between the opposing parties.

The final *interactional* level of analysis is where "flashpoints" occur. This level is concerned with the nature and quality of relations between the police and/or relevant segments of the public, which are likely in both parties to vary in respect, cooperation, provocation, and restraint.[25] The nature of these relations are conditioned by several factors located at the previous level of analysis (e.g., the strength of collective grievances, the degree to which protesters are vilified, the tenor of recent police-community relations, etc). Here it is likely that a "flashpoint" incident, or succession of incidents (i.e., forcibly dispersing a crowd, throwing a brick at an officer, etc.), will trigger disorder. While there may be a rationale for such actions, it is generally invisible to the other side and the "flashpoint" is often interpreted as a refusal by one or both sides to accommodate the rights and interests of the other party.[26]

Applying the Flashpoint Model: Ferguson Unrest

This section will determine if the constructs laid out in the Flashpoints Models of Public Disorder can explain the occurrence of the unrest in Ferguson in 2014 and Baltimore in 2015. What follows is an analysis of the Ferguson and Baltimore incidents according to the Flashpoint model's seven integrated levels, including structural, political/ideological, cultural, institutional, contextual, situational, and interactional.

Structural

Focused on the macrosociological factors that are tied to the distribution of power and resources, we will see that several structural factors served as the backdrop to the public disorder that occurred in Ferguson. The St. Louis Metropolitan area, including St. Louis City and St. Louis County (which is comprised of ninety-one municipalities), remains one of the most racially segregated places in the United States.[27] Much of the isolation of Blacks in the city of St. Louis is the result of decades of government policies and real estate practices: the institutionalization of racial segregation through racially explicit zoning decisions, race-restricted deed covenants, suburban finance, public housing, and urban renewal plans that sought to shift Black populations from central cities like St. Louis to inner ring suburbs like Ferguson.

At a time when cities were examining the legality of zoning, the city of St. Louis formalized racial segregation during the era of World War I.[28] In the early twentieth century, a racial zoning ordinance made it illegal to purchase a house on a block unless the majority—75 percent—of current residents were of the same race as the buyer.[29] Although St. Louis voters codified segregation with an ordinance that prohibited racially integrated neighborhoods, that ordinance was struck down when the Supreme Court ruled against a similar law in Louisville, Kentucky.[30] The court's decision relied primarily on the premise that racial zoning ordinances infringed on property owners right to sell to whom they wished.[31] Yet, in an effort to control Black population movement in the second decade of the twentieth century, the city of St. Louis turned to restrictive deed covenant that prohibited home sales to Blacks and kept segregation intact.[32]

Restricted covenants attach specific restrictions to the use and resale of property and clauses to property deeds.[33] Racial occupancy was the central element of original deed covenants and restrictive agreements in St. Louis.[34] Assuming that Blacks posed a threat to property values, race-restrictive covenants came about as private agreements to exclude Blacks from White neighborhoods in 1910.[35] Specifically, the St. Louis Real Estate Exchange drafted a uniform contract for neighborhood associations, which took two forms. The first ensured that homeowners would not sell their property to Blacks or permit the property to be occupied by them.[36] The second required associations of homeowners to sign mutual agreements that no member would sell or permit occupancy by Blacks.[37] Race-restricted deed covenants that were "written into deeds bound [W]hites together in a racial cartel pledged to keep dwellings in [W]hite hands in perpetuity."[38] Restricted covenants formalized racial policies among realtors in St. Louis, which in turn shaped the practice of real estate in Greater St. Louis.[39]

In the early years of the New Deal, restricted covenants were adopted as explicit public policy, as the Federal Housing Authority (FHA) subsidized suburban development and continued the racial covenant conditions of mortgage insurance during the late 1930s to the late 1950s.[40] Since the FHA (and private banks and realtors) perceived racial, ethnic, and economic heterogeneity as risky, they underwrote the efforts by White suburbanites to segregate White suburban areas by race and class.[41] Concerned with racial occupancy, American historian Richard Rothstein argues that "this FHA policy began a half-century of federal government efforts to move St. Louis's families to newly growing exclusive white suburbs."[42] It was only after civil rights groups persistently identified FHA policies as a source of racial segregation and housing shortage that the FHA's 1947 Underwriting Manual removed explicit references to race.[43] Even still, FHA privately assured lenders and developers that there would be no real change in policy and continued to promote racial restrictions in their loan insurance programs until the 1960s.[44] Consequently, government-supported and -administered redlining policies denied loans to Black and mixed neighborhoods while FHA mortgage insurance flowed primarily to the suburbs, subsidizing White flight and contributing to a suburban sprawl that left the City and Black residents behind.[45] While government housing policies promoted White home ownership and asset accumulation, they relegated Blacks to public housing and vouchers.

Following the Great Depression, federal support for low-income public housing held out the possibility of thwarting or amending discriminatory patterns of private real estate in St. Louis. However, federal housing policy hardened residential segregation patterns.[46] St. Louis city government constructed subsidized public housing in poor, ghetto neighborhoods, while St. Louis County officials relied on zoning to curtail public housing and minimize the number of units available to low-income home-seekers.[47] In 1949, public housing was attached to the strategy of "slum clearance," the use of urban renewal funds to shift ghetto locations in the guise of cleaning up ghetto neighborhoods.[48] The redevelopment program resulted in "both the formal requirement that each newly constructed unit be accompanied by the destruction of a 'substandard' unit and the implicit assumption that a primary purpose of public housing was to warehouse those displaced by renewal projects."[49] Most displaced families relocated to public housing or to apartments adjoining the original substandard home from which they were displaced, creating new, overcrowded slums that received little investment in city infrastructure and amenities.[50] When public housing became unavailable and the St. Louis Housing Authority issued Section 8 rent supplement vouchers to eligible families, many Blacks still were denied the opportunity to rise into better communities, as many landlords refused to accept Section 8 vouchers.[51] The refusal to accept vouchers contributed to a large concentration of Blacks residing in overcrowded, run-down neighborhoods on the north side of the city.[52] These areas were denied adequate city services, such as trash collection, street lighting, and emergency response.[53] Because their demand for apartments was greater relative to supply, Blacks paid 25-percent higher rent than Whites.[54] To pay their exorbitantly high rent, many Black families took in occupants, or subdivided or sublet their place of residence, intensifying overcrowding. In general, Blacks were "racially segregated into crowded, high-rent slum housing or certain sections of town."[55]

Government policies and real estate practices played a central role in supporting racial stereotypes, resulting in the flight of the middle classes and Whites from central areas in the 1970s.[56] Though the exodus of Whites from the city of St. Louis ended in the 1980s, since then many Blacks have left the inner city—which is characterized by high levels of concentrated poverty and severe racial disparity—for nearby suburbs such as Ferguson. Located twelve miles west of downtown St. Louis, Ferguson was incorporated in 1894.[57] In its early years, Ferguson was a White enclave with virtually no Black presence, even though it bordered Kinloch, a small, majority-Black city.[58] Until the mid-1960s, Ferguson blocked off the main road that connected it to the city of Kinloch with a chain, causing some commentators to speculate that Ferguson was a "sundown town" that banned Black people after dark.[59]

This state of affairs was maintained by discriminatory local government and real estate practices, which prohibited the distribution of mortgages to Blacks.[60] After the passage of the FHA in 1968, Black families moved to Ferguson and other all-White municipalities in North St. Louis County. This triggered White flight, resulting in a population that was 85-percent White and 14-percent Black.[61] In the 1980s, the Lambert International Airport sought to expand, which involved the appropriation of land in Kinloch, causing many residents to migrate to

Ferguson—specifically, in the Canfield Green apartment complex where Michael Brown resided.[62] The new arrivals were generally poor, with one-quarter of the residents living below poverty, 14 percent unemployed, and two-thirds of school children qualifying for free or reduced lunch.[63] The four school districts that serve Ferguson, which are disproportionately Black, have performed poorly; for instance, Normandy School district, where Michael Brown attended, borders Ferguson and ranks last in overall academic performance in the entire state.[64] In fact, the school lost its accreditation a few days after Brown graduated.[65]

As discussed earlier, despite the fact that the majority of residents in Ferguson are Black, at the time of Brown's death the municipal government was virtually all White, including the mayor, six of the seven school board members, five of the six city council members, and fifty out of fifty-four police officers.[66] Consequently, Black residents in Ferguson enjoyed little in the way of political representation. Adding to the fact that the demographics were not represented in Ferguson's seats of authority and power, the average value for Ferguson's real estate was estimated at only one-third of that for the county as a whole.[67] According to scholars John Mollenkopf and Todd Swanstron, if Ferguson "increases tax rates (to raise revenues to meet needs), it will drive home values down further; but if it does not increase tax rates, it will slowly starve municipal services and the schools."[68]

While none of these structural factors directly explain the public disorder that occurred in Ferguson, it does tell us something about the residents, many of whom engaged in protest events following Brown's death and who faced few promising prospects as a result of the segregation, discriminatory housing policies, and social deprivation in Ferguson.

Political/Ideological

The political/ideological level is concerned with the ways in which political institutions influence police attitudes and conduct toward those who are aggrieved. City officials in Ferguson placed increasing political pressure on the police and local courts to maximize revenue from traffic tickets, fines, and court fees as a means to finance municipal operations.[69] Ferguson received one-quarter of its revenue from court fees alone.[70] For example, between July 1, 2010, and June 30, 2014, the FPD issued approximately ninety thousand citations and summons for municipal violations.[71] The city issued 50 percent more citations in 2014 than it did in 2010, even though the number of charges for serious offenses covered by the municipal code (i.e., assault, stealing, driving while intoxicated) remained relatively constant.[72] When citizens failed to appear in court because they could not pay the fine, additional fees were imposed and warrants issued for their arrest.[73] Consequently, "violations that would normally not result in a penalty of imprisonment can, and frequently do, lead to municipal warrants, arrests, and jail time."[74] In Ferguson, maximizing revenue served as the central priority in every branch of Ferguson government, including police, municipal court, and city hall. The nature of implication of the political direction of police policy generated extreme mistrust of the police among Ferguson residents.

Cultural and Institutional/Organizational

Recall that the cultural level focuses on the contrasting ways of life and norms that groups develop on the basis of mutual experience, socialization, and their place in the social structure. The institutional/organizational level is concerned with variables such as traditions and philosophies of policing, formal systems of accountability, training regimes, operating principles, and mission statements. Both the local police culture and the institutional structure of the FPD played a critical role in shaping an atmosphere conducive to public disorder.[75] The increasing number of citations and summons in Ferguson fell disproportionately to Black residents. City officials worked with the primarily White police force, which aggressively stopped, cited, and arrested Black residents for numerous infractions, as discussed in chapter 2.[76] Despite comprising 67 percent of the Ferguson population, Blacks accounted for 85 percent of vehicle stops, 90 percent of citations, and 93 percent of arrests from 2012 to 2014.[77] Moreover, certain charges were filed exclusively against Black individuals. From 2011 to 2013, Blacks accounted for 95 percent of individuals charged with "manner of walking in roadway," 94 percent of individuals charged with failure to comply, 92 percent of individuals charged with resisting arrest, 92 percent of individuals charged with "peace disturbance," and 89 percent of individuals charged with failure to obey.[78] Blacks also accounted for 92 percent of cases in which an arrest warrant was issued and were 68 percent less likely than others to have their cases dismissed by the municipal judge.[79] Essentially, Blacks were disproportionately represented at every stage of Ferguson law enforcement, from initial police contact to final disposition of a case in municipal court.[80] In fact, the federal investigation from the DOJ claimed that Ferguson police and municipal court staff engaged in racially biased practices.[81] The report asserted:

> Racial bias and stereotyping is evident from the facts, taken together. This evidence includes: the consistency and magnitude of the racial disparities throughout Ferguson's police and court enforcement actions; the selection and execution of police and court practices that disproportionately harm African Americans and do little to promote public safety; the persistent exercise of discretion to the detriment of African Americans; the apparent consideration of race in assessing threat; and the historical opposition to having African Americans live in Ferguson, which lingers among some today. We have also found explicit racial bias in the communications of police and court supervisors and that some officials apply racial stereotypes, rather than facts, to explain the harm African Americans experience due to Ferguson's approach to law enforcement. . . . Based on this evidence as a whole, we have found that Ferguson's law enforcement activities stem in part from a discriminatory purpose and thus deny African Americans equal protection of the laws in violation of the Constitution.[82]

Consequently, the disproportionate harm caused to Black residents was driven by intentional discrimination, which is in violation of the Equal Protection Clause of the Fourteenth Amendment. Ultimately, systemic police and judicial court practices in Ferguson balanced the city budgets on the backs of poor Black citizens. As a result, those who were unable to pay their fines and fees for what amounted to civil violations faced collateral consequences: a suspended driver's license, loss of a job, or further marginalization from civic and political participation. These aspects of police culture and the institutional character of the FPD not only resulted in extreme mistrust and cynicism among Black residents and the police, but also in resistance to law enforcement, as many residents perceived officers' ultimate goal was revenue generation rather than to meet public safety needs. All this came to a head when Michael Brown died at the hands of Officer Darren Wilson.

Flashpoint: The Shooting of Michael Brown

The immediate flashpoint for the Ferguson uprising of 2014 occurred on August 9, when Michael Brown and his friend Dorian Johnson were stopped by Officer Wilson as they turned onto Canfield Drive. According to the report by the DOJ, as described earlier, when Wilson passed the young men who were walking in the street, he told them to move to the sidewalk and they refused.[83] Johnson asserted that Wilson started a scuffle in the vehicle by grabbing Brown by the neck, and that Brown tried to pull away as Wilson drew his gun and shot Brown in the hand. Johnson stated that Brown ran, was shot in the back, and then turned around and raised his hands to surrender but the officer again opened fire. Wilson and the FPD disputed these claims, alleging that, after Wilson told the teens to move to the sidewalk, he realized Brown was a robbery suspect. Wilson testified that, as he tried to exit his vehicle, Brown pushed him back into the car, punched him, reached for his gun, and a struggle for the gun ensued, during which Wilson fired two shots. At some point, Brown ran, and Wilson chased him and shot him after he turned and charged toward him. Reports show that Wilson fired twelve bullets, six of which hit Brown, including two in the head.

Although the immediate catalyst of the protests in Ferguson was the killing of Michael Brown, we have seen that the underlying cause was years of racial tension between Black residents, police, and the local government. We will see that, a "lull" fell after the flashpoint that resulted in Brown's death, followed the next day by a disorderly incident, which sparked two weeks of protests and public disorder.[84] In order to understand why there was a lull in advance of public disorder, it is vital to take into consideration the nature of the communication context before Brown's death and how it framed the uprising.

Contextual

The contextual level of analysis is concerned with the dynamic communication processes occurring in the build-up to an event, which can fuel or suppress the potential for disorder. The communication context before and after Brown's death played a central role in shaping mass protests in Ferguson. Prior to Brown's shooting, Americans were already heatedly discussing the issues of police violence against Black civilians, deeply rooted racial disparities in the criminal justice system, and racism in general. This conversation resonated as the deaths of Trayvon Martin, Alton Sterling, Philandro Castile, and Tamir Rice saturated the national media. A few weeks prior to Brown's death, the world watched when a New York officer put Eric Garner in a chokehold for selling cigarettes, heard him state eleven times that he couldn't breathe, and consequently died. A few days before Brown was killed, the world learned that John Crawford was shot down in an Ohio Walmart for carrying a pellet gun. Americans were not just hearing about these incidents; with the advent of technology, they saw these events transpire as raw video broadcast on social media and that the footage disproved what officers alleged had happened.[85] These incidents would inform discussions about what had happened to Brown. To many, Brown's death signified the calamity of the many unarmed Black men who died at the hands of police. With the cumulative effect of cases of police force against Black civilians nationwide, it's not surprising that Ferguson—a city steeped in inequality, segregation, and unfair policing practices—erupted in unrest.[86]

This was further exacerbated by the failure of the FPD to proactively communicate with local residents in the aftermath of Brown's death. Although the FPD provided a statement to the media the day of the shooting, after that it was not forthcoming with information, leading many community residents to believe that the police were withholding information about Brown's shooting.[87] Because then Ferguson Police Chief Thomas Jackson did not speak to the press until the day after the shooting, some believed that the reason for the delay was to allow the police to derive an alternate explanation for the shooting.[88] Six days after Brown's death, Jackson called a press conference to release the name of the officer who had shot him; however, he also released surveillance footage of a strong-armed robbery at a convenience store, showing Brown shoving the shop owner and stealing a pack of cigarillos.[89] To many, the footage implied that this helped to explain and excuse the shooting by Wilson, even though Jackson acknowledged that the "robbery does not relate to the initial contact between the officer [Darren Wilson] and Michael

Brown."[90] Although the DOJ later reported that Wilson claimed he was
aware of the incident at Ferguson Market and suspected that Brown was
involved, Jackson's failure to frame the information objectively invali-
dated his statements as an attempt to communicate with the community,
which exacerbated the severe mistrust between law enforcement and
neighborhood residents.[91] Moreover, the police released information
from an initial autopsy stating that Brown had marijuana in his system.
Many, including Brown's family, believed that the piecemeal manner in
which police released information about Brown was an attempt to smear
his reputation in order to justify his death. Overall, police-media relations were poor, and the public information released by law enforcement
was slow and reactionary. The communication context, coupled with
other factors, all served to stoke the flames that had been smoldering for
quite some time among Black Ferguson residents.

Situational

Recall that the situational level deals with the physical and social elements of order or disorder pertaining to the setting of relevant social
interaction. The spatial location where Brown was fatally shot held
symbolic significance for members of the community. On the night of
Brown's death, his mother, Leslie McSpadden, set up a makeshift memorial at the site of the shooting, while others lighted candles and scattered
flowers on the ground where Brown had died.[92] Some reported that
police ran over the memorial with their cars, smashing candles and
flowers, and that one officer permitted his police dog to urinate on the
memorial.[93] Much of the crowd viewed this course of action as disrespectful and reprehensible, further inflaming tensions.[94]

In the midst of the Ferguson unrest, there existed a wide range of
situational objectives, including varying commitment to the use of violence as a means to an end. According to the Ferguson After-Action
Report, police reported that, on August 11, 2014,

> demonstrators were throwing rocks, bottles, frozen bottles of water,
> Molotov cocktails, and other objects. The mass gatherings became more
> vocal and aggressive with burning of businesses and other property
> damage, including looting and breaking windows. Law enforcement

responded with the use of armored vehicles, tear gas, PepperBall projec-
tiles, bean bag rounds, and Stingerballs to disperse the crowds.[95]

Law enforcement responded to the angry crowd with a massive show
of force, deploying tear gas for several nights, relying on police dogs
to control the crowd, using a police sniper to monitor the crowd, and
patrolling the city streets in an armored vehicle. Not only did such
actions further the sentiments that police were responding in a militarized manner, but the DOJ concluded that the equipment was misused:
tear gas was improperly fired, an armored vehicle was deployed in
situations that did not warrant it, and the use of snipers was deemed
inappropriate as a crowd control measure.[96] While protesters and police
were undoubtedly emotional, the heavy-handed action of the police
served to aggravate mounting racial tension between demonstrators and
law enforcement. Consequently, many communities of color, including
residents in Ferguson, viewed the militarization of police as an occupying army who perceive residents as the enemy.

Interactional

The interactional level of analysis is concerned with the nature and
quality of social interactions between the police and relevant sections
of the public. The highly emotive and symbolically significant incident
involving Brown's death on August 9, 2014, and the immediate outrage
it generated, provided the initial flashpoint for the Ferguson uprising.
Nearly two hundred bystanders were present at the crime scene where
Brown's dead body lay for nearly four hours, a fact that was circulated
via texting and social media.[97] While this fueled the anger and tension,
the flashpoint did not immediately ignite, as a "lull" fell, which was ultimately followed by two weeks of unrest.

News of Brown's death circulated swiftly through the neighborhood.
The day after Brown's killing, a substantial crowd of nearly one thousand
people amassed by the vigil area, on West Florissant Avenue, and in front
of the FPD, for hours.[98] That night, St. Louis County Police Chief Jon
Belmar gave a press conference and shared some facts of the case. He
announced that Michael Brown physically assaulted an officer, who shot
him after a struggle ensued over the officer's weapon.[99] He informed the

public that the officer had no history of similar incidents and that he was on paid leave pending the investigation by St. Louis County. The comments did not satisfy demonstrators, who chanted "no justice, no peace."[100] This, coupled with some residents witnessing police trample Brown's memorial site, resulted in tensions boiling over. Some took it upon themselves to loot QuikTrip, a convenience store on West Florissant Avenue, where much of the community believed that a store employee called the police in the first place.[101] The store was set on fire, numerous local businesses were looted and vandalized, and several police cars were damaged.[102] In an attempt to contain the situation, several agencies deployed police in riot gear, armored vehicles, canines, and tear gas.[103] From here, the situation escalated and drew national attention as anger at police and their militarized response toward largely peaceful demonstrations boiled over into violence.

The rousing effect of this incident and police response to mass demonstrations was intensified by an attempt by the FPD to implicate Brown in a strong-armed robbery and clear the police of any blame. As already mentioned, when Chief Jackson disclosed the officer's identity who shot Brown, he released surveillance footage implicating Brown in the robbery that took place minutes before he was shot by Wilson. Lawyers of Brown's family argued that this was a strategic move to smear Brown.[104] The relevance of the contextual level is evident here, as it antagonized the issue and further increased the divide between police and protesters.

Such, then, were the main features of the unrest in Ferguson. I will turn now to a corresponding analysis of the key arrangements and activities involved in the unrest in Baltimore.

Applying the Flashpoint Model: Baltimore Unrest

Structural

Like Ferguson, the city of Baltimore has a deep history of racial and economic inequality, which is the result of purposeful government (in)action. Several structural factors served as the backdrop to the unrest that occurred in Baltimore: discriminatory government-sponsored policies and practices that played a central role in creating a segregated housing market in the early 1900s, including racial zoning, racial covenants, redlining, public housing, and urban development.

In 1910, the first "racial zoning" ordinance was passed that established block-by-block segregation in Baltimore.[105] In other words, Blacks were prohibited from encroaching into White neighborhoods and Whites were prohibited from residing in Black neighborhoods. Baltimore's segregation law was short-lived. In 1917, the US Supreme Court found ordinances like Baltimore's segregation rule unconstitutional, not because they curtailed Black people's rights as to where they could live, but because they restricted the property rights of (White) homeowners to sell to whomever they wished.[106] As a result, the mayor instructed Baltimore City building instructors and Health Department investigators to cite anyone who rented or sold to Blacks in predominantly White neighborhoods for code violations.[107] In 1925, eighteen Baltimore neighborhood associations formed the "Allied Civic and Protective Association" to encourage local property owners to sign restricted covenants, committing to never sell, rent, or lease their property to Blacks.[108] These covenants, however, were not simply private agreements between homeowners; rather, they were enforced by the city sponsor "Commission on Segregation," which organized neighborhood associations that could circulate and enforce racial covenants.[109]

Such policies were also supported at the national level. The FHA, which was created by Congress, openly supported racial covenants that excluded Blacks (regardless of their socioeconomic status) from the home ownership boom between the 1930s and the 1960s.[110] The FHA prohibited suburban subdivision developers from qualifying for federally subsidized construction loans unless the developers agreed to exclude Blacks from the neighborhood.[111] This federal program also prevented Blacks from acquiring bank mortgages for purchasing a home in suburban subdivisions that were privately financed without federal construction loan guarantees.[112] Because the FHA reflected racist ideology regarding racial separation, Blacks were often denied housing. Consequently, generations of Blacks were prevented from gaining wealth typically generated from home ownership.

In addition to racial covenants, the federal housing policy adopted regulations that established the practice of redlining—a policy that reviewed mortgages based on neighborhood districts essentially denied government subsidized mortgages to people of color.[113] In the mid-1930s, the Home Owner's Loan Corporation (HOLC) was established and made responsible for assessing the financial risk of investing in a geographical area. A red color was assigned to the least desirable neighborhoods, a designation which was linked to race, making it challenging for Black homeowners to secure home loans to purchase property or real estate in traditionally White neighborhoods.[114]

Since Blacks were unable to obtain mortgages and were constrained in overcrowded neighborhoods, it was common for them to rent apartments at substantially higher rates than those similar residents in White neighborhoods or to purchase homes in installment plans.[115] These procedures, also known as contract sales, differed from mortgages in that monthly payments were not amortized (i.e., loan amount is spread into a series of scheduled fixed payments over time) so that a single missed payment resulted in the loss of a home with no accumulated equity.[116] Since many Black contract buyers struggled to make their inflated monthly payments, it was common for married couples to work double shifts, neglect basic housing maintenance, subsidize their apartments, cram in extra tenants, and charge their tenants substantial rent when possible.[117] Contract buying was common among Blacks residing in Baltimore and was solely due to the federal government's policy of denying mortgages to Blacks.

Moreover, during the New Deal (1932–39), federal public housing policy reinforced residential segregation. From the inception of the public housing program, sites were selected and designated for Blacks and Whites.[118] For instance, housing projects for low-income Blacks were all built on slum clearance sites in the central city.[119] While Blacks lived all over the city of Baltimore and surrounding cities before the implementation of the federal housing policies, those programs restricted them to economically disadvantaged and segregated neighborhoods around downtown Baltimore.[120] In contrast, projects for middle-income Whites were placed in White neighborhoods. By the mid-1930s, the government had enticed White families out of public housing with federally insured mortgages that subsidized relocation to new single-family homes in the suburban communities.[121]

Between 1950 and 1964, Baltimore also embarked on aggressive urban renewal programs.[122] Many Blacks protested because, according to the Urban League, these programs gave "official sanctions to segregation in the name of redevelopment."[123] Likewise, the Racial Relations

Office warned that the Baltimore renewal project would result in the displacement of Blacks into a highly segregated housing market, the transfiguration of a racially flexible area to one of racial exclusion, and the reduction of land available to Black residents.[124] However, the city ignored protests and proceeded with the urban development, which resulted in the displacement of twenty-five thousand Baltimoreans, 85 percent of whom were Black.[125] While officials maintain that displaced individuals moved to better housing, the reality is that there were fewer housing units built that were available to Black residents.[126] Consequently, many Black Baltimoreans remained subject to local, state, and federal policies that clustered them in dense, isolated slums characterized by poverty and segregation.

Like in Ferguson, Missouri, the structural factors did not directly cause the unrest that took place in Baltimore. However, they underscore the limited prospects many residents faced as a result of government actions.

Political/Ideological

For decades, Baltimoreans withstood a highly coercive system of policing, which was driven by political influence. In the attack against drugs in the 1990s, Baltimore city officials and the BPD, like much of the nation, adopted and embraced aggressive order-maintenance policing tactics such as "zero-tolerance" street enforcement. Developed by the New York Police Department, the policing strategy prioritized making considerable numbers of unconstitutional stops, searches, and arrests for minor misdemeanor offenses in which police have substantial discretion; their aggressive use resulted in 301,000 pedestrian stops from January 2010 to May 2014.[127] Despite the attempts of the BPD to combat violent crime in the city, from 2010 to 2014 more than 25,000 arrests were made for minor, nonviolent violations.[128] Specifically, approximately 6,500 people were arrested for disorderly conduct, 4,000 for failure to obey an officer, 6,500 for trespassing, 1,000 for "hindering" or impeding, 3,200 for "interference" with law enforcement, 760 for "rogue and vagabond,"[129] and 650 for playing cards or dice.[130] Consequently, zero-tolerance policing tactics contributed to a pervasive pattern of constitutional violations, which, over the years, served to erode the community's trust in the police. The political/ideological climate generated feelings of anger and resentment among many Ferguson residents, which erupted upon Freddie Gray's death.

Cultural and Institutional/Organizational

The cultural and organizational structures and processes buttressing the daily operations of the BPD played a central element in the build-up of tension before the outbreak of collective disorder in Baltimore in April and May of 2015. Unconstitutional policing was aimed at and disproportionately impacted Black Baltimoreans. Despite comprising only 63 percent of the population in Baltimore, Blacks accounted for 84 percent of stops from January 2010 to June 2015.[131] Specifically, BPD officers made 520 stops for every 1,000 Black Baltimore residents compared to 180 stops for White Baltimoreans.[132] Black individuals were more likely to be stopped multiple times, accounting for 95 percent of the 410 people stopped 10 or more times by BPD officers from 2010 to 2015. Not only were Blacks more likely to be stopped, but they were also more likely to be searched compared to other racial/ethnic groups. During the same period, BPD officers were more likely to search Blacks during pedestrian (37 percent) and vehicular (23 percent) stops than other racial/ethnic groups, suggesting that police search practices in the police department discriminated against Black individuals.[133]

Despite the fact that Black Baltimoreans were more likely to be searched by police, searches of Black Baltimore residents resulted in *lower* hit rates of contraband—such as drugs or illegal guns—than searches of non-Blacks. From 2010 to 2015, Baltimore officers found contraband in 3.9 percent of searches of Blacks compared to 8.5 percent of searches of drivers who were not Black.[134] Regarding pedestrian stops, officers found contraband in 2.6 percent of searches of Black people, compared to 3.9 percent from searches of individuals from other racial/ethnic backgrounds.[135] Thus, the disparity is *not* because Blacks violate the law more than White Baltimoreans; rather, they are the result of unconstitutional and racially biased policing.

Moreover, Blacks account for the majority of misdemeanor offenses, such as making a false statement and disobeying an officer. According to the 2010–15 DOJ report, Blacks accounted for:

87 percent of the 3,400 charges for resisting arrest; 89 percent of 1,350 charges for making a false statement to an officer; 84 percent of the 4,000 charges for failing to obey an order; 86 percent of the more than 1,000 charges for hindering or obstruction; 83 percent of the roughly 6,500 arrests for disorderly conduct; and 88 percent of the nearly 3,500 arrests for trespassing on posted property.[136]

Many of these charges are subjective in nature, as officers have substantial discretion in deciding whether to enforce these rules. Although Baltimore police are more likely to arrest Black civilians for minor offenses, booking officers and prosecutors are more likely to decline to pursue these charges. The DOJ report stated that:

> Officials dismissed charges against African Americans for trespassing at a rate 52 percent higher than the rate at which they dismissed other trespassing arrests; dismissed African American resisting arrest charges at a 57 percent higher rate; failure to obey charges at a 33 percent higher rate; false statement charges at a 231 percent higher rate; disorderly conduct charges at a 17 percent higher rate; and disturbing the peace charges at a 370 percent higher rate.[137]

The rates at which charges for such offenses were dropped suggest that police were arresting Blacks on insufficient evidence, which indicates that those officers' standards for arresting Blacks were much lower than that of other racial/ethnic groups.[138] Clearly, racial bias permeated every stage of law enforcement activity in Baltimore, further creating a divide among Black Baltimore residents and the police.

Flashpoint: The Death of Freddie Gray

The unrest in Baltimore can be traced to the contentious conditions surrounding the arrest and subsequent death of Freddie Gray. On April 12, 2015, Gray was chased and arrested by BPD officers who maintained they did so because he fled unprovoked. Upon searching him, they found Gray in possession of a switchblade.

Eyewitness accounts and video footage suggest that the six BPD officers involved in Gray's arrest used excessive force while detaining him;

his legs did not appear to be functioning and he was dragged into the police van. En route to the Western Police District station, Gray's requests for medical attention because of his difficulty breathing were ignored. It was also reported that the officers failed to safely secure Gray inside the transport van, resulting in lethal injuries to his larynx and spinal cord. As in Ferguson, we will see that, despite the flashpoint that resulted in Brown's death, a weeklong "lull" occurred, followed by a couple of days of outbreak and the escalation of public disorder.

Contextual Factors

Against the backdrop of structural challenges, political/ideological climate, and tense police-public relations, additional contextual factors must be taken into account. Following Freddie Gray's death on April 19, 2015, the communication processes in Baltimore stoked the potential for unrest. As Gray lay in a coma at the University of Maryland Shock Trauma Center and died shortly after, protesters peacefully demonstrated, calling for the police officers who were suspected in his death to be charged. However, on April 23, the President of the Baltimore Police Union, Gene Ryan, denounced protesters as "lynch mobs." He stated:

> The images seen on television look and sound much like a lynch mob in that they are calling for the immediate imprisonment of these officers without them ever receiving the due process that is the Constitutional right of every citizen, including law enforcement officers.[139]

His words drew outrage given the history of Blacks as the victims of lynchings by police. From 1880 to 1940, the fear of Blacks led White mobs to turn to "lynch laws" as a means of social control in the segregated South. In fact, lynch mobs served as de jure law enforcement for decades that was defined by its lack of due process for Black civilians.[140] Between 1877 and 1950, approximately four thousand individuals were murdered in twelve Southern states, including Alabama, Kentucky, North Carolina, and Virginia.[141] Most Black people's lives were taken for "minor transgressions against segregationist mores—or simply for demanding basic human rights or refusing to submit to unfair treatment."[142] Consequently, the racially inflammatory language of referring to Baltimore protesters as a "lynch mob" not only underscored a level of ignorance regarding the history of Black America, but it also sharpened the divide between protesters and the BPD and fanned the flames of unrest.

Moreover, poor public communication exacerbated tensions between police and protesters during mass demonstrations. According to the report provided by Johns Hopkins University Office of Critical Event Preparedness and Response, the city leadership provided infrequent, inconsistent, and insufficient communication to the public.[143] This occurred because the city did not use the Joint Information System (JIS) or properly activate a Joint Information Center (JIC); consequently, community stakeholders did not have a clear path for acquiring and disseminating public information.[144]

This proved problematic. Specifically, the BPD learned that city high school students planned to "purge" (commit criminal activity) at Mondawmin Mall—the local transportation hub—in West Baltimore during the afternoon of April 27, 2015.[145] As a result, the police department, in partnership with the Baltimore City Schools Police and the Maryland Transit Administration, made the decision to divert bus services around the mall and secure entrance to the Metro station.[146] This decision was made to ensure the safety of passengers and transit personnel and minimize the risk of escalating the event.[147] However, hundreds of students who were not involved in the "purge" were left without any adequate transportation to get home, as police prevented them from getting on other buses.[148] Moreover, the crowd was not informed when the last departing buses would leave the mall.[149] As a result, deficient communication to the public only exacerbated the situation and fostered public mistrust in city government.[150]

Situational and Interactional

The Police Executive Research Forum report establishes that on Saturday, April 25, 2015, a mass demonstration began in the Western District and moved to a planned rally at City Hall, which included thousands of protesters. Although protests remained peaceful for much of the day, approximately two hundred demonstrators marched toward Camden Yards, home of the Orioles baseball team, where thousands of fans were attending a game. Police maintain that violence erupted because protesters attacked baseball fans, pedestrians, and motorists in the area.[151] However, Brandon Soderberg, a White journalist for Baltimore's *City Paper*, who was at Camden Yards when violence broke out, reported that

> a small group of protesters and a small group of baseball fans started whipping bottles at one another and brawling. When the protesters turned the corner onto Washington Boulevard from Camden Street chanting "black lives matter," some baseball fans applauded and a few angrily chanted back, "We don't care"—someone who worked at The Bullpen confirmed this for me. He also said that some patrons chanted "run them over," and one yelled "go get them." Other protesters, including City Paper contributor D. Watkins and gang members interviewed on WBAL, recall bar patrons calling them "nig*ers," among other racist epithets.[152]

As a result, this situation became hostile: a scuffle ensued between Black protesters and White suburban fans and bar patrons, and violence erupted on the street.[153] The scene was now set for separate flashpoints to occur.

Demonstrators confronted fifty police officers, who were wearing patrol uniforms, and pelted them with rocks, bricks, and debris.[154] When the crowd began destroying parked police cars, additional police—wearing riot gear for the first time since the protests began—swept down Howard Street to protect the police cruisers.[155] As a result, twelve people were ultimately arrested that day and the crowd eventually dispersed.[156]

Police accounts maintained that the disorder two days later, on April 27, started amid rumors of a "purge" by high school students that would begin at Mondawmin Mall and end downtown on the day of Gray's viewing.[157] These accounts insist that as dozens of officers attempted to manage the crowd of school-aged students, the students threw rocks, bricks, and debris at police.[158] However, Baltimore teachers and parents in the area contended that the incident ignited when police in riot gear *prevented* students from getting home, as they forced riders off buses, shut down the subway stop, and blocked roads near the mall and Frederick Douglass High School.[159] They assert that police actions inflamed the tense situation, and that it was only after they prevented students from leaving the area and ultimately left them stranded without a means to get home that some students vented their frustration by throwing rocks and water bottles at police.[160]

As students protested, police held the line and retreated without making any arrests for an hour and a half because they were outnumbered.[161] While the disorder eventually spread across Baltimore and resulted in looting and arson,[162] the report submitted by Johns Hopkins's Office of Critical Event Preparedness and Response credited initial force restraint by the police as *preventing* subsequent escalation.[163] Consider the LA riots of 1992, which resulted in the death of 53 people, and the Baltimore riots of 1968 that left 600 injured.[164] Although the Baltimore uprising resulted in 155 police officer injuries and an estimated $13 million in property damage, during the week of civil unrest no civilians died.[165] This occurred despite gaps in Baltimore City's preparedness for mass demonstration events. In fact, the Police Executive Research Forum reviewed the police's response to the civil unrest and their findings were bleak. They concluded that planning was inadequate, command roles changed without notice, arrest policies were unclear, and there was confusion about definition of orders, among many other problems.

Clearly, key institutional/organizational factors had bearings on the public disorder that arose in Baltimore. Additionally, the communication context compounded interactional factors. Yet, despite no clear policy, inconsistent communications, and an unclear strategy on use-of-force in mass demonstrations, for the most part, officers displayed restraint at the onset of escalations, which likely prevented further escalation of crowd activity and long-term damage to BPD-community relationships.[166]

Conclusion

Uprisings and public disorder are not new occurrences. Yet the Ferguson unrest of 2014 and the Baltimore unrest of 2015, particularly in Baltimore's Inner Harbor, constituted a unique social, cultural, and political phenomenon that is central to our understanding of the build-up and outbreak of collective disorder. The systematic application of the flashpoint model shows that unrest in both cities was the result of a complex set of causal factors that ignited years of pent-up tension.

Both the Ferguson and Baltimore incidents underscored the deep racial divide in the United States. Discrimination and segregation occurred along racial lines, highlighting constraints at the structural level, such as unemployment, poverty, and academic problems. Sweeping patterns of racial discrimination also proved to be a systemic problem in the FPD and BPD, which undermined their legitimacy among Black residents. The issue of race was a powerful driver to the development of the Ferguson and Baltimore protests into a social movement, which was fueled by social media. During protests in Ferguson, the Black Lives Matter movement transformed from a Twitter hashtag to a political issue. Because of increased interaction with social media, the story spread to local activists and news outlets and was picked up by national news organizations.

Both the cultural environment and institutional features of the FPD and BPD were also driven by a political context that prioritized repression, largely for financial profit. These factors set the stage for public disorder. In Ferguson, a poor communication context also impacted violent outbreaks. Though the police made some conciliatory effort to appease the public (i.e., marching with protesters, removing barricades), it was offset by incendiary actions (i.e., calling protesters a "lynch mob," trampling makeshift vigils, smearing Brown's name) that were interpreted by protesters as disrespectful. In Baltimore, public communication from leadership was both infrequent and inconsistent in relaying timely information and maintaining public calm.[167]

Overall, the flashpoint model offers a conceptual framework to further our understanding of the nature and causes of the large-scale disorder that occurred in Ferguson and Baltimore. The conceptual framework shows that collective disorder can also appear in different geographical places, and that there are common factors that inform the initiation of public uprising.

Conclusion

We are living in an age of protest. Certainly protest has always been part of the fabric of human civilization. But the past couple of years has seen a wave of protest movements with distinctive causes. A culture of resistance has arisen, as people are determined to make themselves heard and fight against social injustice. Students walked out of classrooms, rallying for more restrictive gun laws. The day after Trump's inauguration, protesters demonstrated across the country. Hundreds of thousands of women around the world took to the streets for the Women's March in 2017 and 2018. Trump's temporary ban on entrants from seven Muslim-majority countries led to demonstrations in airports. Thousands protested Trump's immigration policies separating families at the border. Teachers have packed statehouses demanding raises. Activists proclaiming #MeToo have called out those who have engaged in sexual harassment and assaults. Football players have taken a knee during the national anthem to protest the killing of unarmed Black people by the police.

These movements have spread like wildfire, as far too many people believe that the system is not working for them; they not only decry systemic racial bias by police, but also the broader systems, practices, and structures that marginalize and disenfranchise Black people. It is a fact that one in three Black men can expect to spend some time behind bars in his lifetime. One in ten Black men in his thirties is imprisoned on any given day. The imprisonment ratio for Black women is twice that of White women.[1] Upon release from prison, most return to economically distressed communities with little prospect for education and employment, and many are denied public assistance and the right to vote.

This book has shown that historical context impacts contemporary police-race relations and that adverse police experiences have driven many to protest. In this new wave of demonstrations, we see different types of activists, including "revolutionary," "intermediate," and "tourists." We've observed that revolutionary and intermediate protesters in particular take direct action to disrupt the status quo and dismantle an unjust system, demanding an end to the killing, criminalization, and incarceration of Black people. But too often there is a tendency to call for police reform that entails more police technology, surveillance equipment, manpower, and increased training in diversity, implicit bias, and de-escalation. While there is certainly a need for new training regimes, the elimination of militarized tactics on civilians, greater oversight of the police, and enhanced accountability, we are mistaken if we think that these are adequate solutions to reducing abusive policing and racial subordination of Black people. The focus cannot solely be on investing more dollars in law enforcement. Millions have been pumped into police departments over the past four decades, which has only led to greater surveillance of Black and Latino people. After Michael Brown's death in August 2014, 95 percent of police departments in large cities reported they were using body cameras or had committed to doing so in the near future.[2] Many police officials have turned to cameras as a way to improve policing and build trust, as the use of such devices are believed to minimize the use of force in police-civilian encounters, reduce citizens' complaints, and increase the accountability and legitimacy of the police.[3] However, studies give evidence that their effect is limited. Scholars used a randomized controlled trial involving 2,224 Metropolitan Police Department officers in Washington, DC, who were randomly assigned to wear or not wear a body camera.[4] They found that officers with cameras used force and faced civilian complaints at approximately the same rates as officers without cameras. The use of body cameras is not, nor should it be viewed as, a panacea to deeply rooted issues such as police legitimacy and excessive force.

In addition to the advent of body and dashboard cameras, citizens have taken the upgraded technology on their cell phones to document what would otherwise have gone unseen. As a result, we have all borne witness to Black people being tortured and killed by police. We watched as Eric Garner was choked to death by a New York officer. We watched as twelve-year-old Tamir Rice was shot and killed by a Cleveland police officer for playing with a toy gun. We watched as Floyd Dent was brutally beaten and choked by a Michigan officer during a traffic stop. We watched Walter

Scott try to escape a North Charleston officer who shot him eight times in the back before planting evidence near his body to support a false account of the incident. We watched as Alton Sterling was shot six times at close range by a Louisiana officer. We watched the immediate aftermath of Philando Castile being shot in his car multiple times by a Minnesota police officer after reaching for his driver's license.

While such graphic images have spurred civic protests and led to legal action and more media attention to the issue, in many ways the footage of shootings, assaults, and dead Black bodies has become a public spectacle in America, which has a long history of state-sanctioned violence against Black Americans. In the post-Emancipation period, lynchings were crowd events that included children. The destruction of Black bodies in extrajudicial racial hangings were exhibitions for White viewers: socializing events that reinforced White supremacist cultural and institutional systems.[5] Back then, photos and postcards illustrating Black people being suffocated, maimed, and burned were widely circulated.

Today, this is being played out through technology. Millions of people watch, share, retweet, and email recordings of Black people being physically assaulted or losing their lives. Unfortunately, according to journalist and radio host Jamil Smith, much of our society has become "increasingly numb to the spectacle of black death."[6] For much of the public, this has served as a form of entertainment in which corporate media outlets, which grasp the consumer appeal of such footage, have generated large amounts of capital.

While many have become numb, witnessing the gruesome final moments of Black individuals at the hands of law enforcement has been shown to be traumatic for others. In fact, a recent study found that recurring indirect exposure to publicized police killings of unarmed Black men and women is damaging Black Americans' mental health.[7] Interestingly enough, the authors did not find that police killings of White Americans or armed Black Americans had any significant impact on mental health among Black Americans, nor did they find that police killings of unarmed Black Americans had any significant mental health effects among White Americans. The results suggest that "the adverse mental health effects are not simply driven by indirect exposure to violent events and the resulting experience of vicarious trauma."[8] Instead, in the aftermath of police killings of unarmed Black individuals, Black Americans experience collective trauma because such encounters are reflective of structural racism.

Though we have borne witness to the torture and killings of Black individuals, the question is, to what end? The truth is that police killings of unarmed Black citizens still occur. Moreover, police are not being made to be any more accountable. According to criminologist Philip Stinson and the *Washington Post*, fifty-four officers have been charged with fatally shooting someone while on duty since 2005.[9] When officers are charged, they are generally not convicted unless the incident is egregious.[10] Although police often offer an explanation for their actions, many people who view footage of the incident conclude that their actions were not justified. The reality, however, is that judges and jurors rarely find officers liable for criminal charges despite video evidence of the brutalization of Black bodies at the hands of officers.

Although criminal convictions are not common, many cases have produced civil awards. The *New York Times* tracked fifteen high-profile cases from 2014 to 2017, including those of Terence Crutcher, Philando Castile, Keith Scott, Paul O'Neal, Alton Sterling, Samuel DuBose, Sandra Bland, Freddie Gray, Walter Scott, Christian Taylor, Akai Gurley, Laquan McDonald, Tamir Rice, Michael Brown, and Eric Garner.[11] While two cases led to a conviction (cases involving the death of Akai Gurley and Laquan McDonald) and another led to a guilty plea and a prison sentence (case involving the death of Walter Scott), eleven out of the fifteen cases resulted in civil settlements. Together, these cases produced civil awards of nearly $46 million, ranging from $850,000 to $6.5 million in each case. While police shootings are generally found to be legally justified, the size of these civil awards suggests that police have done something wrong. Criminologist Delores Jones-Brown asserts that "the racial divide over how we can prevent these million dollar bodies must be bridged . . . [by taking] seriously the notion that everyone has individual constitutional and human rights."[12] She continues:

> Any indication that a police officer has engaged in violent conduct against a person based on assumptions about the group to which that person belongs, the neighborhood in which he or she is encountered, his or her style of dress, or his or her pattern of speech is a violation of the Bill of

Rights and the Universal Declaration of Human Rights. The right to life cannot be bought off by civil settlements and judgments. Prosecutors, jurors, and judges must revoke the license to kill and condemn rather than accept the use of fatal profiles. In the interest of justice, law enforcement agents must be trained to abandon or control the profiles that some seem inclined to use consciously or subconsciously during interactions with minorities and young black men in particular.[13]

It is clear that when a police officer kills an unarmed Black person, the city (or, at least, the insurance companies) can expect to pay without any admission of wrongdoing by the city's police department. However, these payouts shift the cost of malfeasance onto the public and serve as poor substitutes for police accountability. The reality is that when an officer kills an unarmed Black individual, a similar pattern is followed, regardless of the circumstances. In general, the death will elicit outrage and protests in the city and possibly around the nation. An investigation will be initiated and the accused officer will be placed on (paid) leave. The officer may or may not be indicted, but he or she is rarely convicted and sentenced to a term of imprisonment. If the family sues the police department, they will often receive a civil settlement, but there will be no admission of fault by the city or police department. Perhaps if police officers who shoot and kill an unarmed civilian are required to pay a percentage of these civil settlements, they will think twice about shooting when they know they will be financially liable.

While families often receive a civil award for their suffering, they do not suffer alone. As we have seen, Black Americans who are not directly affected may also experience acute distress from these tragedies. But too often we look at these calamities as individual problems or individual racism among a few officers. We attempt to appease individual people by settling for monetary consolation. In doing so, we have created a system of individual reparations that will never address the systemic police culture that celebrates aggressive, racially framed policing. Consequently, we've locked up more Black and Latino people. And, even upon release, they are legally locked out of the job market because they have a record and are then criminalized for their survival.

What has changed in Ferguson and Baltimore since the deaths of Michael Brown and Freddie Gray? Do residents believe enough has been done? Four years after Brown's highly publicized fatal encounter, I went back to both cities and spoke with seventeen Ferguson and Baltimore residents and citizens who frequented establishments in the area to see what they thought. In Ferguson, residents pointed to a handful of efforts that have been made to bring change, including the installment of a Black police chief, an increasing number of minorities on the police force,[14] three Black people sitting on the seven-member city council, Lezley McSpadden's (Brown's mother) plan to run for a seat on the Ferguson city council, and the ousting of the seven-term county prosecutor Bob McCullough in Missouri's primary election. Many mentioned that the Ferguson case substantially increased Black votes, resulting in Wesley Bell—an attorney, former municipal judge and prosecutor, and reform-minded city council member from Ferguson—declaring victory over McCullough in the Democratic primary for St. Louis County.

Additionally, the municipal court system in Ferguson has gone through some changes. In March 2016, the city of Ferguson entered into a federal consent decree with the DOJ to stop a pattern of unconstitutional racial discrimination against the city's predominantly Black population. Ferguson was required to meet several benchmarks intended to improve community policing, ensure bias-free practices, protect First Amendment rights, prevent excessive use of force, recruit a diverse workforce, and increase officer accountability and transparency. Since the consent decree was ordered, the court has a new prosecutor and a new judge who are independent of each other and the city; these city officials, including a new court staff, are under the authority of the city manager.[15] Moreover, the city has dismissed approximately 39,000 municipal court cases, forgiven $1.8 million in fines, and enrolled an estimated 1,400 individuals in community service projects rather than requiring them to pay a fine.[16] Post-Ferguson, the St. Louis community has also made progress in reducing municipal court abuses.

Like Ferguson, the city of Baltimore entered into a federal consent decree with the DOJ, mandating sweeping police reform in April 2017. The consent decree placed restrictions on when and how police engage those suspected of criminal activity; ordered more police training in de-escalation tactics and interacting with youths and people with mental illness; increased supervision of officers; provided greater civilian oversight and transparency in the police department;

and required new investments in technology and equipment.[17] However, unlike in Ferguson, when asked what has changed in the city of Baltimore since the death of Gray, many Baltimore residents whom I spoke with stated point-blank that "nothing has changed" and they have not seen real, concrete transformation. In fact, a few pointed to cases of police misconduct, unethical use of force, and public corruption scandals involving police figures—for example, the Gun Trace Task Force case, in which eight Black and White officers were convicted of robbery, extortion, and overtime fraud after admitting to abusing their power to steal money, drugs, and guns that they were supposed to take off the streets.[18] Several Baltimore residents referred to a disturbing video in which a Black officer assaulted a Black man—who was not being charged with any crime—until he lost consciousness. This led one Baltimore resident to conclude that "there is just as much police violence and corruption in Baltimore City since Freddie Gray died."

What do we need to do so that police officers stop killing Black people? Based on what I have found in my research, it is clear that doubling down on investment in the police is not the answer. America's long history of state-sanctioned violence against Black Americans reflects persistent inequities in the criminal justice system. Thus, rather than putting more dollars into police and prisons, investments need to be made in individuals and communities. Structural disadvantage, pervasive inequality, social dislocation, joblessness, poverty, and inadequate public services are all common characteristics of poor inner-city communities. Not surprisingly, the most racially segregated and socially isolated cities are also violent. And many cities respond by increasing punitive policing and longer prison sentences. As a nation, the government has been "tough on crime" for decades as a means of solving everyday structural problems that disproportionately affect Black people. This country currently ostracizes, marginalizes, criminalizes, and demonizes those who are poor, homeless, have substance addictions, are mentally ill, and whose lives are considered to matter less than others, with laws and policies.

But what if, instead of being tough on crime, we are tough on the underlying issues that criminalize people? Imagine if resources were distributed away from criminal justice institutions and into communities.

Imagine if funds were spent on prevention and intervention initiatives for at-risk youth and young adults. Imagine if these dollars were spent on addressing mental health, substance abuse, and homelessness. Imagine if resources were spent on bringing more jobs into the communities, paying living wages, and providing quality education.

The Movement for Black Lives calls specifically for the reinvestment of federal grants to education, employment, and social services in Black communities, which has been shown to improve community safety. This framework calls for cities to divest in policing and prison expansion and to invest instead in resources that create safety for Black people and people of color, including quality public schools, affordable housing, and mental health care. Seeking radical transformation of the current system, the movement calls for an end to the war on Black people, reparations for the harms inflicted on them, and efforts to enhance individual, family, and community well-being.

Imagine if this divest/invest model was used as an alternative vision for safety. Imagine if churches and faith-based establishments served as a place for training and handling conflict resolution and crisis intervention. Concepts like restorative justice and victim-offender mediation create spaces to promote healing between the victim and the offender, facilitated by a trained mediator. With the mediator's assistance, the victim and offender begin to resolve the conflict and to construct their own approach to achieving justice in the face of that particular crime. Unlike the adversarial criminal justice system, victim-offender mediation gives both parties the opportunity to express their feelings and perceptions of the offense. Effort to bring about reconciliation is made by attempting to reach agreement as to which steps the offender will take to repair the harm done to the victim. The opportunity to redeem oneself and "make things right" is not far-fetched, as many places of worship are also beginning to have important conversations about community defense against neo-Nazis and White supremacists. In Charlottesville, Virginia, in August 2017, it was antiracist and antifascist activists and clergy members— not police—who stood up to White nationalists and guarded places of worship.[19] Likewise, in Durham, North Carolina, it was hundreds of anti-Klan activists—not police—who organized to successfully prevent a scheduled KKK march.[20]

Ending the killing of Black people requires doubling down on investments in communities—not the police or the criminal justice system. Redistributing resources from the criminal justice system into cultivating institutions within poor communities is vital. When we break these structural systems of oppression and seek an alternative vision for safety that takes power away from the hands of police and puts it into communities, we will begin to put an end to denying many marginalized people their humanity.

ACKNOWLEDGMENTS

Writing a book has been an incredibly intimidating and rewarding experience. This process has truly taken a village. First, I wholly thank the Lord for giving me the strength, wisdom, ability, and opportunity to undertake this research study and to see it all the way through. Without His blessings, this achievement would not have been possible.

I am indebted to the residents and protesters in Ferguson and Baltimore who participated in this research project, as they made this book possible. Despite the challenges many faced, they took time to share their experiences with me. For that, I am grateful. I thank Michael Conteh, Kimberly Bender, and Erin Kerrison, who assisted me with interviewing participants. My editor at New York University Press, Ilene Kalish, has been a tremendous help as I completed the final manuscript. I thank her for believing in this project and walking me through the publishing process. I am also grateful for the anonymous reviewers who provided numerous comments on previous drafts, which only improved the quality of the manuscript. I benefited from funding from Michigan State University, including the Humanities and Arts Research Program, Discretionary Funding Initiative, and the School of Criminal Justice.

A number of individuals helped to facilitate this research. Many thanks to Victor Rios, who sent an email to the Racial Democracy Crime and Justice Network listserv asking if any scholars were interested in interviewing protesters in the wake of Michael Brown's death. That email got me started on this project. I am appreciative of Bishop Jesse Battle, who encouraged me to come to Ferguson even in the midst of much racial tension to pursue this project, and who also got me connected to Chris King, the editor of the *St. Louis American*. Chris King opened his networks for me and shared my flier to his seven-thousand-plus followers on Twitter. I am grateful to Finn Esbensen, former chair of the Department of Criminology and Criminal Justice at the University of Missouri-St. Louis, who allowed me to conduct many interviews in the department's conference room. I also thank Cornell Showell, who arranged for me to conduct interviews in a private office at a local church in Baltimore.

Writing this book would not have been possible without the support of my colleagues and great friends. A special thanks to Jody Miller, whom I consider a mentor and friend, and who was willing to talk through ideas with me, read several drafts, and offer insightful feedback through all stages of the writing process. Several colleagues read and commented on ideas in this book: Rod Brunson, Josh Page, Ruth Peterson, Sanja Kutnjak Ivkovic, Chris Smith, Sharon Oselin, Soma Chaudhuri, Scott Decker, Beth Huebner, Jacqueline Mattis, and Robin Jarrett. I am grateful to them for taking the time to review my book proposal and/or chapters of the book, share their experiences with book publishing, and provide counsel. Thanks also to Matthew Galasso for entering data, providing statistics, and formatting references; Marva Goodson, for assisting with coding and formulating tables; Merry Morash, for assisting with data analysis; and Ashleigh LaCourse, for proofreading the entire work, checking for consistencies within and across chapters. My colleagues in the School of Criminal Justice at Michigan State University have been really supportive. The school's director, Mary Finn, exemplifies outstanding leadership and has been a great mentor to me.

Thanks to my family for their enthusiasm: Ernest Cobbina, Pearl Cobbina, Chris Cobbina, and Cheryl Martinez. I appreciate Bishop Ira Combs, Edrea Kenner, Rhonda Morris, Cheryl Ayler, Kristina Beda, Eric Beda and Ama Larsen for their prayers and encouragement when I needed that extra push. Thank you, Pastor Eric Battle, for inspiring me to pursue this project as a book.

APPENDIX A

Demographic Characteristics of Protesters in Ferguson and Baltimore

	Ferguson N = 100	Baltimore N = 92
Gender		
Male	50	39
Female	50	53
Age		
Mean	36.55	44.06
Range	18–74	18–86
Race		
Black	87	68
White	12	20
Hispanic	1	–
Multiracial	–	3
Asian	–	1
Education*		
Some Elementary	1	10
Some High School	6	8
High School Diploma/GED	22	26
Some College/University	50	17
Associate/Bachelor Degree	14	12
Graduate Degree	6	18
Economic Standing*		
Unemployed	35	49
Part/Full Time	65	42

* 1 respondent from Ferguson did not report education level. 1 respondent from Baltimore did not report education level, employment status, place of residence, or years in residence.

(continued)

	Ferguson N = 100	Baltimore N = 92
Residence*		
Ferguson/Baltimore	65	86
Non-Ferguson/Non-Baltimore	35	5
Years in Residence		
Mean—Ferguson/Baltimore	11.58	9.71
Mean—Non-Ferguson/Non-Baltimore	15.88	5.5

APPENDIX B

Research Methods

As a scholar who studies the role of race in the criminal justice system, I was concerned by the high-profile cases of Michael Brown and Freddie Gray and wanted to contribute to change. Like many people, I witnessed on television and social media Brown's and Gray's communities' great demand for social justice. It was clear to me that history was being made. Part of my desire to do something was due to the fact that I had lived in St. Louis for five years as a doctoral student at the University of Missouri-St. Louis. During my time there, I lived in Normandy, which is only a couple of miles away from Ferguson. Thus, I certainly cared about what was happening in this area that I used to call home.

The opportunity to contribute to change occurred within one month of Brown's death. Sociologist Victor Rios was invited to talk to students at St. Louis Community College about his book *Punished: Policing the Lives of Black and Latino Boys*. In addition to his presentation, Rios wanted to document the history that was being created by everyday people who had become activists. To do so, he invited me, along with a group of scholars who engaged in research promoting social justice, to participate in a project known as the Ferguson Research Action Collaboration. The goal was to respectfully and ethically document the experiences of Ferguson residents after the killing of Michael Brown. The team believed that it was important for scholars to take a stand in the movement for racial justice that had emerged. We believed that quality research and social justice work were not mutually exclusive enterprises; research could be used to support the community in Ferguson.

The team relied on a local sociologist to line up interviews with protesters and local youth about their motivations and clashes with local law enforcement. In addition to understanding the nature of police-citizen interactions, I was interested in how parents prepare their children to interact with the police, as well as how distressed communities mobilized. As a former resident of St. Louis, I tapped into my own networks to conduct individual interviews over five days within two months of Brown's death. The management of data quality is detailed below.

Managing Data Quality

Multiple strategies were used to enhance data quality. The semistructured interview protocol ensured that all participants were asked the same questions, while the open-ended questions allowed participants to respond in ways that reflected their unique perspectives.[1] A research team was assembled of trained, culturally competent interviewers. The research team in Ferguson included myself and an African male research assistant. The research team in Baltimore included myself, a younger White female professor, and a younger Black female professor.

Many reported that they would have taken part in the study for free, as they simply wanted to have their voice heard. I was both an "outsider" and an "insider" in Ferguson. My position as a middle-class researcher who resided in Michigan made me an outsider. However, the very fact that I had lived in St. Louis and simply wanted to listen and document their thoughts not only showed people that I cared but provided them confidence that their voice would have an opportunity to be heard long after the reporters had left.

Moreover, as a Black woman, residents and protesters of color felt comfortable speaking their mind to me. Black residents viewed me as trustworthy: a safe person with whom they could openly converse. When some learned that I had resided in St. Louis a few years earlier, they viewed me as "one of them." This allowed me the opportunity to build rapport, establish familiarity, and foster trust, which is necessary in research of this type.[2] Nevertheless, I had to make sure I did not take what was said by participants for granted. At times, Black participants would gloss over details or make statements like "you know how it is" or "you know what I mean." However, I would always probe for additional details, informing them that I did not want to make assumptions. In addition, I would tell them that, since I no longer resided in St. Louis, it was necessary for them to explain to me "how it is." For that reason, my interviews with Black participants resulted in detailed accounts about their experiences with and perceptions of police.

I did have greater social distance with White participants. Some viewed me with suspicion, which can impact the process of disclosure. However, when participants learned that I was a researcher/professor at Michigan State University, collecting data from a range of people for the purpose of gathering varying perspectives, many let their guards down. However, some, like minority participants, may have chosen to conceal their true opinions, especially if they considered it racist, discriminatory, or shameful. For example, while many White participants spoke directly about their experiences with police, which was often infrequent, it is likely that others chose to hold back their true views.

In Ferguson, an African Black male research assistant aided in conducting interviews. He received training on conducting qualitative interviews and responding to participants' accounts in a nonjudgmental manner. However, as a Black male PhD student who was from Africa and had a notable accent, he remained socially distant from many of the participants. Though he was sociable and personable, many participants had difficulty understanding him, and these interviews were not as rich as the others. However, when participants did understand, they provided meaningful answers to most of the questions he posed.

In Baltimore, the research team consisted of a younger White female professor and a younger Black female professor. Both had prior training and an array of experience conducting interviews with marginalized populations. Given the racial diversity among participants and a general distrust of police, the White interviewer was particularly conscious of her position as a White, middle-class researcher. She made a concerted effort to be especially sensitive when interviewing minority participants, and she encouraged them to tell their stories. Many Black participants relished the opportunity to respond to her questions about race, as it provided an opportunity for them to expound on the inequalities that they saw as the result of race and class. And White participants felt comfortable expressing biases, using derogatory language, or discussing White privilege.

As a seasoned interviewer, the young Black female professor had an easy time building rapport. She encouraged participants to openly share their experiences and viewpoints. Black participants felt comfortable talking with her, as she established good rapport, and the interviews were conversational in nature. Occasionally, Black and White participants would sheepishly say that they have not had negative police encounters and questioned whether they were qualified to participate. The interviewer always told participants that the purpose of the study was not to bash the police, but simply to get a wide array of people to share their experiences with and perceptions of the police.

The team would meet both prior to conducting the interviews and at the end of each day of interviewing to debrief. On the whole, interviews conducted by the female interviewers were the most detailed and rich. They had provided participants with the opportunity to recognize themselves as experts. Such opportunities can be empowering, as they offer a context in which people can speak about their lives in ways that may not often be available to them.

The Research

Study Design, Sampling, and Data Collection

The goal for this study is to provide a nuanced analysis of the lived experiences of protesters and residents of Ferguson and Baltimore during a tumultuous time period, highlighting their complex relationships with the police. Such analyses will expose the interplay of factors, coupled with historical events, which ultimately created the context in which the deaths of Michael Brown and Freddie Gray pushed many outraged Americans to demonstrate. In order to understand the causes and effects of police violence against Black citizens—and any civilians—taking geographical context into account is important. My hope is that such an understanding will also expand the way we think about race, place, and policing.

To achieve these goals, I had to locate individuals who were willing to share some of their life experience with me. A purposive sampling technique was used to recruit participants for the study.[3] Specifically, in Ferguson, I identified individuals who either lived there or who had engaged in some form of community action (e.g., protests, marches, rallies, etc.) after Brown's death. Participants were recruited using several methods. First, my former pastor from St. Louis had several community ties and asked people to contact me if they were interested in being interviewed. Also, he strongly encouraged me to get in touch with the editor of a minority newspaper in St. Louis who subsequently broadcasted information about the study on Twitter to his seven-thousand-plus followers. Second, I posted a flier about the project on my Facebook and Twitter pages, which was shared broadly with others. Third, an ad was placed in the employment section of a minority newspaper in St. Louis. Finally, fliers were handed out to students at a local community college and posted at a St. Louis university. Both social media and word of mouth were instrumental in recruiting people. For instance, I discovered during my interviews that some participants learned of my study while protesting. Evidently, several copies of my flier had been made and passed around during a protest. Though I had scheduled several interviews prior to my arrival, I received numerous calls during my five-day stay in St. Louis from people asking to be part of the study. I ended up making two trips to St. Louis to conduct a total of one hundred interviews. Additionally, I conducted follow-up interviews within one month after the grand jury decided not to indict Darren Wilson for Michael Brown's death.[4]

The initial qualitative interviews were conducted between October 2014 and November 2014 in several locations across the Greater St. Louis metropolitan area, including in a conference room at a local university, in fast food restaurants, coffee shops, and a local public library. Prior to each, the research team outlined the study objectives and assured participants that they would be guaranteed confidentiality.[5] Participation in the study was voluntary and participants were paid forty dollars for their involvement.[6] Many, however, reported that they would have taken part in the study for free.

In all, as illustrated in appendix A, one hundred participants were interviewed in Ferguson: fifty men and fifty women. Study participants ranged in age from eighteen to seventy-four, with a mean age of thirty-seven years. The sample includes eighty-seven African Americans, twelve Whites, and one Latina. As it relates to educational status, the common category is some college education, with participants reporting that they were either currently in college or had attended/taken some college courses.[7] In terms of economic standing, sixty-five participants reported that they were currently working part- or full-time at the time of the interview and the remainder were unemployed. Finally, nearly two-thirds of participants lived in the city of Ferguson for an average of eleven years,[8] while the rest resided in the broader St. Louis area for an average of sixteen years.

Although I had several networks in St. Louis, this was not the case in Baltimore. Fortunately, one week before conducting interviews in June 2015, I was in College Park, Maryland, attending the Intersectional Qualitative Research Methods Institute Consortium on Race, Gender, and Ethnicity. While there, members learned of my study and shared my flier with several of their colleagues and students. As I did in Ferguson, I attempted to recruit individuals to take part in the study if they had participated in community action following Gray's death or resided in Baltimore. A flier was posted on my Facebook and Twitter accounts and in the employment section of a newspaper in Baltimore City. Fliers were also passed out to people at a local library.

Like the Ferguson participants, Baltimore participants were told of the study's objectives before the interview and given informed consent forms, which they signed voluntarily, and were promised privacy and confidentiality.[9] Participation in the study was voluntary and participants were paid forty dollars for their time. Unlike in Ferguson, follow-up interviews were not conducted in Baltimore.

Overall, ninety-two individuals were interviewed in Baltimore for the project: fifty-three women and thirty-nine men.[10] Study participants ranged between eighteen and eighty-six years of age, with an average of forty-four years. Study participants were racially/ethnically diverse, with nearly three-quarters Black, slightly more than one-fifth White, and a smaller proportion identified as multiracial or Asian. More participants reported having completed a high school diploma/GED and just over half reported being unemployed at the time of the interview. A total of eighty-six participants were Baltimore residents who had lived in the city for nearly ten years; the others lived outside of the city for an average of 5.5 years. Interviews were primarily conducted in a local public library and a private office in a neighboring church.

This purposive sampling design targeted a heterogeneous group of individual protesters and residents of Ferguson and Baltimore who varied across race, gender, and age, thus yielding a nonprobability sample. The purpose of this kind of sample design is to provide a diverse and robust view of the Ferguson and Baltimore incidents. Qualitative researcher

Earl Babbie notes the usefulness of a "purposive or judgmental sample" when a subset of a population is easily accessed and highly resembles the greater population from which it is drawn.[11] In my study, a subset of protesters and residents of Ferguson and Baltimore were drawn from the larger population of protesters and residents in the United States. Although the sample was of the convenience variety, no protester or resident was specifically singled out for questioning nor were any purposefully prevented from being drawn into the sample. As with research of this type, it is not possible to draw definitive conclusions about the impact of race, place, policing, and protests. Although not generalizable, the study raises significant issues that may guide future inquiries into the racialized nature of policing and the criminal justice system.

Each interview began with the completion of a brief survey, which collected basic demographic information. This was followed by an in-depth, digitally recorded interview, which is the primary data from which this book draws to provide a rich, contextual examination of race, policing, and protests across geographical contexts. The qualitative interviews were semistructured, with open-ended questions that allowed for considerable probing. All of the interviews, which took approximately one hour, were conducted face-to-face and one-on-one. These interviews afforded me the opportunity to collect firsthand impressions from protesters and residents of Ferguson and Baltimore who were directly or indirectly affected by the deaths of Brown and Gray.

The interview properly started with a discussion of race and policing. Participants were first asked to describe their emotional journey upon hearing the news about Brown's or Gray's death[12] and to expand on what had been happening in their city over the past few months. This was followed by asking participants their perceptions of how police handled the outcry from community members. They were then asked to discuss their experience, both positive and negative, with local police before and after Brown's or Gray's death. When participants reported having had police encounters, they were asked to provide further details about these incidents. They were also questioned about whether or not they were afraid and/or suspicious of police and their reasons for feeling that way. Additionally, participants were questioned about their views of whether and why police officers associate Black, Latino, and White people with criminal offending and whether the race of the officers affected such perceptions. This was followed by questions about whether they them-selves believed that Blacks and Latinos commit more or fewer crimes than Whites. Finally, participants were asked to expand on their beliefs about what would happen if the officer(s) involved in Brown's or Gray's death was not indicted or convicted.

The discussion then turned to questions about parenting. Participants were first asked about advice they had given or would give their children for interacting with the police and why they had given such advice, as well as whether and why this differed for their sons and daughters.[13] Participants were also asked to describe how their lives and that of their children have been affected by Brown's or Gray's death.[14]

The interview shifted next to a discussion on community action. Participants were asked open-ended questions about the types of com-munity action they had participated in since Brown's or Gray's death. Those who reported engaging in protests, marches, or demonstrations were asked to discuss their motivation for getting involved. They were then asked to describe the nature of their community action experi-ence, including the advantages and disadvantages of participating, and whether they would engage in activism efforts three to six months from the interview. Finally, the interview was concluded by asking what par-ticipants hoped to accomplish and what they thought needed to happen for the city to move forward. This basic guideline was followed for each interview; however, when additional topics arose in the course of the interview, we often deviated from the interview guide to pursue them.

The data are limited to residents' and protesters' accounts of their en-counters with police in Ferguson and Baltimore. The analysis does not assume that participants have provided full accounts in all instances. It is possible that participants may misinterpret police officers' motives and behaviors. However, for the current study what matters is *how* residents/protesters describe their experiences with the police.

Data Analysis

These in-depth interviews resulted in a rich dataset on the nature, con-texts, and meanings of police-citizen interactions across geographical areas. This methodological technique provided a method for under-standing the social world from the research participants' point of view.

Rigorous examination of such accounts offers a means of "arriving at meanings or culturally embedded normative explanations [for behavior, because they] represent ways in which people organize views of themselves, of others, and of their social worlds."[15] This is not to say that participants' descriptions of events are always precise or that full disclosure was given in every case. In fact, participants may misinterpret police officers' actions and intent. However, this book is concerned with understanding how participants characterize their experiences with and perceptions of the police. Citizens' perceptions of the police, regardless of their objective reality, are important to understand because they affect police-community relations.[16]

To enhance the validity and reliability of the data, participants were asked to describe their experiences with police at several points during the interview by questioning their observations of police practices as well as their personal experiences.[17] In addition, the interview probed for concrete, detailed descriptions of all recounted events. Transcripts of participants' responses were formatted and read into NVivo 11, a qualitative research software program. Several inductive analytic techniques were used to strengthen the internal validity of the analysis. First, I read the data multiple times to code passages and make note of preliminary analytic observations. Second, I used a constant comparative approach, which involved developing and reworking categories as the data are coded.[18] This permitted further refinement or rejection of initially identified analytic patterns. In the analysis, I made sure that the concepts that were developed reflected the most common patterns in participants' accounts. This was achieved using grounded theory methods, which entailed the search for and illumination of outliers.[19] Finally, basic tabulations were utilized to identify the strength of the patterns uncovered.[20]

Juxtaposing residents' and protesters' accounts provides an important basis for developing insights into the history leading to Brown's and Gray's deaths and how and why both Ferguson and Baltimore became ground zeroes for protests against racially biased policing and broader structural inequalities. The analysis process required teasing apart and weaving back together facets of the data that generated detailed renderings of residents' and protesters' lived experiences and perceptions of police.[22] The findings provide a contextual understanding of the racialized nature, circumstances, and meanings of police-citizen encounters.

NOTES

INTRODUCTION

1 The summary of events is based on a report from the Department of Justice (DOJ) following their criminal investigation into the shooting death of Michael Brown by Darren Wilson. See DOJ, 2015a.

2 Wilson reported being uncertain whether Brown closed the door or if the door rebounded closed after it made contact with Brown's body when he swung it open.

3 Some critics argued that McCulloch was unable to be impartial, as his father, a former police officer, was killed on duty by a Black man when McCulloch was twelve years old. In addition to his father, McCulloch's brother, an uncle, and a cousin all served with the St. Louis Police Department, and his mother worked as a clerk at the department.

4 Mayor's Office of Emergency Management, 2015; Barajas, 2015.

5 Barajas, 2015.

6 Mayor's Office of Emergency Management, 2015.

7 Mayor's Office of Emergency Management, 2015.

8 CBS, 2015.

9 Dyson, 2017.

10 Morrison, 1993.

11 Stevenson, 2017.

12 Stevenson, 2017, p. 5.

13 Bitner, 1972.

14 Withrow, 2004, p. 344.

15 Glaser, 2015, p. 3.

16 Matsueda & Drakulich, 2009.

17 Engel, 2005.

18 Weitzer & Tuch, 2006.

19 Gabbidon & Higgins, 2009; Graziano, Schuck, & Martin, 2010; Weitzer & Tuch, 2004, 2006.

20 Brown & Benedict, 2002; Weitzer & Tuch, 2004.

21 Jones-Brown, 2000; Mastrofski et al., 2002; Terrill & Reisig, 2003; Weitzer, 1999.

22 Brunson & Miller, 2006; Decker, 1981; Huebner et al., 2004; Weitzer & Tuch, 2002.

23 Brunson, 2007; Brunson & Miller, 2006; Weitzer & Tuch, 2002.

24 Kennedy, 1997.

25 Decker, 1981.

26 Boyles, 2015; Brunson, 2007; Brunson, & Miller, 2006; Weitzer & Brunson, 2009.
27 Ritchie, 2017.
28 But see Britton, 2011; Brunson and Weitzer, 2009; Jacques, 2017.
29 Collins, 1990.
30 When social scientists refer to place in people's lives, it indicates the role of geographical context or location.
31 US Census Bureau, 1963.
32 US Census Bureau, 2014.
33 Lichter, Parisi & Taquino, 2015.
34 US Census Bureau, 2014.
35 USCCR, 1970.
36 Baybeck & Jones, 2004.
37 Hamer, 2011.
38 US Census of Population and Housing, 1970–2010.
39 US Census of Population and Housing, 1970–2010.
40 US Census of Population and Housing, 1970–2010.
41 US Census Bureau, 1952; US Census Bureau, 2000.
42 Rusk, 1996, pp. 20–21.
43 Rusk, 1996.
44 DOJ, 2015b, DOJ, 2016.
45 US Census Bureau, 2010.
46 US Census Bureau, 2015.
47 The city of Baltimore officially separated from Baltimore County in 1851. Though the city is not part of a larger county, its city government carries out all the functions and responsibilities of county government. Baltimore is considered the largest independent city in the United States.
48 Judge Barry Williams had prosecuted police misconduct while working for the Justice Department (see Bidgood, 2016; Stolberg and Bidgood).
49 MacDonald, 2003.
50 Brandl et al., 2001.
51 Protest policing refers to the use of police force by the state to control protest events and restore public order. It is the most public and most common form of repression (Earl et al. 2003). The term symbolizes "repression" for the protesters, while for the state, the term represents "law and order" (see della Porta and Diani, 2007:197 for a brief reference to the literature).

CHAPTER 1. RACE AND POLICING

1 Degler, 1959.
2 Handlin & Handlin, 1950.
3 Morgan, 2005.
4 Blackmon, 2008.
5 Baker, 2007, p. 406.
6 hooks, 1995; Madhubuti, 1990.

7 Leary, 2005.
8 Eaton, 1966; Franklin & Schweninger, 1999.
9 Hadden, 2001; Mann, 1993; Williams, 1999.
10 Foner, 1975.
11 Williams & Murphy, 1990, p. 1.
12 Morris, 1996.
13 Barlow & Barlow, 1999; Hadden, 2003.
14 Woodward, 1955, p. 27.
15 Woodward, 1955.
16 Stevenson, 2017.
17 Vitale, 2017.
18 Oshinsky, 1996.
19 Blackmon, 2008.
20 Blackmon, 2008, p. 56.
21 Blackmon, 2008; Oshinsky, 1996.
22 Kennedy, 1997, p. 90.
23 Blackmon, 2008.
24 Oshinski, 1996.
25 Bass, 2001, p. 159.
26 Alexander, 2010.
27 Williams, 2015.
28 Durr, 2015.
29 King, 2012.
30 Alexander, 2010.
31 Woodward, 1968.
32 Williams, 2015.
33 Vitale, 2017.
34 Day & Whitehorn, 2001.
35 Bass, 2001.
36 Walker, 1999; Weitzer & Tuch, 1999.
37 Sampson & Bartusch, 1998; Weitzer, 2000; Weitzer & Tuch, 2002.
38 Brandl, Frank, Worden, & Bynum, 1994; Brunson, 2007; Reiss, 1971; Weitzer, 2000.
39 Crow & Adrion, 2011; Johnson, 2005; Steffensmeier & Demuth, 2001.
40 Chiricos et al., 2004; LaGrange & Silverman, 1999.
41 Welch, 2007.
42 Skolnick, 1966.
43 Browning et al., 1994; Fagan & Davies, 2000; Weitzer & Tuch, 1999.
44 The facts of *Terry* are as follow: On October 31, 1963, Cleveland police detective Martin McFadden was patrolling downtown in plain clothing when he observed two Black men, John Terry and Richard Clinton, standing on a street corner. As McFadden watched the two men, he saw them take turns walking past a store window, peering into the window, and then returning to the corner where they

would reconvene. McFadden witnessed them do this numerous times before a third man joined them. Believing the men were casing the store for a potential robbery, Officer McFadden approached the men for questioning and patted them down. After discovering that both Terry and Clinton had concealed weapons, McFadden arrested the two men. Both were found guilty and filed a certiorari petition in the US Supreme Court (Terri, 392 US 1, 1998). The issue before the US Supreme Court was whether weapons discovered as a result of a stop-and-frisk rather than from probable cause should be excluded. Presented with arguments that a lower standard of probable cause was needed for police to fight crime, the court ruled that preventing crime and ensuring officers' safety outweighed the intrusion experienced by a citizen when stopped.

45 Many states require motorists to have yearly validation stickers, pollution control stickers, and safety inspection stickers.

46 Harris, 1997.

47 Harris, 1997.

48 Epp, Maynard-Moody, & Haider-Markel, 2014.

49 Harris, 1999, p. 291.

50 Harris, 1999.

51 Russell, 1998.

52 Bayley & Mendelsohn, 1969; Werthman & Piliavin, 1967.

53 Werthman & Piliavin, 1967, p. 75.

54 Bayley & Mendelsohn, 1969; Smith, 1986; Hemmens & Levin, 2000.

55 Krivo & Peterson, 1996.

56 Massey & Fischer, 2010; Wilson, 1996.

57 Wilson, 1996.

58 Logan & Stults, 2011.

59 Massey & Fischer, 2010.

60 Farrigan & Parker, 2012.

61 Massey & Denton, 1988.

62 Hotchkiss, 2015

63 Massey & Denton, 1993.

64 Steinmetz et al., 2017.

65 Massey & Denton, 1993.

66 Blauner, 1969, p. 396.

67 Gau et al., 2012; Wu et al., 2009.

68 Bursik & Grasmick, 1993; Sampson, Raudenbush, & Earls, 1997.

69 Anderson, 1999; Cobbina, Like-Haislip, & Miller, 2010; Cobbina, Miller & Brunson, 2008.

70 Gau & Jordan, 2015.

71 Rosenbaum, Schuck, Costello, Hawkins, & Ring, 2005; Weitzer & Tuch, 2006.

72 Reisig & Parks, 2003; Weitzer & Tuch, 2006.

73 Rosenbaum, Schuck, Costello, Hawkins, & Ring, 2005.

74 Gallagher et al., 2001.

CHAPTER 2. "GUILTY UNTIL PROVEN INNOCENT"

1 DOJ, 2015b.
2 DOJ, 2015b, p. 42.
3 Maciag, 2014.
4 Robles, 2014.
5 ArchCity Defender, 2014.
6 ArchCity Defender, 2014.
7 DOJ, 2016.
8 DOJ, 2016.
9 Stanley, 2017.
10 Stanley, 2017.
11 This chapter does not focus on protesters but on residents of Ferguson and Baltimore.
12 Feagin, 1991; Feagin & Sikes, 1994.
13 Though a total of 192 protesters and residents of Ferguson and Baltimore were interviewed in the study, this chapter focuses specifically on 152 residents of Ferguson and Baltimore and their encounters with police.
14 I use chi-square analysis to make comparisons throughout the book. It is important to note, however, that my sample is purposive in nature and therefore violates key assumptions regarding random or representative sampling. While technically statistical methods are not appropriate for my sample, I use these methods not in an attempt to generalize to a larger population but rather to highlight the strength of the patterns I uncovered. Other comparative qualitative work (Miller 2008, 2001) report on patterns in their data the way that I do despite the use of a purposive sample.
15 When chi square analysis is used to compare positive and negative personal incidents for Ferguson and Baltimore, 77.5 percent of the Ferguson incidents were viewed as negative, and 59.8 percent of Baltimore incidents were viewed as negative, but the difference was not statistically significant ($\chi2 = 2.46$, df = 1, p = .117).
16 In Ferguson, 75.5 percent of incidents described by Blacks were seen as negative, and 12.5 percent of incidents described by Whites were seen as negative. Alternatively, 24.5 percent of incidents described by Blacks were seen as positive and 87.5% of those described by Whites were seen as positive. A contingency table analysis of just positive and negative incidents showed a statistically significant difference ($\chi2 = 12.51$, df = 1, p = <.001). In Baltimore, Blacks described 59.7 percent of incidents as negative and Whites described 42.0 percent of incidents as negative, but the difference was not statistically significant ($\chi2 = 2.20$, df = 1, p = .138).
17 A similar sampling strategy was used in both sites; thus, I have no reason to believe that the patterns that I have uncovered are an artifact of sampling. However, a different sampling approach would need to be used to draw a stronger inference so that incidents can be generalizable.

18 DOJ, 2015b, 2016.

19 Visher, 1983.

20 Crenshaw & Ritchie, 2015.

21 Meehan & Ponder, 2002.

22 Brunson & Miller, 2006.

23 Cobbina et al., 2017; Weitzer & Brunson, 2009.

24 Cobbina, Conteh, & Emrich, 2017; Lundman, 1996.

25 Boyles, 2015, p. 47.

26 Kennedy, 1997.

27 Terry v. Ohio, 1968, 393 US 1.

28 Ghandnoosh, 2015: White & Fradella, 2016.

29 ArchCity Defenders, 2014; Office of the Missouri Attorney General, 2014.

30 DOJ, 2016.

31 Gau & Jordan, 2015, p. 11.

32 White & Fradella, 2016.

33 Anderson, 1999.

34 Boyles, 2015; Butler, 1999.

35 Lundman & Kaufman, 2003.

36 DOJ, 2015a.

37 DOJ, 2015b.

38 "Report in Response to HB 771," 2016.

39 Asquith, 2016.

40 Wallace, 2016.

41 In nineteen incidents it remained unclear if police interaction was through voluntary or involuntary contacts, as accounts remained vague. And five accounts that were positive in nature were via vicarious experiences.

42 Richardson, 1974.

43 Hurwitz & Peffley, 1997; Peffley & Hurwitz, 1998; Stevenson, 2017.

44 Cobbina, Awusu-Bempah & Bender, 2016.

CHAPTER 3. "IT'S A BLUE THING"

1 Bolton & Feagin, 2004.

2 Dulaney, 1996; Williams & Murphy, 1990.

3 Walker, Spohn & DeLone, 2000.

4 Williams & Murphy, 1990.

5 The Watts riots left thirty-four people dead, over one thousand injured, nearly four thousand arrested, and an estimated $40 million in property damage (Abu-Lughod, 2007).

6 Bureau of Justice Statistics, 2013; Reaves, 2010.

7 Weitzer, 2000.

8 Bolton & Feagin, 2004.

9 President's Task Force on Twenty-First Century Policing, 2015.

10 DOJ, 2016.

11 Reiss, 1971.

12 Decker & Smith, 1980; Reiss, 1971; Smith & Holmes, 2003.

13 Fyfe, 1988; NAACP, 1995; Walker, 1985.

14 Decker & Smith, 1980; National Advisory Commission on Civil Disorders, 1968; Walker, 1999.

15 Blalock, 1967; Quinney, 1970.

16 Chambliss, 2001.

17 Alex, 1969.

18 Bolton & Feagin, 2004.

19 While residents were asked about their experiences and perceptions of police in their neighborhood, in some cases it remained unclear whether Ferguson residents were referencing police in Ferguson or nearby jurisdictions. With ninety-one municipalities in St. Louis County, most with their own city hall and police force, it was difficult to determine whether or not participants were referring to their perceptions of local law enforcement or more global assessments of police. While this is a limitation of the study, the findings still provide an overall broad view of Ferguson and Baltimore residents' views of Black police.

20 Although residents in the study were asked about their perceptions of whether or not the race of police affects their treatment of civilians, most focused on the behavior of White officers. Hence, substantially fewer residents reported their views of Black officers.

21 Specifically, nine Ferguson residents and seven Baltimore residents reported this theme.

22 Decker & Smith, 1980.

23 Mastrofski et al., 2002; Reisig, McCluskey, Mastrofski & Terrill, 2004.

24 Cobbina, Conteh, & Emrich, 2017.

25 Task Force on the Police, 1967.

26 Alex, 1969.

27 Cochran & Warren, 2012.

28 Nolen, 2011; Weithoff, 2006.

29 Nolen, 2011.

30 Nolen, 2011.

31 Correll et al., 2007; Plant, Peruche & Butz, 2005.

32 Smith & Alpert, 2007.

33 Smith & Alpert, 2007.

34 Brown & Frank, 2006; Wilkins & Williams, 2009.

35 Mosher, 1982.

36 Pitkins, 1967.

37 Romzek, 1990; Simon, 1957; Wilkins & Williams, 2008.

38 Hahn, 1971.

39 Weitzer & Tuch, 2006, p. 99.

40 Brunson & Gau, 2015; Hawkins & Thomas, 1991.

41 Bolton & Feagin, 2004.

42 Bolton & Feagin, 2004.
43 Riksheim & Chermak, 1993; Rozek, 1990; Simon 1957.
44 In the interview, Cassandra disclosed that the officer was suspended for verbally assaulting her, given that she was a minor at the time of the incident.
45 Trautman, 2000.
46 Smith & Holmes, 2003.
47 Sharp, 2014.
48 Wilkins & Williams, 2008.
49 Sun & Payne, 2005.
50 Kappeler, Sluder, & Alpert, 1998, p. 84.
51 Kane, 2005.
52 Kanter, 1977a, 1977b; Nicholson-Crotty, Nicholson-Crotty, & Fernandez, 2017.
53 Nicholson-Crotty, Nicholson-Crotty & Fernandez, 2017, p. 213.
54 Massey & Denton, 1993; Schill & Wachter, 1995; Wilson, 1987.
55 Brunson, 2007; Brunson & Gau, 2015; Weitzer, 1999; Weitzer & Tuch, 1999.

CHAPTER 4. "WE STAND UNITED"

1 Buechler, 2004; Coy, 2001; Dixon & Roscigno, 2003; Stryker, Owens, & White, 2000.
2 Munson, 2010.
3 Klandermans, 1997.
4 McVeigh, 1995.
5 Leach et al., 2006; Van Zomeren et al., 2004.
6 Kelly & Breinlinger, 1996; Runciman, 1966.
7 Foster & Matheson, 1999.
8 Gamson, 1992.
9 Van Stekelenburg & Klandermans, 2013.
10 Van Stekelenburg and Klandermans, 2013, p. 889.
11 Bandura, 1997.
12 Klandermans, 1984, 1997.
13 Van Zomeren et al., 2004.
14 Jenkins, 2004.
15 Klandermans & de Weerd, 2000; Melucci, 1989.
16 Van Stekelenburg & Klandermans, 2013.
17 Smyth, 2002.
18 Simon & Klandermans, 2001; Simons et al., 1998; Van Zomeen et al., 2008.
19 Eleven participants gave two reasons for participating in protests.
20 A small number of protesters in the study mentioned others reasons for engaging in protest efforts; six did so to gather information, six believed history was in the making, five were curious, and five wanted to support young people. However, since they were not dominant themes, they are not discussed.
21 Institute for Intergovernmental Research, 2015.
22 DOJ, 2015a.

23 Hunn & Bell, 2014.

24 DOJ, 2015, p. 9.

25 Hunn & Bell, 2014.

26 DOJ, 2015a.

27 Institute for Intergovernmental Research, 2015.

28 DOJ, 2015a.

29 Hunn & Bell, 2014.

30 The medicolegal death investigator's role is to investigate any death that falls under the jurisdiction of the medical examiner or coroner, including all deaths that are suspicious, violent, or unexplained. While the local law enforcement jurisdiction is responsible for the crime scene, the medicolegal death investigator is responsible for the deceased individual.

31 Ferguson After-Hour Report, 2015.

32 Peterson & Ward, 2015.

33 Stevenson, 2017.

34 Stevenson, 2017.

35 Aymer, 2016; King, 2014; Tolliver et al., 2016.

36 Johnson, 2014; Zagier, 2014.

37 Eligon, 2014.

38 This slang word is short for "going to" or "about to."

39 Several witnesses were interviewed by the FBI agents, St. Louis County Police detectives, and federal prosecutors from the St. Louis County Prosecutor's Office (see DOJ, 2015).

40 Sanburn, 2014.

41 Fishman, 2006; hooks, 2004.

42 Findlay, 2000; Higgs, 1977.

43 Welch, 2007.

44 Hawley & Flint, 2016, p. 208.

45 DOJ, 2015a.

46 Associated Press, 2007.

47 Elinson & Frosch, 2015. The cities include Baltimore, Chicago, Dallas, Houston, Los Angeles, Miami-Dade, New York, Philadelphia, Phoenix, and Washington, DC.

48 Eversley, 2014.

49 Rosenbaum, Schuck, Costello, Hawkings & Ring, 2005.

50 CNN, 2015. "New video shows arrest of Freddie Gray in Baltimore," https://www.youtube.com.

51 Almukhtar et al., 2016.

52 Dance, 2015.

53 Almukhtar et al., 2016.

54 Feron, 2015.

55 Feron, 2015.

56 Wenger & Puente, 2015.

57 Wenger & Puente, 2015.
58 Virginia Slave Codes, 2018.
59 Texas & Oldham, 2015.
60 Weaver, 2017.
61 Kappeler, 2015.
62 Butler, 2017.
63 Comey, 2015.
64 FBI, 2014.
65 Somashekhar & Rich, 2016.
66 Somashekhar & Rich, 2016.
67 *Guardian*, 2015.
68 *Guardian*, 2015.
69 Fryer, 2018.
70 The name of this movement is a pseudonym.
71 Institute for Intergovernmental Research, 2015.
72 Carson, 2018.
73 Carson, 2018.
74 Carson, 2018.
75 Alexander, 2010.
76 Alexander, 2010, p. 17.
77 Carney, 2016.
78 Garza, 2014.
79 Klaus, 2016.
80 McClain, 2017.
81 Sinclair, 2017.
82 The president of the University of Missouri resigned after Black activists and football players protested against his handling of racial tension on campus (Kingkade & Waldron, 2015). After receiving a directive from university administrators instructing students to avoid potentially offensive Halloween costumes, Erika Christakis, a lecturer in early childhood education, responded that students should be able to determine for themselves what constituted appropriate costumes for Halloween parties and should be allowed to wear "offensive" costumes. This was met with a storm of protests on campus and she and her husband, a tenured sociology professor and physician, stepped down from their positions as faculty-in-residence at Silliman College (Hartocollis, 2016).
83 Liebelson & Reilly, 2015.
84 Rhodan, 2016.
85 President's Task Force on Twenty-First-Century Policing, 2015.
86 Nelson, 2015.
87 Lichtblau, 2016.
88 Lichtblau, 2016.
89 DOJ, 2015b.
90 DOJ, 2015b.

91 This thematic pattern was common among nine Ferguson protesters and two Baltimore protesters.

92 Turner, 1999.

93 Tajfel & Turner, 1979; Van Stekelenburg & Klandermans, 2001.

94 It wasn't until two days after Brown's killing that the cable networks devoted any airtime to covering it (Hitlin & Vogt, 2014).

95 LeFebvre & Armstrong, 2016.

96 Smith, 2013.

97 Vissers & Stolle, 2014; Vitak et al., 2011.

98 McCurdy, 2012.

99 Noble, 2015.

100 Alcindor, 2014; Castillo & Ford, 2014.

101 Hyman, 2015.

102 Dance, 2015; Kohn, 2014.

103 Morgan & Waddington, 2016.

104 Morgan & Waddington, 2016, p. 6.

105 Lopez, 2014.

106 Lopez, 2014.

107 Lopez, 2014.

108 James, 2014.

109 McFadyen-Ketchum, 2015.

110 McFadyen-Ketchum, 2015.

111 McFadyen-Ketchum, 2015.

112 Baylor, 1996; Entman & Rojecki, 1993.

113 Pew, 2014.

114 Vega, 2015.

115 Willis & Krauthamer, 2012.

116 Willis & Krauthamer, 2012, p. 2.

117 Willis & Krauthamer, 2012.

118 Kochevar, 2014.

119 Thomas, 2004.

120 Thomas, 2004.

121 Thomas, 2004.

122 Gladwell & Shirky, 2011.

CHAPTER 5. "I WILL BE OUT HERE EVERY DAY STRONG!"

1 Van Zomeren, Spears, Fischer and Leach, 2004.

2 Jasper, 2014; Owens, 2009.

3 Jasper, 2014; McAdams, 1986.

4 Van Stekelenburg & Klandermans, 2013.

5 Jasper, 2014.

6 Della Porta & Fillieule, 2007:217.

7 Earl, 2011; Earl et al., 2003.

8 Earl, 2011.

9 Zwerman & Steinhoff, 2005.

10 The "softer" policing style implies "the tolerance of a large number of protest groups and a wide range of protest activities, with low reliance upon the use of force and illegal tactics, and the development instead of prevention and negotiation with a flexible implementation of the law" (della porta and Fillieule, 2007: 218).

11 Escobar, 1993.

12 Sullivan, 2011.

13 Sullivan, 2011.

14 Earl, 2011.

15 Opp & Roehl, 1990.

16 Hirsch, 1990.

17 Opp & Roehl, 1990.

18 Earl, Soule & McCarthy, 2003.

19 Hughey, 2015.

20 Coyne & Hall-Blanco, 2016; Dansky, 2016.

21 Coyne & Hall-Blanco, 2016; Hughey, 2015.

22 Musgrave et al, 2014.

23 ACLU Report, 2014.

24 Hirschman, 1970.

25 Coyne & Hall-Blanco, 2016.

26 Ananat & Washington, 2007.

27 Ananat & Washington, 2007.

28 Davenport, Soule & Armstrong, 2011.

29 Davenport, Soule & Armstrong, 2011, p. 169.

30 Institute for Intergovernmental Research, 2015.

31 I recognize that categorization as a tool for building theory and/or analyzing data can be considered problematic as it can lead to oversimplification, thereby overlooking tensions that may exist both within and between categories and incorrectly grouping social phenomena/actors which are often fluid in reality as a static entity (see Fujii, 2009). While not dismissing the reality that social phenomena and its actors can move between and/or occupy multiple categories at the same, I argue that categorization can be used as a useful method in social sciences, as an ideal type, particularly when making sense of complex data, such as understanding the motivations involved. To avoid using predetermined categories that could have led to false generalizations, I did not create categories prior to the interviews. I identified the motivation groups during the analysis stage using inductive logic.

32 Although 115 people engaged in some form of collective action, 102 engaged in street protests. They were asked to discuss their perceptions of how police handled the outcry from community members following the deaths of Michael Brown and Freddie Gray and whether they had contact with police after Brown's and Gray's death, and to describe the encounter(s).

33 See also Varon, 2004; Zwerman & Steinhoff, 2005.

34 Freddie Jones, 2014. "Ferguson Police: 'Bring it, You Fucking Animals!' To Protesters," https://www.youtube.com.

35 See also Terrill, 2003.

36 Gau & Brunson, 2010.

37 Police Executive Research Forum, 2015.

38 Police Executive Research Forum, 2015.

39 Police Executive Research Forum, 2015.

40 The only exception was Dylan, a White male intermediate protester, who was a legal observer. After leaving a demonstration and walking toward his car, an officer told him to cross the street. When Dylan tried to explain that he was going to his car, the officer insisted. Dylan disregarded the officer's command and was subsequently arrested and charged for obstructing traffic on the sidewalk.

41 See McAdams, 1982.

42 Only one Baltimore protester reported this theme.

43 See Institute for Intergovernmental Research, 2015.

44 Dansky, 2016.

45 Tyler & Fagan, 2008.

46 Dansky, 2016, p. 62.

47 Only one diligent protester reported this as a theme in Baltimore.

48 Institute for Intergovernmental Research, 2015, p. 56.

49 Institute for Intergovernmental Research, 2015.

50 Eleven revolutionary activists witnessed or experienced physical force from officers compared to three intermediate/tourist protesters.

51 Links et al., 2015.

52 Links et al., 2015, p. 14.

53 Links et al., 2015.

54 Baltimore City Fraternal Order of Police Lodge # 3 After-Action Review, 2015.

55 Links et al., 2015.

56 Links et al., 2015.

57 Police Executive Research Forum, 2015.

58 Of the 102 street protesters in the sample, 85 provided valid responses regarding their subsequent involvement in future protests. Data were missing for 6 participants, and 11 were uncertain about future protest involvement or their response was unclear.

59 Data regarding prior protest participation was missing for 26 Ferguson and 6 Baltimore activists. Among the 39 who responded in Ferguson, 2 radical, 4 intermediate and 1 tourist protester reported prior protest activity. Among the 31 who had valid responses in Baltimore, 3 radical, 10 intermediate, and 5 tourist activists reported previous activism efforts.

60 See Fireman & Gamson 1979; Hirsch 1990.

61 See Earl, 2011, pp. 267–268; Jenkins & Perrow, 1977.

62 Opp & Roehl, 1990; Varon, 2004; Zwerman & Steinhoff, 2005.

63 Two reported being uncertain if they would continue with future activism efforts and one participant's reply was unclear.

64 See also Boykoff, 2006.

CHAPTER 6. PUBLIC DISORDER

1 Moran & Waddington, 2016.
2 Waddington, Jones, & Critcher, 1987.
3 Moran & Waddington, 2016.
4 Moran & Waddington, 2016.
5 Waddington et al., 1987; Waddington, 2010.
6 Moran & Waddington, 2016.
7 Moran & Waddington, 2016.
8 Moran & Waddington, 2016; Waddington et al., 1987.
9 Waddington et al., 1987.
10 Moran & Waddington, 2016.
11 King & Waddington, 2005.
12 Moran & Waddington, 2016.
13 Moran & Waddington, 2016.
14 Waddington et al., 1987.
15 Moran & Waddington, 2016.
16 Waddington et al., 1987.
17 Moran & Waddington, 2016.
18 King & Waddington, 2005.
19 King & Waddington, 2005.
20 Waddington et al., 1987.
21 Moran & Waddington, 2016.
22 Moran & Waddington, 2016, p. 23.
23 Moran & Waddington, 2016.
24 Moran & Waddington, 2016.
25 King & Waddington; 2005; Moran & Waddington, 2016.
26 Waddington et al., 1989.
27 Research & Statistics Division of St. Louis City, 2012.
28 Gordon, 2008.
29 Lipsitz, 2015; Rothstein, 2014.
30 Eligon, 2005; Gordon, 2008.
31 Heathcott 2011.
32 Eligon, 2005.
33 Gordon, 2008; Rothstein, 2014.
34 Gordon, 2008.
35 Rothstein, 2014.
36 Rothstein, 2014.
37 Rothstein, 2014.
38 Lipsitz, 2015, p. 129.

39 Gordon, 2008.

40 Gordon, 2008; Rothstein, 2014.

41 Gordon, 2008.

42 Rothstein, 2014, p. 15.

43 Gordon, 2008.

44 Gordon, 2008.

45 Gordon, 2008, Lipsitz, 2015.

46 Gordon, 2008.

47 Lipsitz, 2015.

48 Rosenstein, 2014.

49 Gordon, 2008, p. 98.

50 Gordon, 2008; Lipsitz, 2015.

51 Eligon, 2015; Rosenstein, 2014.

52 Rosenstein, 2014.

53 Rosenstein, 2014.

54 Rosenstein, 2014.

55 Hamer, 2011, p. 16.

56 Rosenstein, 2014. In the 1950s, more than 850,000 people resided in St. Louis City. By 1990, less than 400,000 of the city population dropped less than 400,000. These declines continued, with the city losing 50,000 additional residents by 2000 and as of 2010 just under 320,000 resided in the city (US Census Bureau, 1995; US Census Bureau, 2001). Although the out-migration from the city included Whites and Blacks, Whites departed at a much faster rate (see Baybeck & Jones, 2004).

57 City of Ferguson, 2018.

58 Gordon, 2008.

59 Rothstein, 2014; Wright, 2005.

60 Rothstein, 2014.

61 Gordon, 2008.

62 Oliveri, 2015.

63 Pinard, 2015.

64 Oliveri, 2015.

65 Oliveri, 2015.

66 DOJ, 2015b.

67 Moran & Waddington, 2016.

68 Mollenkopf & Swanstron, 2015.

69 DOJ, 2015b.

70 Mollenkopf & Swanstrom, 2015.

71 DOJ, 2015b.

72 DOJ, 2015b.

73 DOJ, 2015b.

74 DOJ, 2015b, p. 9.

75 Moran & David Waddington, 2016.

76 DOJ, 2015b.

77 DOJ, 2015b.

78 DOJ, 2015b.

79 DOJ, 2015b.

80 DOJ, 2015b.

81 DOJ, 2015b.

82 DOJ, 2015b, p. 63.

83 DOJ, 2015a.

84 A second wave of unrest, which lasted a week, occurred in Ferguson when the announcement was made that the grand jury would not indict Darren Wilson for Michael Brown's death. A third wave of unrest occurred on the one year anniversary of Brown's fatal shooting, which lasted a couple of days. I utilize the Flashpoint Model of Public Disorder to explain the initial uprising that occurred in Ferguson and Baltimore.

85 Bouie, 2015.

86 Bouie, 2015.

87 Institute for Intergovernmental Research, 2015.

88 Institute for Intergovernmental Research, 2015.

89 Roller, 2014.

90 Bothelo & Lemon, 2014.

91 Institute for Intergovernmental Research, 2015.

92 Follman, 2014.

93 Follman, 2014.

94 Follman, 2014.

95 Institute for Intergovernmental Research, 2015.

96 Institute for Intergovernmental Research, 2015.

97 Institute for Intergovernmental Research, 2015.

98 Institute for Intergovernmental Research, 2015.

99 Institute for Intergovernmental Research, 2015.

100 Suereth, 2015.

101 This emanated from Brown's mother, who mistakenly stated on television that her son was returning from the store in question; see Suereth, 2015.

102 Bosman & Fitzsimmons, 2014; Institute for Intergovernmental Research, 2015.

103 Institute for Intergovernmental Research, 2015.

104 Swaine & Carroll, 2014.

105 Power, 1983.

106 Power, 1983; Rothstein, 2015.

107 Rothstein, 2015.

108 Wood, 2015.

109 Power, 2004.

110 Wood, 2015.

111 Rothstein, 2015.

112 Rothstein, 2015.

113 Wood, 2015.

114 Rothstein, 2015.

115 Rothstein, 2015.

116 Rothstein, 2015.

117 Rothstein, 2015.

118 Samuels, 2008.

119 Samuels, 2008.

120 Gladora, 2006.

121 Rothstein, 2012.

122 Gladora, 2006.

123 Gladora, 2006, p. 2.

124 Samuels, 2008.

125 Gladora, 2006; Samuels, 2008.

126 Samuels, 2008.

127 DOJ, 2016.

128 DOJ, 2016.

129 This is a crime of breaking and entering a motor vehicle and/or stealing its contents.

130 DOJ, 2016.

131 DOJ, 2016.

132 DOJ, 2016.

133 DOJ, 2016.

134 DOJ, 2016.

135 DOJ, 2016.

136 DOJ, 2016, p. 55.

137 DOJ, 2016, p. 57.

138 DOJ, 2016

139 Campbell & George, 2015.

140 Capps, 2015.

141 Gambino, 2015.

142 Gambino, 2015.

143 Links et al., 2015.

144 Links et al., 2015.

145 Links et al., 2015.

146 Links et al., 2015.

147 Links et al., 2015.

148 Links et al., 2015.

149 Links et al., 2015.

150 Links et al., 2015.

151 Baltimore City Fraternal Order of Police Lodge 3, 2015.

152 Soderberg, 2015.

153 Police Executive Research Forum, 2015.

154 Police Executive Research Forum, 2015.

155 Hermann, 2015.

156 Hermann et al., 2015; Police Executive Research Forum, 2015.

157 Griggs, 2015; Police Executive Research Forum, 2015.
158 Police Executive Research Forum, 2015.
159 McLaughlin & Brodey, 2015.
160 Cocking, 2015.
161 Frizell, 2015.
162 Cocking, 2015.
163 Links et al., 2015.
164 Frizell, 2015.
165 Anderson, 2017.
166 Links et al., 2015.
167 Links et al., 2015.

CONCLUSION

1 Bureau of Justice Statistics, 2015.
2 Lafayette Group, 2015.
3 House of Parliament, 2015, Scheindlin & Manning, 2015.
4 Yakum et al., 2017.
5 Petersen & Ward, 2015.
6 Smith, 2015.
7 Bor et al., 2018.
8 Bor et al., 2018.
9 Kindy & Kelly, 2015.
10 Kindy & Kelly, 2015.
11 Lee & Park, 2017.
12 Jones-Brown, 2009.
13 Jones-Brown, 2009.
14 The number of Black officers on the police force jumped from four to ten, and the number of White individuals on the force declined from forty-eight to twenty-six (Mindock, 2018).
15 Patrick, 2017.
16 Williams, 2017.
17 Rector & Anderson, 2018.
18 Lussenhop, 2018.
19 Haft, 2018.
20 Bohatch, 2017.

APPENDIX B

1 Schensul & LeCompte, 2013.
2 Glassner & Loughlin, 1987.
3 The study was approved by the Institutional Review Board at Michigan State University.
4 Follow-up interviewers were conducted very close together due to the anticipation of heightened unrest in the city following the upcoming grand jury decision.

During the first interview, many protesters believed that Wilson would not be indicted and some speculated that violence and riots would erupt as a result.

5 Completed interviews were kept in a locked file cabinet. Interviews were conducted by me and my graduate research assistant. I conducted just over two-thirds of the interviews and a male graduate assistant conducted roughly one-third of the interviews.

6 Study participants were paid $25 during the follow-up interviews.

7 One participant had missing data.

8 Three particpants had missing data.

9 Completed interviews were kept in a locked file cabinet.

10 Interviews conducted in Baltimore were conducted by me, a former female graduate assistant, and a female colleague.

11 Babbie, 2007, p. 184.

12 Ferguson participants were asked to discuss their emotional journey for Michael Brown and Baltimore participants were questioned about their emotional journey upon hearing the news of Freddie Gray's death.

13 Baltimore participants were asked a slightly different question. They were asked: "What do you think kids should know when it comes to interacting with the police? Does that advice differ for girls and boys?"

14 In April 2015, a video went viral of a mother hitting her son after she witnessed him throwing rocks at the police. Because it received national attention, we asked Baltimore participants their personal thoughts as to how the mother handled the situation.

15 Orbuch 1997, p. 455.

16 Brandl et al., 2001; Weitzer & Tuch, 2002.

17 While we asked about participants' experiences with police at different points in the interview, we did not use multiple sources to confirm information.

18 Glaser & Strauss, 1967.

19 Strauss, 1987.

20 Despite the use of a purposive sample in the current study, other scholars that have done comparative qualitative work likewise report on patterns in their data in the way that I do (see Miller, 2001, 2008; Silverman, 2006).

21 Throughout the book, I use the words "the vast majority" to indicate approximately three-quarters or more; "most" or "the majority" to indicate more than one-half; "many" to indicate more than one-third; "a number" to indicate approximately one-quarter or more; and "several" or "a few" to highlight themes mentioned by a small number of women but more than two.

REFERENCES

Abu-Lughod, Janet L. 2007. *Race, Space, and Riots in Chicago, New York, and Los Angeles*. New York: Oxford University Press.

Alex, Nicholas. 1969. *Black in Blue*. New York: Appleton-Century-Crofts.

Alexander, Michelle. 2010. *The New Jim Crow: Mass Incarceration in the Age of Colorblindness*. New York: New Press.

Allport, Gordon W. 1954. *The Nature of Prejudice*. Cambridge: Addison-Wesley.

Almukhtar, Sarah, Larry Buchanan, K. K. Rebecca Lai, Haeyoun Park, Tim Wallace, and Karen Yourish. 2016. Freddie Gray Case Ends With No Convictions of Any Police Officers. *New York Times* (July 27), https://www.nytimes.com.

American Civil Liberties Union (ACLU). 2014. *Comment on Ferguson Grand Jury Decision*. http://www.aclu.org/news/aclu-comment-ferguson-grand-jury-decision.

Amnesty International. 2014. *On the Streets of America: Human Rights Abuses in Ferguson*. New York: Amnesty International.

Ananat, Elizabeth Oltmans, and Ebonya Washington. 2009. Segregation and Black Political Efficacy. *Journal of Public Economics* 93: 807–822.

Anderson, Elijah. 1999. *Code of the Street*. New York: Norton.

Anderson, Jessica. 2017. Baltimore Businesses Destroyed During Riots Sue City Officials for Failing to Prevent Violence. *Baltimore Sun* (June 21), http://www.baltimoresun.com.

Anderson, Margaret L., and Patricia H. Collins, eds. 2007. *Race, Class, and Gender: An Anthology*. 7th ed. Belmont: Wadsworth.

ArchCity Defenders. 2014. Municipal Courts White Paper. http://s3.documentcloud.org.

Ariel, Barak, Alex Sutherland, Darren Henstock, Josh Young, Paul Drover, Jayne Sykes, Simon Megicks, and Ryan Henderson. 2016. "Contagious Accountability": A Global Multisite Randomized Controlled Trial on the Effect of Police Body-Worn Cameras on Citizens' Complaints Against the Police. *Criminal Justice and Behavior* 44: 293–316.

Associated Press. 2017. Ferguson Attorney: Michael Brown's Family Settles with City for $1.5 Million. *Los Angeles Times* (June 23), http://www.latimes.com.

Aymer, Samuel R. 2016. "I Can't Breathe": A Case Study—Helping Black Men Cope with Race-Related Trauma Stemming from Police Killing and Brutality. *Journal of Human Behavior in the Social Environment* 26: 367–376.

Babbie, Earl R. 2007. *The Practice of Social Research*. Belmont: Wadsworth.

Baker, Al, J. David Goodman, and Benjamin Mueller. 2015. Beyond the Chokehold: The Path to Eric Garner's Death. *New York Times* (June 13), https://www.nytimes.com.

Baker, David. 2007. Systematic White Racism and the Brutalization of Executed Black Women in the United States. In *It's a Crime: Women and Justice*, 4th ed., edited by Roslyn Muraskin, 398–443. Upper Saddle River: Pearson.

Baltimore City Fraternal Order of Police Lodge #3. 2015. After-Action Review: A Review of the Management of the 2015 Baltimore Riots.

Bandura, Albert. 1997. *Self-efficacy: The Exercise of Control*. New York: Freeman.

Barajas, Joshua. 2015. Freddie Gray's Death Ruled a Homicide. PBS NewsHour (May 1), http://www.pbs.org.

Barkan, Steven E., Steven F. Cohn, and William H. Whitaker. 1995. Beyond Recruitment: Predictors of Differential Participation in a National Antihunger Organization. *Sociological Forum* 10: 113–134.

Barlow, David E., and Melissa Hickman Barlow. 1999. A Political Economy of Community Policing. *Policing: An International Journal of Police Strategies & Management* 22: 646–674.

Barry, Dan. 2000. The Diallo Case: The Police; One Legacy of a 41-Bullet Barrage Is a Hard Look at Aggressive Tactics on the Street. *New York Times* (February 26), http://www.nytimes.com.

Bass, Sandra. 2001a. Out of Place: Petit Apartheid and the Police. In *Petit Apartheid in the US Criminal Justice System*, edited by Dragan Milovanovic and Katheryn K. Russell, 43–54. Durham: Carolina Academic.

Bass, Sandra. 2001b. Policing Space, Policing Race: Social Control Imperatives and Policy Discretionary Decisions. *Social Justice* 28: 156–176.

Baybeck, Brady, and Endsley Terrence Jones, eds. 2004. *St. Louis Metromorphosis: Past Trends and Future Directions*. St. Louis: Missouri Historical Society.

Bayley, David H., and James Garofalo. 1989. The Management of Violence by Police Patrol Officers. *Criminology* 27: 1–27.

Bayley, David H., and Harold Mendelsohn. 1969. *Minorities and the Police*. New York: Free Press.

Baylor, Tim. 1996. Media Framing of Movement Protest: The Case of American Indian Protest. *Journal of Social Science* 33: 241–255.

Benedict, William Reed, Ben Brown, and Douglas J. Bower. 2000. Perceptions of the Police and Fear of Crime in a Rural Setting: Utility of a Geographically Focused Survey for Police Services, Planning, and Assessment. *Criminal Justice Policy Review* 11: 275–298.

Benford, Robert D., and David Snow. 2000. Framing Processes and Social Movements: An Overview and Assessment. *Annual Review of Sociology* 26: 611–639.

Berkowitz, Leonard. 1972. Frustrations, Comparisons, and Other Sources of Emotion Aroused as Contributors to Social Unrest. *Journal of Social Issues* 28: 77–91.

Berman, Mark. 2014. No Indictment After Police Shoot and Kill Man at an Ohio Wal-Mart; Justice Dept. Launches Investigation. *Washington Post* (September 24), https://www.washingtonpost.com.

Bidgood, Jess. 2016. In Freddie Gray Trials, Baltimore Judge Sets High Bar for Prosecution. *New York Times* (June 24), http://www.nytimes.com.

Biekart, Kees, and Alan Fowler. 2013. Transforming Activisms 2010+: Exploring Ways and Waves. *Development and Change* 44: 527–546.

Bitner, Egon. 1972. *The Functions of the Police in Modern Society.* 2nd ed. Washington: National Institute of Mental Health.

Blackmon, Douglas. 2008. *Slavery by Another Name: The Re-enslavement of Black People in America from the Civil War to World War II.* New York: Doubleday.

Blalock, Hubert M., Jr. 1967. *Toward a Theory of Minority-Group Relations.* New York: John Wiley & Sons.

Blauner, Robert. 1969. Internal Colonialism and Ghetto Revolt. *Social Problems* 16: 393–408.

Blee, Kathleen M. 1998. *No Middle Ground: Women and Radical Protest.* New York: New York University Press.

Bohatch, Emily. 2017. Counter-protesters Rally Against Potential KKK March in Durham, North Carolina. *USA Today* (August 18), https://www.usatoday.com.

Bolton, Kenneth, and Joe R. Feagin. 2004. *Black in Blue: African American Police Officers and Racism.* New York: Routledge.

Bonner, Kideste Mariam Wilder. 2014. Race, Space, and Being Policed: A Qualitative Analysis of Residents' Experiences with Southern Patrols. *Race and Justice* 4: 124–151.

Bor, Jacob, Atheendar S. Venkataramani, David R. Williams, and Alexander C. Tsai. 2018. Police Killings and Their Spillover Effects on the Mental Health of Black Americans: A Population-based, Quasi-experimental Study. *Lancet* 392: 302–310.

Bosman, Julie, and Emma Fitzsimmons. 2014. Grief and Protests Follow Shooting of a Teenager. *New York Times* (August 10), https://www.nytimes.com.

Botelho, Greg. 2012. What Happened the Night Trayvon Martin Died. CNN (May 23), http://www.cnn.com.

Botelho, Greg, and Don Lemon. 2014. Ferguson Police Chief: Officer Didn't Stop Brown as Robbery Suspect. CNN (August 15), https://www.cnn.com.

Bouffard, Leana Allen, and Nicole Leeper Piquero. 2010. Defiance Theory and Life Course Explanations of Persistent Offending. *Crime & Delinquency* 56: 227–252.

Bouie, Jamelle. 2015. How Ferguson Changed America. *Slate* (August 2), http://www.slate.com.

Boykoff, Jules. 2006. *The Suppression of Dissent: How the State and Mass Media Squelch US American Social Movements.* New York: Routledge.

Boyles, Andrea S. 2015. *Race, Place, and Suburban Policing: Too Close for Comfort.* Oakland: University of California Press.

Brady, Henry E., Sidney Verba, and Kay Lehman Schlozman. 1995. Beyond SES: A Resource Model of Political Participation. *American Political Science Review* 89: 271–294.

Brandl, Steven G., James Frank, Robert E. Worden, and Timothy S. Bynum. 1994. Global and Specific Attitudes Toward the Police: Disentangling the Relationship. *Justice Quarterly* 11: 119–134.

Brandl, Steven G., Meghan S. Stroshine, and James Frank. 2001. Who Are the Complaint-Prone Officers? An Examination of the Relationship Between Police Officers' Attributes, Arrest Activity, Assignment, and Citizens' Complaints About Excessive Force. *Journal of Criminal Justice* 29: 521–529.

Brown, Robert A., and James Frank. 2006. Race and Officer Decision Making: Examining Differences in Arrest Outcomes Between Black and White Officers. *Justice Quarterly* 23: 96–126.

Brundage, William Fitzhugh, ed. 1997. *Under Sentence of Death: Lynching in the South.* Chapel Hill: University of North Carolina Press.

Brunson, Rod K. 2007. "Police Don't Like Black People": African American Young Men's Accumulated Police Experiences. *Criminology & Public Policy* 6: 71–102.

Brunson, Rod K., and Jody Miller. 2006. Gender, Race, and Urban Policing: The Experience of African American Youths. *Gender and Society* 20: 531–552.

Brunson, Rod K., and Jody Miller. 2006. Young Black Men and Urban Policing in the United States. *British Journal of Criminology* 46: 613–640.

Brunson, Rod K., and Jacinta Gau. 2015. Officer Race Versus Macro-Level Context: A Test of Competing Hypotheses About Black Citizens' Experiences with and Perceptions of Black Police Officers. *Crime & Delinquency* 61: 213–242.

Buechler, Steven M. 2004. The Strange Career of Strain and Breakdown Theories of Collective Action. In *The Blackwell Companion to Social Movements*, edited by David A. Snow, Sarah A. Soule, and Hanspeter Kriesi, 47–66. Malden: Blackwell.

Bureau of Justice Statistics. 2015. Local Police Departments, 2013: Personnel, Policies, and Practices, table 5, http://www.bjs.gov.

Bureau of Justice Statistics. 2015. Prisoners in 2014, table 10 and appendix table 3, https://www.bjs.gov.

Bursik, Robert J., Jr., and Harold G. Grasmick. 1993. *Neighborhoods and Crime: The Dimensions of Effective Community Control.* New York: Lexington.

Butler, Paul. 2017. *Chokehold.* New York: New Free Press.

Butler, Paul. 1995. Racially Biased Jury Nullification: Black Power in the Criminal Justice System. *Yale Law Journal* 105: 677–725.

Cahill, Teddy, Wesley Lowery, and Niraj Chokski. 2015. Calls for Calm after Grand Jury Declines to Indict Officers in Death of Tamir Rice. *Washington Post* (December 29), https://www.washingtonpost.com.

Campbell, Colin, and Justin George. 2015. Baltimore Police Union President Likens Protests to "Lynch Mob." *Baltimore Sun* (April 22), http://www.baltimoresun.com.

Cao, Liqun, James Frank, and Francis T. Cullen. 1996. Race, Community Context and Confidence in the Police. *American Journal of Police* 15: 3–22.

Capps, Kriston. 2015. What Does It Mean When Police Unions Denounce Protesters as "Lynch Mobs"? *CityLab* (April 23), https://www.citylab.com.

Carney, Nikita. 2016. All Lives Matter, but So Does Race: Black Lives Matter and the Evolving Role of Social Media. *Humanity and Society* 40: 180–199.

Carroll, Leo, and M. Lilliana Gonzalez. 2014. Out of Place: Racial Stereotypes and the Ecology of Frisks and Searches Following Traffic Stops. *Journal of Research in Crime and Delinquency* 51: 559–584.

CBS. 2015. NYC Protests Over Freddie Gray Get Heated. CBS (April 29), http://www.cbsnews.com.

Chambliss, William J. 2001. *Power, Politics and Crime*. Boulder: Westview.

Chen, David W., and Al Baker, 2010. New York to Pay $7 Million for Sean Bell Shooting. *New York Times* (July 27), http://www.nytimes.com.

Chiricos, Ted, Kelly Welch, and Marc Gertz. 2004. Racial Typification of Crime and Support for Punitive Measures. *Criminology* 42: 359–389.

CNN Library. 2016. Trayvon Martin Shooting Fast Facts. CNN (February 7), http://www.cnn.com.

Cobbina, Jennifer E., Michael Conteh, and Colin Emrich. 2017. Race, Gender, and Responses to the Police among Ferguson Residents and Protesters. *Race and Justice*, https://doi.org/10.1177/2153368717699673.

Cobbina, Jennifer E., Toya Z. Like-Haislip, and Jody Miller. 2010. Gang Fights Versus Cat Fights: Urban Young Men's Gendered Narratives of Violence. *Deviant Behavior* 31: 596–624.

Cobbina, Jennifer E., Jody Miller, and Rod Brunson. 2008. Gender, Neighborhood Danger, and Risk Avoidance Strategies Among Urban African American Youth. *Criminology* 46: 501–538.

Cobbina, Jennifer E., Akwasi Owusu-Bempah, and Kimberly Bender. 2016. Perceptions of Racialization of Crime Among Ferguson Residents and Protesters. *Journal of Crime and Justice* 39: 210–229.

Cochran, Joshua C., and Patricia Y. Warren. 2014. Racial, Ethnic, and Gender Differences in Perceptions of the Police: The Salience of Officer Race Within the Context of Racial Profiling. *Journal of Contemporary Criminal Justice* 28: 206–227.

Cocking, Chris. 2015. What Led to the Baltimore Riots? *Conversation* (April 28), https://theconversation.com.

Cohen, William. 1976. Negro Involuntary Servitude in the South, 1865–1940: A Preliminary Analysis. *Journal of Southern History* 42: 31–60.

Collins, Patricia. 2000. *Black Feminist Thought: Knowledge, Consciousness, and the Politics of Empowerment*. New York: Routledge.

Comey, James B. 2015. Hard Truths: Law Enforcement and Race (speech), https://fbi.gov.

Correia, Mark E., Michael D. Reisig, and Nicholas P. Lovrich. 1996. Public Perceptions of State Police: An Analysis of Individual-Level and Contextual Variables. *Journal of Criminal Justice* 24: 17–28.

Correll, Joshua, Bernadette Park, Charles M. Judd, Bernd Wittenbrink, Melody S. Sadler, and Tracie Keesee. 2007. Across the Thin Blue Line: Police Officers and Racial Bias in the Decision to Shoot. *Journal of Personality and Social Psychology* 92: 1006–1023.

Corrigall-Brown, Catherine. 2012. *Patterns of Protest: Trajectories of Participation in Social Movements*. Stanford: Stanford University Press.

Coy, Patrick G. 2001. An Experiment in Personalist Politics: The Catholic Worker Movement and Nonviolent Direct Action. *Peace and Change: A Journal of Peace Research* 26: 78–94.

Coyne, Christopher J., and Abigail R. Hall-Blanco. 2016. Foreign Intervention, Police Militarization, and Minorities. *Peace Review: A Journal of Social Justice* 28: 165–170.

Cox, Erin, Justin Fenton, and Luke Broadwater. 2015. Critics Question Delay in Calling out the Guard. *Baltimore Sun* (April 28), http://www.baltimoresun.com.

Cress, Remy, and David A. Snow. 2011. Radicalism within the Context of Social Movements: Processes and Types. *Journal of Strategic Security* 4: 115–130.

Cress, Daniel M., and David A. Snow. 2000. The Outcomes of Homeless Mobilization: The Influence of Organization, Disruption, Political Mediation, and Framing. *American Journal of Sociology* 105: 1063–1104.

Crenshaw, Kimberlé, Neil Gotanda, Gary Peller, and Kendall Thomas, eds. 1995. *Critical Race Theory: The Key Writings That Formed the Movement*. New York: New Press.

Crenshaw, Kimberlé, and Angela Ritchie. 2015. *Say Her Name: Resisting Police Brutality Against Black Women*. New York: African American Policy Forum, Center for Intersectionality and Social Policy Studies.

Cross, Remy, and David A. Snow. 2011. Radicalism Within the Context of Social Movements: Processes and Types. *Journal of Strategic Security* 4: 115–130.

Crow, Matthew S., and Brittany Adrion. 2011. Focal Concerns and Police Use of Force: Examining the Factors Associated with Taser Use. *Police Quarterly* 14: 366–387.

Dance, Scott. 2015. Freddie Gray's Spinal Injury Suggests "Forceful Trauma," Doctors Say. *Baltimore Sun* (April 21), http://www.baltimoresun.com.

Dansky, Kara. 2016. Local Democratic Oversight of Police Militarization. *Harvard Law & Policy Review* 10: 59–75.

Davenport, Christian, Sarah A. Soule, and David A. Armstrong. 2011. Protesting While Black? The Differential Policing of American Activism, 1960–1990. *American Sociological Review* 76: 152–178.

Davis, Gerald F., Doug McAdam, W. Richard Scott, and Mayer N. Zald, eds. 2005. *Social Movements and Organization Theory*. New York: Cambridge University Press.

Day, Susie, and Laura Whitehorn. 2001. Human Rights in the United States: The Unfinished Story of Political Prisoners and COINTERPRO. *New Political Science* 23: 285–297.

Decker, Scott H. 1981. Citizen Attitudes Toward the Police: A Review of Past Findings and Suggestions for Future Policy. *Journal of Police Science and Administration* 9: 81–87.

Decker, Scott H., and Russell L. Smith. 1980. Police Minority Recruitment: A Note on its Effectiveness in Improving Black Evaluations of the Police. *Journal of Criminal Justice* 8: 387–393.

Degler, Carl. 1959. Slavery and the Genesis of American Race Prejudice. *Comparative Studies in Society and History* 2: 49–66.

Delgado, Richard, and Jean Stefancic, eds. 2000. *Critical Race Theory: The Cutting Edge.* 2nd ed. Philadelphia: Temple University Press.

della Porta, Donatella. 1995. *Social Movements, Political Violence and the State: A Comparative Analysis of Italy and Germany.* Cambridge: Cambridge University Press.

della Porta, Donatella, and Mario Diani. 2007. The Policing of Protest and Political Opportunities of Social Movements. In *Social Movements: An Introduction,* edited by Donatella della Porta and Mario Diani, 193–222. Malden: Blackwell.

della Porta, Donatella, and Olivier Fillieule. 2007. Policing Social Protests. In *The Blackwell Companion to Social Movements,* edited by David A. Snow, Sarah A. Soule, and Hanspeter Kriesi, 216–241. Malden: Blackwell.

della Porta, Donatella, and Herbert Reiter. 1998. *Policing Protests: The Control of Mass Demonstration in Western Democracies.* Minneapolis: University of Minnesota Press.

Desmond, Matthew, and Mustafa Emirbayer. 2009. *Racial Domination, Racial Progress: The Sociology of Race in America.* New York: McGraw-Hill.

Dixon, Marc, and Vincent J. Roscigno. 2003. Status, Networks, and Social Movement Participation: The Case of Striking Workers. *American Journal of Sociology* 108: 1292–1327.

Downton, James V., and Paul Ernest Wehr. 1997. *The Persistent Activist: How Peace Commitment Develops and Survives.* Boulder: Westview.

Downton, James V., and Paul Ernest Wehr. 1991. Peace Movements: The Role of Commitment and Community in Sustaining Member Participation. *Research in Social Movements, Conflict and Change* 13: 113–134.

Du Bois, W. E. B. 1910. Reconstruction and Its Benefits. *American Historical Review* 15: 781–799.

Dulaney, W. Marvin. 1996. *Black Police in America.* Bloomington: Indiana University Press.

Durose, Matthew R., Erica L. Smith, and Patricia A. Langan. 2007. Contacts Between Police and the Public, 2005. Bureau of Justice Statistics, https://www.bjs.gov.

Durr, Marlese. 2015. What is the Difference Between Slave Patrols and Modern Day Policing? Institutional Violence in a Community of Color. *Critical Sociology* 41: 873–879.

Earl, Jennifer. 2011. Political Repression: Iron Fists, Velvet Gloves, and Diffuse Control. *Annual Review of Sociology* 37: 261–284.

Earl, Jennifer, Sarah A. Soule, and John McCarthy. 2003. Protest Under Fire? Explaining the Policing of Protest. *American Sociological Review* 68: 581–606.

Eaton, Clement. 1966. *A History of the Old South.* New York: Macmillan.

Eligon, John. 2014. Michael Brown Spent Last Weeks Grappling with Problems and Praise. *New York Times* (August 24), https://www.nytimes.com.

Elinson, Zusha, and Dan Frosch. 2015. Cost of Police Misconduct Cases Soars in Big US Cities: Data Show Rising Payouts for Police Misconduct Settlements and Court Judgments. *Wall Street Journal* (July 15), http://www.wsj.com.

Engel, Robin Shepard. 2005. Citizens' Perceptions of Injustice During Traffic Stops with Police. *Journal of Research in Crime and Delinquency* 42: 445–481.

Engel, Robin Shepard, and Jennifer M. Calnon. 2004. Examining the Influence of Drivers' Characteristics During Traffic Stops with Police: Results from a National Survey. *Justice Quarterly* 1: 1–36.

Entman, Robert M., and Andrew Rojecki. 1993. Freezing Out the Public: Elite and Media Framing of the US Anti-Nuclear Movement. *Political Communication* 10: 155–173.

Epp, Charles R., Steven Maynard-Moody, and Donald Haider-Markel. 2014. *Pulled Over: How Police Stops Define Race and Citizenship*. Chicago: University of Chicago Press.

Escobar, Edward. 1993. The Dialectics of Repression: The Los Angeles Police Department and the Chicano Movement, 1968–1971. *Journal of American History* 79: 1483–1514.

Eversley, Melanie. 2014. More Protests in Wake of Grand Jury Decision on Ferguson. *USA Today* (November 25), http://www.usatoday.com.

Fagan, Jeffrey, and Garth Davies. 2000. Street Stops and Broken Windows: Terry, Race and Disorder in New York City. *Fordham Urban Law Journal* 28: 457.

Farrigan, Tracey, and Timothy Parker. 2012. The Concentration of Poverty is a Growing Rural Problem. Amber Waves (December 5), https://www.ers.usda.gov.

Feagin, Joe R., and Melvin P. Sikes. 1994. *Living with Racism: The Black Middle-Class Experience*. Boston: Beacon.

Federal Bureau of Investigation. 2015. Crime in the United States, 2014, Expanded Homicide Data, table 14, https://www.fbi.gov.

Fenton, Justin, and Erica L. Green. 2015. Baltimore Rioting Kicked Off with Rumors of "Purge." *Baltimore Sun* (April 27), http://www.baltimoresun.com.

Ferron, Karl. 2015. Timeline: Freddie Gray's Arrest, Death and the Aftermath. *Baltimore Sun* (April 12), http://data.baltimoresun.com.

Findlay, James A. 2000. *Drapetomania—A Disease Called Freedom: An Exhibition of 18th-, 19th-, and Early 20th-Century Material Culture from the Collection of Derrick Joshua Beard*. Fort Lauderdale: Bienes Center for the Literary Arts.

Fireman, Bruce, and William A. Gamson. 1979. Utilitarian Logic in Resource Mobilization Perspective. In *Dynamics of Social Movements: Resource Mobilization, Social Control and Tactics*, edited by Myer Zald and John McCarthy, 8–44. Cambridge: Winthrop.

Fishman, Laura T. 2006. The Black Bogeyman and White Self-Righteousness. In *Images of Color, Images of Crime*, edited by Coramae Richey Mann, Marjorie S. Zatz, and Nancy Rodriguez, 192–211. New York: Oxford University Press.

Flanigan, Daniel J. 1973. Criminal Procedures in Slave Trials in the Antebellum South. *Journal of Southern History* 42: 47–48.

Follman, Mark. 2014. Michael Brown's Mom Laid Flowers Where He Was Shot—and Police Crushed Them. *Mother Jones* (August 27), https://www.motherjones.com.

Foner, Philip S. 1975. *History of Black Americans: From Africa to the Emergence of the Cotton Kingdom*. Westport: Greenwood.

Foster, Mindi D., and Kimberly Matheson. 1999. Perceiving and Responding to the Personal/Group Discrimination Discrepancy. *Personality and Social Psychology Bulletin* 25: 1319–1329.

Frank, James, Brad W. Smith, and Kenneth J. Novak. 2005. Exploring the Basis of Citizens' Attitudes Toward the Police. *Police Quarterly* 8: 206–228.

Franklin, John Hope, and Loren Schweninger. 1999. *Runaway Slaves: Rebels on the Plantation 1790–1860*. New York: Oxford University Press.

Frizell, Sam. 2015. How Baltimore Police Lost Control in 90 Minutes. *Time* (April 29), http://time.com.

Fryer, Roland. 2018. "An Empirical Analysis of Racial Differences in Police Use of Force." NBER Working Papers 22399, National Bureau of Economic Research, Inc.

Fujii, Lee Ann. 2011. *Killing Neighbors: Webs of Violence in Rwanda*. Ithaca: Cornell University Press.

Fyfe, James J. 1988. Police Use of Deadly Force: Research and Reform. *Justice Quarterly* 5: 165–205.

Gamson, William A. 1992. *Talking Politics*. New York: Cambridge University Press.

Gau, Jacinta M., and Rod K. Brunson. 2010. Procedural Justice and Order Maintenance Policing: A Study of Inner-City Young Men's Perceptions of Police Legitimacy. *Justice Quarterly* 27: 255–279.

Gau, Jacinta M., and Kareem Jordan. 2015. Profiling Trayvon: Young Black Males, Suspicion, and Surveillance. In *Deadly Injustice: Trayvon Martin, Race, and the Criminal Justice System*, edited by Devon Johnson, Patricia Y. Warren, and Amy Farrell, 7–22. New York: New York University Press.

Gabbidon, Shaun L., and George E. Higgins. 2009. The Role of Race/Ethnicity and Race Relations on Public Opinion Related to the Treatment of Blacks by the Police. *Police Quarterly* 12: 102–115.

Gallagher, Catherine, Edward Maguire, Stephen D. Mastrofski, and Michael D. Reisig. 2001. *The Public Image of the Police*. Gaithersburg: International Association of Chiefs of Police.

Gambino, Lauren. 2015. Jim Crow Lynchings More Widespread Than First Thought, Report Concludes. *Guardian* (February 10), https://www.theguardian.com.

Gamson, William A. 1992a. *Talking Politics*. New York: Cambridge University Press.

Gamson, William A. 1992b. The Social Psychology of Collective Action. In *Frontiers in Social Movement Theory*, edited by Aldon D. Morris and Carol McClurg Mueller, 53–76. New Haven: Yale University Press.

Garza, Alicia. 2014. A Herstory of the #BlackLivesMatter Movement by Alicia Garza. Feminist Wire (October 7), http://thefeministwire.com.

Gau, Jacinta, and Rodney K. Brunson. 2010. Procedural Justice and Order Maintenance Policing: A Study of Inner-city Young Men's Perceptions of Police Legitimacy. *Justice Quarterly* 27: 255–279.

Gau, Jacinta M., Nicholas Corsaro, Eric A. Stewart, and Rod K. Brunson. 2012. Examining Macro-level Impacts on Procedural Justice and Police Legitimacy. *Journal of Criminal Justice* 40: 333–343.

Ghandnoosh, Nazgol. 2015. *Black Lives Matter: Eliminating Racial Inequity in the Criminal Justice System*. Washington: Sentencing Project.

Gillham, Patrick F. 2011. Securitizing America: Strategic Incapacitation and the Policing of Protest since the 11 September 2001 Terrorist Attacks. *Sociology Compass* 5: 636–652.

Gillham, Patrick F., and John Noakes. 2007. "More Than a March in a Circle": Transgressive Protests and the Limits of Negotiated Management. *Mobilization: An International Quarterly* 12: 341–357.

Gladora, Chris. 2006. History: Housing Policy and Segregation in Baltimore. *Indypendent Reader*, https://indyreader.org.

Gladwell, Malcolm, and Clay Shirky. 2011. From Innovation to Revolution: Do Social Media Make Protests Possible? *Foreign Affairs* 90: 153–154.

Glaser, Barney G., and Anselm L. Strauss. 1967. *The Discovery of Grounded Theory: Strategies for Qualitative Research*. Chicago: Aldine.

Glaser, Jack. 2015. *Suspect Race: Causes and Consequences of Racial Profiling*. New York: Oxford University Press.

Glass, Pepper. 2010. Everyday Routines in Free Spaces: Explaining the Persistence of the Zapatistas in Los Angeles. *Mobilization: An International Quarterly* 15: 199–216.

Glassner, Barry, and Julia Loughlin. 1987. *Drugs in Adolescent Worlds: Burnouts to Straights*. New York: St. Martin's.

Goffman, Erving. 1974. *Frame Analysis: An Essay on the Organization of Experience*. Cambridge: Harvard University Press.

Goodman, J. David. 2015. Eric Garner Case is Settled by New York City for $5.9 Million. *New York Times* (July 13), https://www.nytimes.com.

Gordon, Colin. 2008. *Mapping Decline: St. Louis and the Fate of the American City*. Philadelphia: University of Pennsylvania Press.

Graham, Sandra, and Brian S. Lowery. 2004. Priming Unconscious Racial Stereotypes about Adolescent Offenders. *Law and Human Behavior* 28: 483–504.

Grand Jury for the Circuit Court of St. Louis County. 2014. State of Missouri v. Darren Wilson: Transcript of Grand Jury Proceedings.

Graziano, Lisa, Amie Schuck, and Christine Martin. 2010. Police Misconduct, Media Coverage, and Public Perceptions of Racial Profiling: An Experiment. *Justice Quarterly* 27: 52–76.

Greenwald, Anthony G., and Linda H. Krieger. 2006. Implicit Bias: Scientific Foundations. *California Law Review* 94: 945–967.

Griggs, Brandon. 2015. Baltimore's Riots and "The Purge." CNN (April 29), https://www.cnn.com.

Guardian. 2015. The Counted. *Guardian* (December 31), https://www.theguardian.com.

Guynes, Randall, and Russell Wolff. 2004. *Un-served Arrest Warrants: An Exploratory Study*. Washington: National Institute of Justice.

Hadden, Sally E. 2001. *Slave Patrols: Law and Violence in Virginia and the Carolinas*. Cambridge: Harvard University Press.

Haft, Lara. 2018. It's Time for Jewish Communities to Stop Investing in the Police. *Forward* (March 23), https://forward.com.

Hager, Greg, Kara Daniel, Rick Graycarek, and Van Knowles. 2005. *Improved Coordination and Information Could Reduce the Backlog of Un-served Warrants.* Frankfort: Legislative Research Commission.

Hahn, Harlan. 1971. A Profile of Urban Police. *Law and Contemporary Problems* 36: 449–466.

Hamer, Jennifer F. 2011. *Abandoned in the Heartland: Work, Family, and Living in East St. Louis.* Berkeley: University of California Press.

Handlin, Oscar, and Mary Handlin. 1950. Origins of the Southern Labor System. *William and Mary Quarterly* 7: 199–222.

Hardin, Curtis D., and Mahzarin R. Banaji. 2013. The Nature of Implicit Prejudice: Implications for Personal and Public Policy. In *The Behavioral Foundations of Public Policy*, edited by Eldar Shafir, 13–30. Princeton: Princeton University Press.

Harris, David A. 1999. The Stories, the Statistics and the Law: Why "Driving While Black" Matters. *University of Minnesota Law Review* 84: 265–326.

Hartocollis, Anemona. 2016. Yale Professor and Wife, Targets of Protests, Resign as College Heads. *New York Times* (May 26), https://www.nytimes.com.

Hawkins, Homer, and Richard Thomas. 1991. White Policing of Black Populations: A History of Race and Social Control in America. In *Out of Order? Policing Black People*, edited by Ellis Cashmore and Eugene McLaughlin, 65–86. London: Routledge.

Hawley, Jamie, and Staycie L. Flint. 2016. "It Looks Like a Demon": Black Masculinity and Spirituality in the Age of Ferguson. *Journal of Men's Studies* 24: 208–212.

Heathcott, Joseph. 2011. "In the Nature of a Clinic": The Design of Early Public Housing in St. Louis. *Journal of the Society of Architectural Historians* 70: 82–103.

Hemmens, Craig, and Daniel Levin. 2000. Resistance Is Futile: The Right to Resist Unlawful Arrest in an Era of Aggressive Policing. *Crime & Delinquency* 46: 472–496.

Henderson, Martha L., Francis T. Cullen, Liqun Cao, Sandra Lee Browning, and Renee Kopache. 1997. The Impact of Race on Perceptions of Criminal Justice. *Journal of Criminal Justice* 25: 447–462.

Hermann, Peter, John Woodrow Cox, and Ashley Halsey. 2015. After Peaceful Start, Protest of Freddie Gray's Death in Baltimore Turns Violent. *Washington Post* (April 25), https://www.washingtonpost.com.

Hirsch, Eric. 1990. Sacrifice for the Cause: Group Processes, Commitment and Recruitment in a Student Social Movement. *American Sociological Review* 55: 243–54.

Higgs, Robert. 1977. *Competition and Coercion: Blacks in the American Economy, 1865–1914.* New York: Cambridge University Press.

Hitlin, Paul, and Nancy Vogt. 2014. Cable, Twitter Picked up Ferguson Story at a Similar Clip. Pew Research Center, http://www.pewresearch.org.

hooks, bell. 2004. *We Real Cool.* New York: Routledge.

hooks, bell. 1995. *Killing Rage: Ending Racism.* New York: Henry Holt.

Horowitz, Alana. 2014. Ferguson, Missouri Protest of Michael Brown Death Swarmed by SWAT Team. Huffington Post (August 13), https://www.huffingtonpost.com.

Hotchkiss, Michael. 2015. Hypersegregated Cities Face Tough Road to Change. Princeton University (May 18), https://www.princeton.edu.

House of Parliament. 2015. *Body-worn Video in UK Policing.* http://researchbriefings.parliament.uk.

Huebner, Beth M., Joseph A. Schafer, and Timothy S. Bynum. 2004. African American and White Perceptions of Police Services: Within- and Between-Group Variation. *Journal of Criminal Justice* 32: 125–135.

Hughey, Matthew. 2015. The Five I's of Five-O: Racial Ideologies, Institutions, Interests, Identities, and Interactions of Police Violence. *Critical Sociology* 41: 857–871.

Hunn, David, and Kim Bell. 2014. Why Was Michael Brown's Body Left There for Hours? *St. Louis Post-Dispatch* (September 14), http://www.stltoday.com.

Hurwitz, Jon, and Mark Peffley. 1997. Public Perceptions of Race and Crime: The Role of Racial Stereotypes. *American Journal of Political Science* 41: 375–401.

Institute for Intergovernmental Research. 2015. *After-Action Assessment of the Police Response to the August 2014 Demonstrations in Ferguson, Missouri.* Washington: Office of Community Oriented Policing Services.

Jacques, Scott. 2017. A Run-in with the Cops Is Really Few and Far Between: Negative Evidence and Ethnographic Understanding of Racial Discrimination by Police. *Sociological Focus* 50: 7–17.

James, Brendan. 2014. Fox News: Ferguson Protesters "Forgetting MLK's Message." TPM LiveWire (August 14), http://talkingpointsmemo.com.

Jasper, James M. 2014. Constructing Indignation: Anger Dynamics in Protest Movements. *Emotions Review* 6: 208–213.

Jenkins, Craig A., and Charles Perrow. 1977. Insurgency of the Powerless: Farm Worker Movements (1946–1972). *American Sociological Review* 42: 249–268.

Jenkins, Richard. 2004. *Social Identity.* London: Routledge.

Johnson, Brian D. 2005. Contextual Disparities in Guidelines Departures: Courtroom Social Contexts, Guidelines Compliance, and Extralegal Disparities in Criminal Sentencing. *Criminology* 43: 761–796.

Johnson, Charles C. 2014. LAWSUIT: Why We Sued St. Louis County Court to Get Michael Brown's Juvenile Arrest Records. Got News (August 22), http://gotnews.com.

Jones-Brown, Delores. 2009. The Right to Life? Policing, Race and Criminal Injustice. *Human Rights* 36: 6.

Jones-Brown, Delores. 2007. Forever the Symbolic Assailant: The More Things Change, the More They Remain the Same. *Criminology & Public Policy* 6: 103–121.

Jones-Brown, Delores D. 2000. Debunking the Myth of Officer Friendly: How African American Males Experience Community Policing. *Journal of Contemporary Criminal Justice* 16: 209–29.

Kane, Robert J. 2005. Compromised Police Legitimacy as a Predictor of Violent Crime in Structurally Disadvantaged Communities. *Criminology* 43: 469–498.

Kane, Robert J. 2002. The Social Ecology of Police Misconduct. *Criminology* 40: 867–896.

Kanter, Rosabeth Moss. 1977a. *Men and Women of the Corporation.* New York: Basic.

Kanter, Rosabeth Moss. 1977b. Some Effects of Proportions on Group Life. *American Journal of Sociology* 82: 965–990.

Kappeler, Victor E. 2015. *Community Policing: A Contemporary Perspective*. New York: Routledge.

Kappeler, Victor E., Richard D. Sluder, and Geoffrey P. Alpert. 1998. *Forces of Deviance: Understanding the Dark Side of Policing*. Prospect Heights: Waveland.

Kelly, Caroline, and Sara Breinlinger. 1995. Identity and Injustice: Exploring Women's Participation in Collective Action. *Journal of Community & Applied Social Psychology* 5: 41–57.

Kennedy, Randall. 1997. *Race, Crime, and the Law*. New York: Pantheon.

Kindy, Kimberly, and Kimbriell Kelly. 2015. Thousands Dead, Few Prosecuted. *Washington Post* (April 11), https://www.washingtonpost.com.

King, Gilbert. 2012. *Devil in the Grove: Thurgood Marshall, the Groveland Boys, and the Dawn of a New America*. New York: HarperCollins.

King, Mike, and David Waddington. 2005. Flashpoints Revisited: A Critical Application to Policing of Anti-Globalisation Protest. *Policing and Society* 15: 255–282.

King, Shaun. 2014. Five Ugly and Uncanny Parallels Between Lynchings and Police Killings in America. Daily Kos (November 13), https://www.dailykos.com.

Kingkade, Tyler, and Travis Waldron. 2015. Embattled University Of Missouri President Tim Wolfe Resigns. Huffington Post (November 9), https://www.huffingtonpost.com.

Klandermans, Bert. 1997. *The Social Psychology of Protest*. Cambridge: Blackwell.

Klandermans, Bert. 1984. Mobilization and Participation: Social-Psychological Expansions of Resource Mobilization Theory. *American Sociological Review* 49: 583–600.

Klandermans, Bert, and Marga de Weerd. 2000. Group Identification and Political Protest. In *Self, Identity, and Social Movements*, edited by Sheldon Stryker, Timothy J. Owens, and Robert W. White, 68–90. Minneapolis: University of Minnesota Press.

Klandermans, Bert, Jojanneke van der Toorn, and Jacquelien van Stekelenburg. 2008. Embeddedness and Identity: How Immigrants Turn Grievances into Action. *American Sociological Review* 73: 992–1012.

Klaus, Tom. 2016. Leaderlessness? The Lessons in Black Live's Matter's Resilience. *Non-Profit Quarterly* (January 5), https://nonprofitquarterly.org.

Klinger, David A. 1997. Negotiating Order in Patrol Work: An Ecological Theory of Police Response to Deviance. *Criminology* 35: 277–306.

Krivo, Lauren J., and Ruth D. Peterson. 1996. Extremely Disadvantaged Neighborhoods and Urban Crime. *Social Forces* 75: 619–650.

Kubrin, Charis E. 2005. Gangstas, Thugs, and Hustlas: Identity and the Code of the Street in Rap Music. *Social Problems* 52: 360–378.

Lafayette Group. 2015. *Major Cities Chiefs and Major County Sheriffs Survey of Technology Needs—Body Worn Cameras*. Washington: Homeland Security, Office of Emergency Communications.

LaGrange, Teresa C., and Robert A. Silverman. 1999. Low Self-Control and Opportunity: Testing the General Theory of Crime as an Explanation for Gender Differences in Delinquency. *Criminology* 37: 41–72.

Leach, Colin Wayne, Aarti Iyer, and Anne Pedersen. 2006. Anger and Guilt About In-Group Advantage Explain the Willingness for Political Action. *Personality and Social Psychology Bulletin* 32: 1232–1245.

Leary, Joy DeGruy. 2005. *Post Traumatic Slave Syndrome: America's Legacy of Enduring Injury and Healing.* Milwaukee: Uptone.

LeBlanc, Paul. 2017. Settlement Reached in Michael Brown Civil Lawsuit. CNN (June 21), http://www.cnn.com.

Lee, Jasmine C., and Haeyoun Park. 2017. In 15 High-Profile Cases Involving Deaths of Blacks, One Officer Faces Prison Time. *New York Times* (December 7), https://www.nytimes.com.

Lichter, Daniel T., Domenico Parisi, and Michael C. Taquino. 2015. Toward a New Macro-Segregation? Decomposing Segregation within and between Metropolitan Cities and Suburbs. *American Sociological Review* 80: 843–873.

Liebelson, Dana, and Ryan J. Reilly. 2015. Inside Hillary Clinton's Meeting With Black Lives Matter. Huffington Post (October 9), https://www.huffingtonpost.com.

Lind, E. Allen, and Tom R. Tyler. 1988. *The Social Psychology of Procedural Justice.* New York: Plenum.

Links, Jonathan, Katie O'Conor, and Lauren Sauer. 2015. *Recommendations for Enhancing Baltimore City's Preparedness and Response to Mass Demonstration Events: Based on a Review and Analysis of the Events of April 2015.* Baltimore: Johns Hopkins University Press.

Lipsitz, George. 2015. From Plessy to Ferguson. *Cultural Critique* 90: 119–139.

Liptak, Kevin, and Athena Jones. 2016. Obama on Police Shootings: "This is Not Just a Black Issue." CNN (July 7), http://www.cnn.com.

Loewan, James W. 2005. *Sundown Towns: A Hidden Dimension of American Racism.* New York: New Press.

Logan, John R., and Brian J. Stults. 2011. The Persistence of Segregation in the Metropolis: New Findings from the 2010 Census, Project US2010 Census Brief, https://s4.ad.brown.edu.

Lum, Lydia. 2009. The Obama Era: A Post-Racial Society? *Diverse Issues in Higher Education* 25: 14–16.

Lundman, Richard J. 1996. Demeanor and Arrest: Additional Evidence from Previously Unpublished Data. *Journal of Research in Crime and Delinquency* 33: 306–323.

Lundman, Richard, and Robert Kauffman. 2003. Driving While Black: Effects of Race, Ethnicity, and Gender on Citizen Self-Reports of Traffic Stops and Police Action. *Criminology* 41: 195–220.

Lussenhop, Jessica. 2018. Who Were the Corrupt Baltimore Police Officers? BBC News (February 13), https://www.bbc.com.

MacDonald, Heather. 2003. *Are Cops Racist?* Chicago: Ivan R. Dee.

Maciag, Mike. 2014. Skyrocketing Court Fines Are Major Revenue Generator for Ferguson. *Governing* (August 22), http://www.governing.com.

MacKinnon, Rebecca. 2012. The Netizen. *Development* 55: 201–204.

Madhubuti, Haki R. 1990. *Black Men: Obsolete, Single, Dangerous? The African American Family in Transition: Essays in Discovery, Solution and Hope.* Chicago: Third World.

Mann, Cora Mae. 1993. *Unequal Justice: A Question of Color.* Bloomington: Indiana University Press.

Marable, Manning. 1983. *How Capitalism Underdeveloped Black America: Problems in Race, Political Economy, and Society.* Boston: Allyn & Bacon.

Massey, Douglas S., and Nancy A. Denton. 1993. *American Apartheid: Segregation and the Making of the Underclass.* Cambridge: Harvard University Press.

Massey, Douglas S., and Nancy A. Denton. 1988. The Dimensions of Residential Segregation. *Social Forces* 67: 281–315.

Massey, Douglas S., and Mary J. Fischer. 2000. How Segregation Concentrates Poverty. *Ethnic and Racial Studies* 23: 670–691.

Mastrofski, Stephen D., Michael D. Reisig, and John D. McCluskey. 2002. Police Disrespect Toward the Public: An Encounter-Based Analysis. *Criminology* 40: 515–551.

Matsueda, Ross L., and Kevin Drakulich. 2009. Perceptions of Criminal Justice, Symbolic Racism, and Racial Politics. *Annals of the American Academy of Political and Social Science* 623: 163–178.

Mayor's Office of Emergency Management. 2015. Timeline of Events, http://mayor.baltimorecity.gov.

McAdam, Doug. 1988. *Freedom Summer.* New York: Oxford University Press.

McAdam, Doug. 1986. Recruitment to High-Risk Activism: The Case of Freedom Summer. *American Journal of Sociology* 92: 64–90.

McAdam, Doug, John D. McCarthy, and Mayer N. Zald. 1988. Social Movements. In *Handbook of Sociology*, edited by Neil J. Smelser, 695–737. Newbury Park: Sage.

McCarthy, John D., and Clark McPhail. 1998. The Institutionalization of Protest in the United States. In *The Social Movement Society: Contentious Politics for a New Century*, edited by David S. Meyers and Sidney Tarrow, 83–110. Lanham: Rowman & Littlefield.

McCarthy, Tom. 2014. Ferguson Protests: Michael Brown Family Calls for Calm amid Criticism of Video Release—As It Happened. *Guardian* (August 15), https://www.theguardian.com.

McClain, Dani. 2017. Can Black Lives Matter Win in the Age of Trump? *Nation* (October 9), https://www.thenation.com.

McCurdy, Patrick. 2012. Social Movements, Protest and Mainstream Media. *Sociology Compass* 6: 244–255.

McFadyen-Ketchum, Andrew. 2015. Is Mainstream Media to Blame for Riots in Ferguson and Baltimore? Good Men Project (October 25), https://goodmenproject.com.

McIntyre, Charshee. 1984. *Criminalizing a Race: Free Blacks During Slavery.* Queens: Kayode.

McLaughlin, Eliott. 2016. Ex-North Charleston Officer Indicted on Federal Charges in Walter Scott Death. CNN (May 11), http://www.cnn.com.

McLaughlin, Jenna, and Sam Brody. 2015. Eyewitnesses: The Baltimore Riots Didn't Start the Way You Think. *Mother Jones* (April 28), http://www.motherjones.com.

McPhail, Clark, and John D. McCarthy. 2005. Protest Mobilization, Protest Repression, and Their Interaction. In *Repression and Mobilization*, edited by Christian Davenport, Hank Johnston, and Carol McClurg Mueller, 3–32. Minneapolis: University of Minnesota Press.

McPhail, Clark, David Schweingruber, and John D. McCarthy. 1998. Protest Policing in the United States: 1960–1995. In *Policing Protests: The Control of Mass Demonstrations in Western Democracies*, edited by Donatella della Porta and Herbert Reiter, 49–60. Minneapolis: University of Minnesota Press.

McVeigh, Rory. 1995. Social Structure, Political Institutions, and Mobilization Potential. *Social Forces* 74: 465–481.

Mecklin, John. 1914. The Black Codes. *South Atlantic Quarterly* 16: 248–259.

Meehan, Albert J., and Michael C. Ponder. 2002. Race and Place: The Ecology of Racial Profiling African American Motorists. *Justice Quarterly* 19: 399–430.

Melucci, Alberto. 1989. *Nomads of the Present: Social Movements and Individual Needs in Contemporary Society*. Philadelphia: Temple University Press.

Metzler, Christopher. 2009. The Myth of a Post-racial America. *Diverse Issues in Higher Education* 25: 16.

Middlemass, Keesha. 2017. *Convicted and Condemned: The Politics and Policies of Prisoner Reentry*. New York: New York University Press.

Miller, Jody. 2008. *Getting Played: African American Girls, Urban Inequality, and Gendered Violence*. New York: New York University Press.

Miller, Jody. 2001. *One of the Guys: Girls, Gangs and Gender*. New York: Oxford University Press.

Miller, Kirk. 2009. Race, Driving, and Police Organization: Modeling Moving and Nonmoving Traffic Stops with Citizen Self-Reports of Driving Practices. *Journal of Criminal Justice* 37: 564–575.

Mindock, Clark. 2018. Ferguson Shooting: Four Years After Michael Brown's Death, How Have Things Changed? *Independent* (August 8), https://www.independent.co.uk.

Moon, Melanie. 2014. Police Keep Watch Over Protesters in Ferguson. Fox2Now (August 10), http://fox2now.com.

Moran, Matthew, and David Waddington. 2016. *Riots: An International Comparison*. London: Palgrave Macmillan.

Morgan, Philip D. 2005. Origins of American Slavery. *OAH Magazine of History* 19: 51–56.

Morris, Thomas D. 1996. *Southern Slavery and the Law, 1619–1860*. Chapel Hill: University of North Carolina Press.

Morrison, Denton E. 1971. Some Notes Toward Theory on Relative Deprivation, Social Movements, and Social Change. *American Behavioral Scientist* 14: 675–690.

Morrison, Toni. 1993. On the Backs of Blacks. *Time* (December 2), http://content.time.com.

Mosher, Frederick C. 1982. *Democracy and the Public Service*. 2nd ed. New York: Oxford University Press.

Munson, Ziad W. 2002. *The Making of Pro-Life Activists: How Social Movement Mobilization Works*. Chicago: University of Chicago Press.

Musgrave, Shawn, Tom Meagher, and Gabriel Dance. 2014. The Pentagon Finally Details its Weapons-for-Cops Giveaway. Marshall Project (December 3), https://www.themarshallproject.org.

Myrdal, Gunnar. 1944. *An American Dilemma: The Negro Problem and Modern Democracy*. New York: Harper & Row.

National Advisory Commission on Civil Disorders. 1968. *Report of the National Advisory Commission on Civil Disorders*. Washington: US Government Printing Office.

National Association for the Advancement of Colored People and the Criminal Justice Institute at Harvard Law School. 1995. *Beyond the Rodney King Story: An Investigation of Police Conduct in Minority Communities*. Boston: Northeastern University.

Nelson, Colleen. 2015. Obama Calls for Restricting Military Gear to Local Police. *Wall Street Journal* (May 18), https://www.wsj.com.

Nepstad, Sharon Erickson. 2008. *Religion and War Resistance in the Plowshares Movement*. New York: Cambridge University Press.

Nepstad, Sharon Erickson. 2004. Persistent Resistance: Commitment and Community in the Plowshares Movement. *Social Problems* 51: 43–60.

Nepstad, Sharon Erickson, and Christian Smith. 1999. Rethinking Recruitment to High-Risk/Cost Activism: The Case of the Nicaragua Exchange. *Mobilization: An International Quarterly* 4: 25–40.

Nicholson-Crotty, Sean, Jill Nicholson-Crotty, and Sergio Fernandez. 2017. Will More Black Cops Matter? Officer Race and Police-Involved Homicides of Black Citizens. *Public Administration Review* 77: 206–216.

Nolen, Claude H. 2001. *African American Southerners in Slavery, Civil War and Reconstruction*. Jefferson: McFarland.

Office of the Missouri Attorney General. 2014. Racial Profiling Data/2013, Ferguson Police Department, http://ago.mo.gov/.

Oliveri, Rigel C. 2015. Setting the Stage for Ferguson: Housing Discrimination and Segregation in St. Louis. *Missouri Law Review* 80: 1053–1075.

Opp, Karl-Dieter, and Wolfgang Roehl. 1990. Repression, Micromobilization, and Political Protest. *Social Forces* 69: 521–547.

Orbuch, Terri L. 1997. People's Accounts Count: The Sociology of Accounts. *Annual Review of Sociology* 23: 455–478.

Oshinsky, David M. 1996. *Worse than Slavery: Parchman Farm and the Ordeal of Jim Crow Justice*. New York: Free Press.

Owen, Barbara, and Barbara Bloom. 1995. Profiling Women Prisoners: Findings from the National Surveys and the California Sample. *Prison Journal* 75: 165–185.

Owens, Lynn. 2009. *Cracking Under Pressure: Narrating the Decline of the Amsterdam Squatters' Movement*. Amsterdam: Amsterdam University Press.

Passy, Florence. 2001. Socialization, Connection, and the Structure/Agency Gap: A Specification of the Impact of Networks on Participation in Social Movements. *Mobilization: An International Quarterly* 6: 173–192.

Patrick, Robert. 2017. Federal Judge Lauds Progress So Far on Ferguson Consent Decree. *St. Louis Post-Dispatch* (September 19), https://www.stltoday.com.

Paxton, Pamela. 2002. Social Capital and Democracy: An Interdependent Relationship. *American Sociological Review* 67: 254–277.

PBS. Virginia's Slave Codes 1705. 2018. http://www.pbs.org.

Peffley, Mark, and Jon Hurwitz. 1998. Whites' Stereotypes of Blacks: Sources and Political Consequences. In *Perception and Prejudice: Race and Politics in the United States*, edited by Jon Hurwitz and Mark Peffley, 996–1012. New Haven: Yale University Press.

Petersen, Nick, and Geoff Ward. 2015. The Transmission of Historical Racial Violence: Lynching, Civil Rights-Era Terror, and Contemporary Interracial Homicide. *Race and Justice* 5: 114–143.

Peterson, Ruth, and Lauren Krivo. 2009. Race, Residence, and Violent Crime: A Structure of Inequality. *Kansas Law Review* 57: 303–333.

Pew Research Center. 2014. Cable, Twitter Picked Up Ferguson Story at a Similar Clip. http://www.pewresearch.org.

Pinard, Michael. 2015. Poor, Black, and "Wanted": Criminal Justice in Ferguson and Baltimore. *Howard Law Journal* 58: 1–16.

Pitkin, Hannah Fenichel. 1967. *The Concept of Representation*. Berkeley: University of California Press.

Plant, E. Ashby, B. Michelle Peruche, and David A. Butz. 2005. Eliminating Automatic Racial Bias: Making Race Non-Diagnostic for Responses to Criminal Suspects. *Journal of Experimental Social Psychology* 41: 141–156.

Police Executive Research Forum. 2015. *Lessons Learned from the 2015 Civil Unrest in Baltimore*. Washington: Police Executive Research Forum.

Power, Garrett. 2004. Meade v. Dennistone: The NAACP's Test Case to ". . . Sue Jim Crow Out of Maryland with the Fourteenth Amendment." *Maryland Law Review* 63: 773–810.

Power, Garrett. 1983. Apartheid Baltimore Style: The Residential Segregation Ordinances of 1910–1913. *Maryland Law Review* 42: 289–328.

President's Task Force on 21st Century Policing. 2015. *Interim Report of the President's Task Force on 21st Century Policing*. Washington: Office of Community Oriented Policing Services.

Putnam, Robert. 2000. *Bowling Alone: The Collapse and Revival of American Community*. New York: Simon & Schuster.

Quillian, Lincoln, and Devah Pager. 2001. Black Neighbors, Higher Crime? The Role of Racial Stereotypes in Evaluations of Neighborhood Crime. *American Journal of Sociology* 107: 717–767.

Quinney, Richard. 1970. *The Social Reality of Crime*. Boston: Little, Brown.

Ramirez, Deborah A., Jack McDevitt, and Amy Farrell. 2000. *A Resource Guide on Racial Profiling Data Collection: Promising Practices and Lessons Learned.* Washington: US Department of Justice.

Ratliff, Thomas. 2011. *On the Stage of Change: A Dramaturgical Approach to Violence, Social Protest and Policing Styles in the US.* Doctoral dissertation. Blacksburg: Virginia Tech.

Reaves, Brian A. 2010. *Local Police Departments, 2007.* Washington: US Department of Justice.

Rector, Kevin, and Jessica Anderson. 2018. One Year into Consent Decree, Baltimore Police Reforms Move Forward Slowly and Behind the Scenes. *Baltimore Sun* (April 6), http://www.baltimoresun.com.

Reisig, Michael D., John D. McCluskey, Stephen D. Mastrofski, and William Terrill. 2004. Suspect Disrespect Toward the Police. *Justice Quarterly* 21: 241–268.

Reisig, Michael D., and Roger B. Parks. 2000. Experience, Quality of Life, and Neighborhood Context: A Hierarchical Analysis of Satisfaction with Police. *Justice Quarterly* 17: 607–629.

Reiss, Albert J. 1971. *The Police and the Public.* New Haven: Yale University Press.

Reitzel, John D., Stephen K. Rice, and Alex R. Piquero. 2004. Lines and Shadows: Perceptions of Racial Profiling and Hispanic Experience. *Journal of Criminal Justice* 32: 607–616.

Report in Response to HB 771 (CH 133), Baltimore Police Department, Reporting on Community Policing. 2016. https://www.baltimorepolice.org.

Research & Statistics Division of the St. Louis City. 2007. *St. Louis County, Missouri: 2007–2012 Fact Book.* St. Louis: St. Louis County Department of Planning.

Reveal Media. 2015. http://revealmedia.com/news.

Rhodan, Maya. 2016. Black Lives Matter Activist Says Obama Meeting was Positive. *Time* (February 18), http://time.com.

Richardson, L. Song. 2011. Arrest Efficiency and the Fourth Amendment. *Minnesota Law Review* 95: 2035–2098.

Richie, Beth E. 2001. Challenges Incarcerated Women Face as They Return to Their Communities: Findings from Life History Interviews. *Crime and Delinquency* 47: 368–389.

Riksheim, Eric C., and Steven M. Chermak. 1993. Causes of Police Behavior Revisited. *Journal of Criminal Justice* 21: 353–382.

Ritchie, Andrea J. 2017. *Invisible No More: Police Violence Against Black Women and Women of Color.* Boston: Beacon.

Roller, Emma. 2014. The Character Assassination of Michael Brown. *Atlantic* (August 19), https://www.theatlantic.com.

Romzek, Barbara S. 1990. Employee Investment and Commitment: The Ties That Bind. *Public Administration Review* 50: 374–382.

Rory, Carroll, and Jon Swaine. 2014. Missouri Governor Declares State of Emergency and Curfew in Ferguson. *Guardian* (August 17), https://www.theguardian.com.

Rosenbaum, Dennis P., Amie M. Schuck, Sandra K. Costello, Darnell F. Hawkins, and Marianne K. Ring. 2005. Attitudes Toward the Police: The Effects of Direct and Vicarious Experience. *Police Quarterly* 8: 343–365.

Rothstein, Richard. 2015. From Ferguson to Baltimore: The Fruits of Government-Sponsored Segregation. Working Economics Blog (April 29), https://www.epi.org.

Rothstein, Richard. 2014. *The Making of Ferguson: Public Policies at the Root of its Troubles.* Washington: Economic Policy Institute.

Rothestein, Richard. 2012. Public Housing: Government-Sponsored Segregation. *American Prospect* (October 11), http://prospect.org.

Runciman, Walter Garrison. 1966. *Relative Deprivation and Social Justice: A Study of Attitudes to Social Equality in Twentieth Century England.* London: Routledge.

Russell, Katherine. 1998. *The Color of Crime.* New York: New York University Press.

Rusk, David. 1996. *Baltimore Unbound: A Strategy for Regional Renewal.* Baltimore: Johns Hopkins University Press.

Ryals, Mitch. 2014. Ferguson Protesters, Including the Lost Voices, Get Kicked Out of Protest Sites. *Riverfront Times* (September 29), http://www.riverfront times.com.

Sampson, Robert J., and Dawn Jeglum Bartusch. 1998. Legal Cynicism and (Subcultural?) Tolerance of Deviance: The Neighborhood Context of Racial Differences. *Law and Society Review* 32: 777–804.

Sampson, Robert J., Stephen W. Raudenbush, and Felton Earls. 1997. Neighborhoods and Violent Crime: A Multilevel Study of Collective Efficacy. *Science* 277: 918–924.

Samuels, Barbara. 2008. Segregation and Public Housing Development in Cherry Hill and Westport: Historical Background. Middle Branch Community Listening Session, Maryland State Commission on Environmental Justice and Sustainable Communities.

Sanchez, Claudio G. V., and Dennis P. Rosenbaum. 2011. Racialized Policing: Officers' Voices on Policing Latino and African American Neighborhoods. *Journal of Ethnicity in Criminal Justice* 9: 152–178.

Sanchez, Raf, and David Lawler. 2015. Ferguson: Timeline of Events Since Michael Brown's Death. *Telegraph* (August 10), https://www.telegraph.co.uk.

Santayana, George. 1906. *Reason in Common Sense: Life of Reason.* Vol. 1. Woodbridge: Charles Scribner's Sons.

Scheindlin, Shira A., and Peter K. Manning. 2015. Will the Widespread Use of Police Body Cameras Improve Police Accountability? *Americas Quarterly* 9: 24–27.

Schensul, Jean J., and Margaret LeCompte. 2013. *Essential Ethnographic Methods: A Mixed Methods Approach.* Lanham: Rowman & Littlefield.

Schill, Michael H., and Susan M. Wachter. 1995. The Spatial Bias of Federal Housing Law and Policy: Concentrated Poverty in Urban America. *University of Pennsylvania Law Review* 143: 1285–1342.

Schussman, Alan, and Sarah A. Soule. 2005. Process and Protest: Accounting for Individual Protest Participation. *Social Forces* 84: 1083–1108.

Sharp, Elaine B. 2014. Minority Representation and Order Maintenance Policing: Toward a Contingent View. *Social Science Quarterly* 95: 1155–71.

Shoichet, Catherine, Ben Brumfield, and Tristan Smith. 2014. Tear Gas Fills Ferguson's Streets Again. CNN (August 13), https://www.cnn.com.

Silverman, D. 2006. *Interpreting Qualitative Data: Methods for Analyzing Talk, Text and Interaction.* 3rd ed. London: Sage.

Simon, Bernd, and Bert Klandermans. 2001. Politicized Collective Identity: A Social Psychological Analysis. *American Psychologist* 56: 319–331.

Simon, Bernd, Michael Loewy, Stefan Stürmer, Ulrike Weber, Peter Freytag, Corinna Habig, Claudia Kampmeier, and Peter Spahlinger. 1998. Collective Identification and Social Movement Participation. *Journal of Personality and Social Psychology* 74: 646–658.

Simon, Herbert A. 1957. *Administrative Behavior: A Study of Decision-Making Processes in Administrative Organizations.* 2nd ed. New York: Macmillan.

Sinclair, Harriett. 2017. Black Lives Matter Calls for US to Ban Confederate Symbols after Charlottesville Violence. *Newsweek* (August 15), http://www.newsweek.com.

Skogan, Wesley G. 1979. Citizen Satisfaction with Police Services. In *Evaluating Alternative Law Enforcement Policies,* edited by Ralph Baker and Fred A. Meyer Jr., 29–42. Lexington: Lexington Books.

Skolnick, Jerome H. 1966. *Justice Without Trial: Law Enforcement in a Democratic Society.* New York: John Wiley & Sons.

Skolnick, Jerome H., and James J. Fyfe. 1993. *Above the Law: Police and the Excessive Use of Force.* New York: Free Press.

Smith, Aaron. 2013. Smartphone Ownership 2013. Pew Research Center (June 5), http://www.pewinternet.org.

Smith, Brad W., and Malcolm D. Holmes. 2003. Community Accountability, Minority Threat, and Police Brutality: An Examination of Civil Rights Criminal Complaints. *Criminology* 41: 1035–1063.

Smith, Douglas A. 1986. The Neighborhood Context of Police Behavior. In *Communities and Crime,* edited by Albert J. Reiss Jr. and Michael Tonry, 313–341. Chicago: University of Chicago Press.

Smith, Douglas A., and Christy A. Visher. 1981. Street-Level Justice: Situational Determinants of Police Arrest Decisions. *Social Problems* 29: 167–177.

Smith, Jamil. 2015. Videos of Police Killings are Numbing Us to the Spectacle of Black Death. *New Republic* (April 13), https://newrepublic.com.

Smith, Michael R., and Geoffrey P. Alpert. 2007. Explaining Police Bias: A Theory of Social Conditioning and Illusory Correlation. *Criminal Justice and Behavior* 34: 1262–1283.

Smyth, Leo F. 2002. Identity-Based Conflicts: A Systemic Approach Evaluation Project. *Negotiation Journal* 18: 147–161.

Sniderman, Paul M., and Thomas Leonard Piazza. 1993. *The Scar of Race.* Cambridge: Harvard University Press.

Snow, David A., and Robert D. Benford. 1988. Ideology, Frame Resonance, and Partici-pant Mobilization. *International Social Movement Research* 1: 197–217.

Snow, David A., Sarah A. Soule, and Hanspeter Kriesi. 2004. Mapping the Terrain. In *The Blackwell Companion to Social Movements*, edited by David A. Snow, Sarah A. Soule, and Hanspeter Kriesi, 3–16. Maldon: Blackwell.

Soderberg, Brandon. 2015. How Drunk Sports Fans Helped Spark Saturday Night's Post-Protest Violence. *City Paper* (April 28), http://www.citypaper.com.

Somashekhar, Sandhya, and Steven Rich. 2016. Final Tally: Police Shot and Killed 986 People in 2015. *Washington Post* (January 6), http://www.washingtonpost.com.

Spohn, Cassia C. 2000. Thirty Years of Sentencing Reform: The Quest for a Racially Neutral Sentencing Process. In *Policies, Processes, and Decisions of the Criminal Justice System*, Vol. 3, 427–501. Washington: US Department of Justice.

St. Louis County Planning. 2012. Policy Brief: The Dynamics of Population Change in St. Louis County, Missouri. https://www.stlouisco.com.

Steffensmeier, Darrell, and Stephen Demuth. 2001. Ethnicity and Judges' Sentencing Decisions: Hispanic-Black-White Comparisons. *Criminology* 39: 145–178.

Steinmetz, Kevin F., Brian P. Schaefer, and Howard Henderson. 2017. Wicked Over-seers: American Policing and Colonialism. *Sociology of Race and Ethnicity* 3: 68–81.

Stevenson, Bryan. 2017. A Presumption of Guilt: A Legacy of America's History of Racial Injustice. In *Policing the Black Man*, edited by Angela Davis, 3–30. New York: Pantheon Books.

Stolberg, Sheryl, and Jesse Bidgood. 2016. All Charges Against Baltimore Officers Dropped in Freddie Gray Case. *New York Times* (July 27), http://www.nytimes.com.

Strauss, Anselm L. 1987. *Qualitative Analysis for Social Scientists*. New York: Cambridge University Press.

Stryker, Sheldon, Timothy Joseph Owens, and Robert W. White, eds. 2000. *Self, Iden-tity, and Social Movements*. Minneapolis: University of Minnesota Press.

Suereth, Tim. 2015. *Ferguson: America's Breaking Point*. Elwood: Elwood.

Sullivan, Christopher. 2011. Police Will Repress-But Will it Demobilize? Mobilizing Ideas (December 19), https://mobilizingideas.wordpress.com.

Sun, Ivan Y., and Brian K. Payne. 2004. Racial Differences in Resolving Conflicts: A Comparison Between Black and White Police Officers. *Crime and Delinquency* 50: 516–541.

Swanstrom, Todd, and John Mollenkopf. 2015. The Ferguson Moment: Race and Place. New York University Furman Center (January), http://furmancenter.org.

Tajfel, Henry, and John C. Turner. 1979. An Integrative Theory of Intergroup Conflict. In *The Social Psychology of Intergroup Relations*, edited by William G. Austin and Stephen Worchel, 33–47. Chicago: Nelson-Hall.

Tarrow, Sidney, and James W. Tollefson. 1994. *Power in Movement: Social Movements, Collective Action and Politics*. New York: Cambridge University Press.

TASER. 2015. The #1 On-Officer Video Platform: Axon Cameras are Built Strong for Law Enforcement. https://www.taser.com/products/on-officer-video.

Task Force on the Police, President's Commission on Law Enforcement and Administration of Justice. 1967. *Task Force Report: The Police*. Washington: Government Printing Office.

Taxman, Faye S. 2005. Brick Walls Facing Reentering Offenders. *International Journal of Comparative and Applied Criminal Justice* 29: 5–18.

Taylor Greene, Helen. 2000. Understanding the Connections Between Race and Police Violence. In *The System in Black and White: Exploring the Connections Between Race, Crime and Justice*, edited by Michael Markowitz and Delores Jones-Brown, 73–84. Westport: Praeger.

Terrill, Willam. 2003. Police Use of Force and Suspect Resistance: The Micro Process of the Police-Suspect Encounter. *Policy Quarterly* 6: 51–83.

Terrill, William, and Michael D. Reisig. 2003. Neighborhood Context and Police Use of Force. *Journal of Research in Crime and Delinquency* 40: 291–321.

Texas, Par, and Williamson S. Oldham. 2015. *A Digest of the General Statute Laws of the State of Texas: To Which Are Subjoined the Repealed Laws of the Republic and State of Texas, By, Through, or Under Which Rights Have Accrued: Also, the Colonization Laws of Mexico, Coahuila and Texas, Which Were*. N.p.: Sagwan.

Thibaut, John, and Laurens Walker. 1975. *Procedural Justice: A Psychological Analysis*. Hillsdale: Erlbaum.

Tilly, Charles. 1978. *From Mobilization to Revolution*. Reading: Addison-Wesley.

Tobin, Gary. 1982. Deposition in *Liddell et al. v. Board of Education of the City of St. Louis*. United States District Court, Eastern District of Missouri, Eastern Division, Civil Action 72–100C (4), December 13.

Tolliver, Willie F., Bernadette R. Hadden, Fabienne Snowden, and Robyn Brown-Manning. 2016. Police Killings of Unarmed Black People: Centering Race and Racism in Human Behavior and the Social Environment Content. *Journal of Human Behavior in the Social Environment* 26: 279–286.

Tolnay, Stewart Emory, and Elwood M. Beck. 1995. *A Festival of Violence: An Analysis of Southern Lynchings, 1882–1930*. Champaign: University of Illinois Press.

Trautman, Neal. 2000. Police Code of Silence Facts Revealed. Legal Officers Section Annual Conference, International Association of Chiefs of Police. http://www.aele.org/loscode2000.html.

Turner, John C. 1999. Some Current Themes in Research on Social Identity and Self-Categorization Theories. In *Social Identity: Context, Commitment, Content*, edited by Naomi Ellemers, Russell Spears, and Bertjan Doosje, 634. Malden: Blackwell.

Turvey, Catherine. 2015. With Racial Segregation Declining Between Neighborhoods, Segregation Now Taking New Form (news release). American Sociological Association Public Information Office, http://asanet.org.

Tyler, Tom R., and Jeffrey Fagan. 2008. Legitimacy and Cooperation: Why Do People Help the Police Fight Crime in Their Communities? *Ohio State Journal of Criminal Law* 6: 231–275.

Tyler, Tom R., Jonathon Jackson, and Ben Bradford. 2014. Procedural Justice and Co-operation. In *Encyclopedia of Criminology and Criminal Justice*, edited by Gerben Bruinsma and David Weisburd, 4011–4024. New York: Springer.

Tyler, Tom R., and Heather J. Smith. 1998. Social Justice and Social Movements. In *Handbook of Social Psychology*, edited by Susan T. Fiske, Daniel T. Gilbert, and Gardner Lindzey, 595–629. New York: McGraw-Hill.

Tyler, Tom R., and Cheryl J. Wakslak. 2004. Profiling and Police Legitimacy: Procedural Justice, Attributions of Motive, and Acceptance of Police Authority. *Criminology* 42: 253–281.

US Census Bureau. State and County QuickFacts, http://www.census.gov.

US Census Bureau. 2015. American Factfinder. http://factfinder.census.gov.

US Census Bureau. 2014. American FactFinder. http://www.census.gov.

US Census Bureau. 2001. Census 2000 PHC-T-4. Ranking Tables for Counties: 1990 and 2000. http://www.census.gov.

US Census Bureau. 2000. American FactFinder. http://factfinder.census.gov.

US Census Bureau. 1995. Population of Counties by Decennial Census. http://www.census.gov.

US Census Bureau. 1963. Vol. I, Characteristics of the Population: Part 27, Missouri. US Census of Population, 1960. http://www2.census.gov.

US Census Bureau. 1952. *United States Census of Population, 1950*. Washington: US Government Printing Office.

USCCR (US Commission on Civil Rights). 1970. *Hearing before the US Commission on Civil Rights, St. Louis, Missouri, January 14–17, 1970*. Washington: US Government Printing Office.

US Department of Justice. 2016. *Advancing Diversity in Law Enforcement*. Washington: Equal Employment Opportunity Commission.

US Department of Justice Civil Rights Division. 2016. Investigation of the Baltimore City Police Department. https://www.justice.gov.

US Department of Justice. 2015a. Department of Justice Report Regarding the Criminal Investigation into the Shooting Death of Michael Brown by Ferguson, Missouri Police Officer Darren Wilson. https://www.justice.gov.

US Department of Justice Civil Rights Division. 2015b. Investigation of the Ferguson Police Department. https://www.courts.mo.gov.

van Stekelenburg, Jacquelien, and Bert Klandermans. 2013. The Social Psychology of Protest. *Current Sociology Review* 61: 886–905.

van Stekelenburg, Jacquelien, and Bert Klandermans. 2007. Individuals in Movements: A Social Psychology of Contention. In *Social Movements Across Disciplines*, edited by Bert Klandermans and Conny Roggeband, 157–204. New York: Springer.

van Zomeren, Martijn, Russell Spears, Agneta H. Fischer, and Colin Wayne Leach. 2004. Put Your Money Where Your Mouth Is! Explaining Collective Action Tendencies Through Group-Based Anger and Group Efficacy. *Journal of Personality and Social Psychology* 87: 649–664.

Varon, Jeremy Peter. 2004. *Bringing the War Home: The Weather Underground, the Red Army Faction, and Revolutionary Violence in the Sixties and Seventies.* Berkeley: University of California Press.

Vega, Tanzina. 2015. How Baltimore Police, Protesters Battle on Twitter. CNN (April 28), http://www.cnn.com.

Verba, Sidney, Kay L. Schlozman, and Henry E. Brady. 1995. *Voice and Equality: Civic Voluntarism in American Politics.* Cambridge: Harvard University Press.

Visher, Christy A. 1983. Gender, Police Arrest Decisions, and Notions of Chivalry. *Criminology* 21: 5–28.

Vissers, Sara, and Dietlind Stolle. 2014. The Internet and New Modes of Political Participation: Online versus Offline Participation. *Information, Communication, and Society* 17: 937–955.

Vitak, Jessica, Paul Zube, Andrew Smock, Caleb T. Carr, Nicole Ellison, and Cliff Lampe. 2011. It's Complicated: Facebook Users' Political Participation in the 2008 Election. *Cyberpsychology, Behavior, and Social Networking* 14: 107–114.

Vitale, Alex S. 2017. *The End of Policing.* Brooklyn: Verso.

Waddington, David. 2010. Applying the Flashpoints Model of Public Disorder to the 2001 Bradford Riot. *British Journal of Criminology* 50: 342–359.

Waddington, David, Karen Jones, and Chas Critcher. 1987. Flashpoints of Public Disorder. In *The Crowd in Contemporary Britain,* edited by George Gaskell and Robert Benewick, 155–189. London: Sage.

Walker, Samuel. 2001. *Police Accountability: The Role of Citizen Oversight.* Belmont: Wadsworth.

Walker, Samuel. 1999. *The Police in America: An Introduction.* 3rd ed. Boston: McGraw-Hill.

Walker, Samuel. 1985. Racial Minority and Female Employment in Policing: The Implications of Glacial Change. *Crime & Delinquency* 31: 555–572.

Walker, Samuel. 1980. *Popular Justice: A History of American Criminal Justice.* New York: Oxford University Press.

Walker, Samuel, Cassia Spohn, and Miriam Delone. 2000. *The Color of Justice: Race, Ethnicity, and Crime in America.* 2nd ed. Belmont: Wadsworth.

Wallach, Irving A., and Collette C. Jackson. 1973. Perception of the Police in a Black Community. In *The Urban Policeman in Transition: A Psychological and Sociological Review,* edited by John R. Snibbe and Homa M. Snibbe, 382–403. Springfield: Charles C. Thomas.

Weaver, Jessica. 2017. Police Training Should Start with a History Lesson on Slavery Laws. Root (June 10), https://www.theroot.com.

Webb, Vincent J., and Chris E. Marshall. 1995. The Relative Importance of Race and Ethnicity on Citizen Attitudes Toward the Police. *American Journal of Police* 14: 45–66.

Websdale, Neil. 2001. *Policing the Poor: From Slave Plantation to Public Housing.* Boston: Northeastern University Press.

Weithoff, William E. 2006. Enslaved Africans' Rivalry with White Overseers in Plantation Culture: An Unconventional Interpretation. *Journal of Black Studies* 36: 429–455.

Weitzer, Ronald. 2000. Racializing Policing: Residents' Perceptions in Three Neighborhoods. *Law and Society Review* 34: 129–155.

Weitzer, Ronald. 1999. Citizen Perceptions of Police Misconduct: Race and Neighborhood Context. *Justice Quarterly* 16: 819–846.

Weitzer, Ronald, and Rodney Brunson. 2009. Strategic Responses to the Police Among Inner-City Youth. *Sociological Quarterly* 50: 235–256.

Weitzer, Ronald, and Steven Tuch. 2006. *Race and Policing in America: Conflict and Reform.* New York: Cambridge University Press.

Weitzer, Ronald, and Steven A. Tuch. 2005. Racially Biased Policing: Determinants of Citizen Perceptions. *Social Forces* 83: 1009–1030.

Weitzer, Ronald, and Steven A. Tuch. 2004. Race and Perceptions of Police Misconduct. *Social Problems* 51: 305–325.

Weitzer, Ronald, and Steven A. Tuch. 2002. Perceptions of Racial Profiling: Race, Class and Personal Experience. *Criminology* 40: 435–457.

Weitzer, Ronald, and Steven A. Tuch. 1999. Race, Class and Perceptions of Discrimination by the Police. *Crime and Delinquency* 45: 494–507.

Weitzer, Ronald, Steven A. Tuch, and Wesley G. Skogan. 2008. Police-Community Relations in a Majority-Black City. *Journal of Research in Crime and Delinquency* 45: 398–428.

Welch, Kelly. 2007. Black Criminal Stereotypes and Racial Profiling. *Journal of Contemporary Criminal Justice* 23: 276–288.

Wenger, Yvonne, and Mark Puente. 2015. Baltimore to Pay Freddie Gray's Family $6.4 Million to Settle Civil Claims. *Baltimore Sun* (September 8), http://www.baltimoresun.com.

Werthman, Carl, and Irving Piliavin. 1967. Gang Members and the Police. In *The Police: Six Sociological Essays*, edited by David Bordua, 56–98. New York: John Wiley.

White, Michael D., and Henry F. Fradella. 2016. *Stop and Frisk: The Use and Abuse of a Controversial Policing Tactic.* New York: New York University Press.

Wilkins, Vicky M., and Brian N. Williams. 2009. Representing Blue: Representative Bureaucracy and Racial Profiling in the Latino Community. *Administration and Society* 40: 775–798.

Wilkins, Vicky M., and Brian N. Williams. 2008. Black or Blue: Racial Profiling and Representative Bureaucracy. *Public Administration Review* 68: 654–664.

Williams, Hubert, and Patrick V. Murphy. 1990. *The Evolving Strategy of Police: A Minority View.* Washington: National Institute of Justice.

Williams, Kristina. 2015. *Our Enemies in Blue: Police and Power in America.* Oakland: AK.

Williams, Marcia. 1999. *Soul Survivors: The Definitive Anthology of Female Slave Narratives.* London: X.

Williams, Timothy. 2017. A Persistent Case in Ferguson Raises Doubts About Reform. *New York Times* (September 4), https://www.nytimes.com.

Willis, Deborah, and Barbara Krauthamer. 2013. *Envisioning Emancipation: Black Americans and the End of Slavery*. Philadelphia: Temple University Press.

Wilson, William Julius. 1996. *When Work Disappears: The World of the New Urban Poor*. New York: Knopf.

Wilson, William Julius. 1987. *The Truly Disadvantaged*. Chicago: University of Chicago Press.

Wilson, William Julius. 1978. *The Declining Significance of Race*. Chicago: University of Chicago Press.

Wiltfang, Gregory, and Doug McAdam. 1991. Distinguishing Cost and Risk in Sanctuary Activism. *Social Forces* 69: 987–1010.

Withrow, Brian L. 2004. Driving while Different: A Potential Theoretical Explanation for Race-Based Policing. *Criminal Justice Policy Review* 15: 344–364.

Withrow, Brian L. 2002. Race-Based Policing. In *Encyclopedia of Crime and Justice*, edited by David Levinson, n.p. Thousand Oaks: Sage.

Wood, George A. 1914. The Black Code of Alabama. *South Atlantic Quarterly* 13: 350–360.

Wood, Maxine. 2015. *Highlighting the History of Housing Segregation in Baltimore, Maryland and its Impact on the Events of April 27, 2015 and Beyond*. 3rd Colloquium. Baltimore: Center for Social Organizations of Schools at Johns Hopkins School of Education.

Woodward, C. Vann. 1955. *The Strange Career of Jim Crow*. New York: Oxford University Press.

Wright, John A. 2005. *St. Louis: Disappearing Black Communities*. Charleston: Arcadia.

Wu, Yuning, Ivan Y. Sun, and Ruth A. Triplett. 2009. Race, Class or Neighborhood Context: Which Matters More in Measuring Satisfaction with Police? *Justice Quarterly* 26: 125–156.

Yakum, David, Anita Ravishankar, and Alexander Coppock. 2017. Evaluating the Effects of Police Body-Worn Cameras: A Randomized Controlled Trial (working paper). Washington, LAB @ DC.

Zagier, Alan Scher. 2014. Did Michael Brown Have a Juvenile Record? Is It Televant? *Christian Science Monitor* (September 3), https://www.csmonitor.com.

Zwerman, Gilda, and Patricia Steinhoff. 2005. When Activists Ask for Trouble: State-Dissident Interactions and the New Left Cycle of Resistance in the United States and Japan. In *Repression and Mobilization*, edited by Christian Davenport, Hank Johnston, and Carol McClurg Mueller, 85–107. Minneapolis: University of Minnesota Press.

INDEX

accountability, 67, 157–58; community accountability, 60; enhanced, 154; formal systems of, 130, 136
Advancing Diversity in Law Enforcement, 55
Alex, Nicholas, 63
Alexander, Michelle, 89–90
Alliance for a Just Society, 73
Allied Civic and Protective Association, 143
All Lives Matter, 90
Angelou, Maya, 26
armored vehicles, 141
Armstrong, David, 107
arrest: Black civilians arrested for minor offenses, 147; laws, 83; from protesting, 112–13; resisting, 40; warrants, 28, 137; Wilson, demands for arrest of, 88
at-risk youth, 160

Babbie, Earl, 173
Baker, David, 15
Baltimore, 125–26, 178n47; Baltimore riots of 1968, 151; Black population of, 10; changes since killing of Gray, 157–59; Committee on Segregation, 143; contextual level analysis of, 148; cultural level analysis of, 146–47; decline in population of, 10; demographic and socioeconomic indicators of, 8–9, 9; demographic characteristics of protesters in, 165–66; economic inequality in, 142; experiences with and perceptions of Black police officers in, 57, 57; Inner Harbor, 151; interactional level analysis of, 149–51; large-scale disorder in, 98; legacy of racism in, 5; negative experiences with police in, 30; participants interviewed in, 172; personal and vicarious experiences of Black and White residents in, 29, 29–30; political/ideological level analysis of, 145–46; positive police interactions in, 49; protesters reaction to militarization of police in, 118; racial bias in, 147; racial zoning in, 143; research team in, 168, 169; situational level analysis of, 149–51; size of, 12; socioeconomic indicators for Blacks and Whites in, 10–11, 11; structural level analysis of, 142–45; uprisings in, 6; White residents of, 43
Baltimore City Schools Police, 149
Baltimore Police Department (BPD), 2, 11; drugs planted by, 28; gender and, 49; Gray and, 147; institutional features of, 152; militarization of, 119–20; use of excessive force by, 147–48
Baumgartner, Frank, 21
Bell, Wesley, 158
Belmar, Jon, 76
Black bodies, 155; brutalization of, 156; policing of, 17
Black citizens: Black police officers and, 60; KKK and, 19; personal and vicarious experiences and, 29, 29–30; targeted for extralegal reasons, 38

ABOUT THE AUTHOR

Jennifer E. Cobbina is Associate Professor in the School of Criminal Justice at Michigan State University.